A Garland Series

Nineteenth-Century Book Arts and Printing History

Twenty-Six Texts reprinted in
Twenty-Three Volumes, mostly relating to
Papermaking, Book Illustration, Type Design,
Typefounding, and the Practice of Printing
during the Industrial Revolution.

Edited by

John Bidwell

The Printer's Manual

A Practical Guide for Compositors and Pressmen

by

Thomas Lynch

with a new introduction by

Peter M. VanWingen

GARLAND PUBLISHING, INC.

New York   1981   *London*

For a complete list of the titles in this series, see the final pages of this volume.

Introduction copyright © 1981 by Peter M. VanWingen

Bibliographical note: this facsimile has been made from a copy in the possession of the Graphic Arts Technical Foundation.

Library of Congress Cataloging in Publication Data

Lynch, Thomas.
The printer's manual.

(Nineteenth-century book arts and printing history)
Reprint of the 1859 ed. published by Cincinnati Type-Foundry, Cincinnati.
1. Printing, Practical. I. Title. II. Series.
Z244.A2L9 1981   686.2'24   78-74410
ISBN 0-8240-3894-0

The volumes in this series are printed on acid-free, 250-year-life paper.

Printed in the United States of America

Introduction

BY THE MID-NINETEENTH CENTURY Cincinnati was the center for western printing and publishing, and it ranked as the fourth largest publishing center in the United States. Printing had first come to Cincinnati in 1794; two paper mills were operating on the Little Miami River by 1811; and a typefoundry was established there in 1820. Of the city's 132,000 inhabitants in 1851 many were engaged in the book trade: Charles Cist's *Cincinnati in 1851* records 6 publishers, 9 newspaper publishers, 26 editors, 43 booksellers, 298 printers as well as 10 lithographers, 23 typefounders, 4 stereotypers, and 4 woodtype cutters. These figures, of course, do not represent semi-skilled workers, transient journeymen, and others only casually or marginally employed in these professions. *Trübner's Bibliographical Guide to American Literature* (London, 1855) suggests that by 1850 the city had twelve publishing houses employing about 700 people. Cincinnati had come to be known to nineteenth-century writers as the "Athens of the West" or—perhaps more accurately—the "Literary Emporium of the West."

But in a city so strategically located on the route to the frontier, it was job printing that flourished above all else: the demand for it was insatiable. According to the *American Dictionary of Printing and Bookselling* (New York, 1894) "about 1845 railway and steamboat printing became an important

Introduction

element in the business, and in color-work this city [Cincinnati] and Buffalo were the centres until after the beginning of the Civil War." In addition, Cincinnati became the new home for many German immigrants, some of whom were well acquainted with European advances in printing technology. When printing instruction was needed here, it was not so much in book composition as in jobbing work—emphasizing the skills of precise presswork, ornamental typography, and color work for railroads, entertainment advertisers, playing card manufacturers, and so on.

This is what distinguishes Thomas Lynch's *The Printer's Manual: A Practical Guide for Compositors and Pressmen*, first published by the Cincinnati Type-Foundry in 1859. As the distributor of type and printing equipment to printers west of the Alleghenies, the Cincinnati Type-Foundry must have realized that there was a need for a down-to-earth, concise, practical manual for the small jobbing printer. Advertisements for *The Printer's Manual* alongside ads for miscellaneous printers' supplies in the foundry's specimen books of 1862, 1864, and 1872 firmly link the manual with the day-to-day operations of the small jobbing shop. When clients demanded more sophisticated printing from such a shop, the printer would be likely to turn to an up-to-date technical manual for guidance. In Philadelphia the L. Johnson & Co. typefoundry had quite successfully published repeated editions of Thomas F. Adams's *Typographia*: apparently, the Cincinnati Type-Foundry saw enough of a market among their customers to venture one of their own.

Few biographical details can be found about the itinerant Cincinnati printer known to the local trade as "Little Tommy Lynch." The major study of the city's printing and publishing,

Introduction

Walter Sutton's *The Western Book Trade: Cincinnati as a Nineteenth-Century Publishing and Book-Trade Center* (Columbus, 1961), mentions neither Lynch nor his manual, nor is Lynch identified in the excellent "Directory of Cincinnati Publishers, Booksellers, and Members of the Allied Trades, 1796–1880" included in that study. City directories record that Lynch worked at four different shops between 1851 and 1861 alone. This frequent movement probably says as much about the fluid nature of the printing trade in Cincinnati as it does about Lynch's transient working habits. Yet, Lynch must have achieved a certain amount of respect among his peers. An obituary notice in the San Francisco trade magazine *Printing: A Journal of the Graphic Arts* (November, 1889) mentioned that he was "secretary of the old Franklin Society, that preceded the Typographical Union." The *Cincinnati Commercial Gazette* of August 28, 1889, reported that Thomas F. Lynch, aged 68, had recently died of exhaustion. *Printing* had it that he died on August 28, aged 73. This minor discrepancy comprises our basic biographical information on Lynch.

Printers' manuals are notorious for the amount of material borrowed from earlier writers. The printing trade in nineteenth-century America was jealous and conservative, much more interested in reinforcing its traditions than in encouraging original writing on its craft skills. Lynch's manual is extraordinary in this respect, being deliberately outside the Moxon-Stower-Johnson-Adams-MacKellar printing manual tradition. Most noticeably, Lynch differs from the usual east coast manuals by providing absolutely no information on the history of printing. He appends instructions on the "manner of putting together and using printing-machines" but shows no concern for the historical development of the equipment.

Introduction

One presumes that his audience felt the same way. By Lynch's own estimation three fourths of his manual is original—which means that the rest is quoted directly and appears within quotation marks. In fact, there are some unattributed passages as well as certain charts, diagrams, and passages borrowed in part from other works. Still, Lynch's manual is remarkably original. The works that he does credit are current technical publications, not reprinted typographical lore. Since Lynch's references to them in his preface are quite abbreviated, I will list his acknowledged sources as follows:

> William Savage. *Practical Hints on Decorative Printing* (London, 1822).
>
> ———. *On the Preparation of Printing Ink, Both Black and Coloured* (London, 1832).
>
> ———. *A Dictionary of the Art of Printing* (London, 1841).
>
> Théotiste Lefèvre. *Guide pratique du compositeur d'imprimerie* (Paris, 1855).
>
> Wilhelm Hasper. *Handbuch der Buchdruckerkunst* (Carlsruhe and Baden, 1835).
>
> Michel Eugène Chevreul. *De la loi du contraste simultané des couleurs, et de l'assortiment des objets colorés, considéré d'après cette loi* (Paris, 1839).

It is interesting to compare Lynch with the two leading manuals of the period: Thomas F. Adams's *Typographia* (various editions between 1837 and 1864) and Thomas MacKellar's *The American Printer* (eighteen editions between 1866 and 1893). Lynch's manual is strong on technical detail—making composition rollers, printing engravings, cleaning type, thinning inks—but is short on the actual running of the business. For example, Lynch includes no material on bookkeeping, warehouse controls, or management. Adams, on the other hand, devotes separate chapters to the overseer's department and to the warehouse department. Lynch's emphasis is on jobbing work. A section on setting tables and columns (not found in Adams or MacKellar) is evidence that printers, especially those in Cincinnati, had begun to supply railroad and steamship timetables at a significant profit.

This trade also created a demand for color printing. Mixing inks and the techniques of color presswork are major topics for Lynch, who devotes over thirty pages to color printing; Adams and MacKellar have fewer than ten pages each. Although Lynch borrows extensively from Savage, he is breaking new ground simply by including this information in a practical manual. By emphasizing color work Lynch demonstrates the importance of Cincinnati in this field, anticipates a trend in popular taste, and prefigures two important Cincinnati publications with a similar emphasis: Oscar H. Harpel's *Typograph, or Book of Specimens* (1870) and John Earhart's *The Color Printer* (1892).

When the first edition was published in 1859, the copyright was recorded at the Clerk's Office of the District Court for the Southern District of Ohio on March 17, 1859, under the name of the Cincinnati Type-Foundry. The copyright deposit copy at the Library of Congress is dated May 5, 1860. A second edition was brought out in 1864, and this version was reprinted in 1866 and 1872. In the preface to the second edition Lynch remarks: "It was intended to reset the whole work in larger sized types, and to remodel the reading-matter; but, the state of the country being such that we know not what a day may bring forth, it is thought best to make the issue without other than minor alterations." In fact, the alterations were anything but minor. The first edition was abridged by some thirty-six pages, eliminating the greater part of the "Addenda" and with it the section on erecting and using printing presses. Also deleted from the first edition were the paper-use tables on page 235. Lynch inserted a "Table of Signatures," perhaps because the first edition had been criticized for slighting book work.

An intriguing aspect of the preface to the second edition is Lynch's announcement of a supplementary publication containing twenty-six colored diagrams and a series of "practical examples of the best manner of setting up title-pages, cards, rule and figure work, and job work generally." It was designed to be used with either the first or second editions of *The Printer's Manual*. There is no evidence that this volume was ever published, but it again associates Lynch with the color printing tradition in Cincinnati.

The following libraries have reported holding copies of *The Printer's Manual*.

1859 (1st ed.)	Graphic Arts Technical Foundation (Pittsburgh, Pennsylvania); Library of Congress; Columbia University
1864 (2nd ed.)	Harvard University; Kemble Collections of the California Historical Society
1866 (reprint)	New York Public Library; William Andrews Clark Memorial Library
1872 (reprint)	Library of Congress; Harvard University; Cincinnati Public Library; Syracuse University; Columbia University

Although not as often reprinted as Adams or MacKellar, *The Printer's Manual* was received well enough by printers in the west to be kept in print for more than thirteen years. We know little about Lynch, but through his work we have a glimpse of a hardworking journeyman printer who over a lifetime in the trade developed practical printing techniques

Introduction

and then had the good sense to write them down. *The Printer's Manual* speaks well (albeit modestly) for its author—and for itself. In their *Bibliography of Printing* (1880–1886) Bigmore & Wyman sum up the merits of this manual accurately and neatly: "Contains some excellent technical instruction on punctuation, materials, jobbing, imposition, press-work, and inks."

PETER M. VANWINGEN

THE

PRINTER'S MANUAL

A PRACTICAL GUIDE

FOR

COMPOSITORS AND PRESSMEN

BY THOMAS LYNCH

TO WHICH IS APPENDED THE MANNER OF PUTTING TOGETHER AND USING

PRINTING-MACHINES

CINCINNATI
PUBLISHED BY THE CINCINNATI TYPE-FOUNDRY
1859

Entered, according to Act of Congress, in the year 1859, by

THE CINCINNATI TYPE-FOUNDRY,

In the Clerk's Office of the District Court of the United States,
for the Southern District of Ohio.

ELECTROTYPED
At the Cincinnati Type-Foundry.

PREFACE.

In preparing this work the author has been compelled to throw aside almost every typographia that has heretofore appeared, as they have been, with one or two exceptions, mere reprints of the works of Smith and Luckombe, and describe the trade as practiced a hundred years ago. The only books from which any assistance has been derived are Mr. Savage's three works: Decorative Printing, Treatise on the Preparation of Printing Inks, and Dictionary of the Art of Printing; Lefevre's Guide Pratique du Compositeur d'Imprimerie; Hasper's Handbuch der Buchdruckerkunst; and Chevreul on Colors; the remainder, comprising fully three-fourths, having been set up without copy of any kind whatever.

The subjects are arranged, in their proper order, under the following heads :

Punctuation. — Comma, Semi-Colon, Colon, Period, Dash, Interrogation, Exclamation, Words containing *ei* and *ie*, Words ending in *-ing*, *-ed*, and *-er* or *-or*, Retention of *e* in Derivatives, Plurals, Division of Words, and Compound Words.

Phrases and Signs. — Latin and French Phrases, useful Abbreviations, Astronomical Signs, Algebraical Signs, Geometrical Signs, Medical Signs, Roman Numerals, Commercial Abbreviations, Accents and other marks, and Elisions.

Material. — Types, Rules, Mitering, Leads, Quotations, Furniture, etc.

Composition. — Cases, Casing the Letter, Distributing, Copy, and Composing.

Imposing. — Making Margin, Cutting Furniture, Locking Up, Taking Proof, Correcting, and the Schedule.

Job-Work. — Title-Pages, Tables or Columns, Stereotyping, and Electrotyping.

Newspapers. — The european and american methods of getting them out.

Press-Work. — Press, Tympan, Ink, Paper, Making the Form Ready, Washing the Form, Pressing the Sheets, Making Rollers, and Preserving Rollers.

Printing-Inks. — Material and Implements, Black Ink, Colored Inks, Changeable Inks, Indelible Ink, Primary Colors and Compounds, etc.

Dry-Colors. — Metal-Leaf and Bronzes, Smalts, Flock, Printing by the Hot Method, Chromotype-Printing, and Embossed Printing.

Addenda. — Giving out Paper, Dimensions of Printing Paper, Fractional Parts of a Bundle, Fractional Parts of a Ream, the Number of Lines which makes 1000 m in various Measures, Table showing the Proportions of Types in given Dimensions ; and the Composition of Algebra, Music, Greek, Hebrew, and Interlinear Work.

Technical Terms. — None are given but those now in use. This division also makes a General Index to the preceding matter, by giving the page at which any subject may be found.

Printing-Machines. — An article, upon this subject, written by a practical machinist, is inserted at the end of the work.

There are some peculiarities in the execution of the work, which it may be necessary to notice. These are : putting a space between the points and the words which precede them ; because the points belong to the sentences, and not to any particular words ; the use of the hyphen at the end of words which are compound and have the latter part understood ; the leaving capital letters out of proper names when they become adjectives, so as to make the work appear uniform, as usage has made many words of this class take lower-case letters ; and the setting of the title-page without points, to prevent a broken appearance.

PRINTER'S MANUAL.

PUNCTUATION.

THIS being a subject on which no two grammarians can agree, it must not be expected that the rules hereinafter laid down, will be found to suit every body. The reasons for giving them in the concise form in which they appear are twofold: in the first place, it is not likely that, in the present transition-state of the english language, any definite rules can be given; and, in the second, the number of pages which it would occupy can be filled with matter of far more practical use to the trade.

The division of words gives the compositor as much trouble as punctuation; because, the rules laid down are so indeterminate, and the exceptions so numerous that they can not be applied to many other words than those given as examples in the grammars; yet, as divisions must often be made, a few plain and practical rules will be given in this chapter.

On account of the whimsical notions of proof-readers, the compositor is subject to a great amount of annoyance and loss of time, by making needless alteration in both of the above particulars.

The spelling of doubtful words, such as those that form their plurals in *-eys* and *-ies*, the doubling of the consonant in *-ing* and *-ed*, in the present or perfect participles, and the words which contain *ei* and *ie*, will be treated, in this department, in such a manner as to remove all difficulty.

THE COMMA.

The comma (,) is the point most frequently used, and abused; therefore it will be the first treated of.

Rule I.— In a simple sentence, the several words of which it consists have, in general, so close a connection with each other, that no point is necessary, except a period at the close: as, "Every part of matter swarms with living creatures." "The western powers claimed nothing but the independence of Turkey."

Exception.— When the connection between the nominative and verb is broken by a secondary phrase, a comma should be placed before and after the minor sentence: as, "Charity, like the sun, brightens every object on which it shines." "I remember, with gratitude, his goodness to me." When these interruptions are slight and unimportant, the comma should be omitted: as, "Flattery is certainly pernicious."

EXAMPLES.

1. The book is the author's pledge to immortality.
2. The friend of order has made half his way to virtue.

Exception 1.— The weakest reasoners among my acquaintance, especially on the subject of religion, are generally the most positive.

Exception 2.— His style, in point of grammatical construction, is open to endless objection.

Rule II.— Series of words of the same part of speech should be separated by a comma: as, "The husband, wife, and children, suffered extremely." "They took away their furniture, clothes, and stock in trade." "He is alternately supported by his father, his uncle, and his elder brother."

Exception.— There is an exception to this rule; and that is, when two nouns are closely connected by a conjunction: as, "Virtue and vice form a strong contrast to each other." But, if the parts connected are long, the comma may be inserted, though the conjunction is used: as, "Romances may be said to be miserable rhapsodies, or dangerous incentives to evil." "Intemperance destroys the strength of our bodies, and the vigor of our minds."

EXAMPLES.

1. A woman, sensible, well-educated, gentle, and religious.
2. In a letter, we may advise, exhort, comfort, and request.

EXCEPTION. — But Frederic was too old and too cunning to be caught, and the ambitious and far-seeing Catharine had ulterior views of her own.

RULE III. — When words in the same construction are joined in pairs by a conjunction, they are separated in pairs by a comma: as, "Hope and fear, pleasure and pain, diversify our lives."

EXAMPLE.

A christian spirit may be manifested either to Greek or Jew, male or female, friend or foe.

RULE IV. — Expressions in a direct address, the nominative absolute, and the participle absolute, are separated by commas from the remainder of the sentence: as, "Come hither, William." "His father dying, he succeeded to the estate." "To do her justice, she was a good-natured, sensible, reasonable woman." "Properly speaking, he is guilty of falsehood."

EXAMPLES.

1. John, will you obtain the work from the library?
2. The city being taken, we fortified it with great care.

RULE V. — Nouns in apposition, when accompanied with adjuncts, and nouns qualified by participles or adjectives with dependent words, should be separated by a comma: as, "Paul, the apostle of the gentiles, was eminent for his zeal and knowledge." "The president, approving the plan, put it in execution." "But he, anxious to refer the cause to arbitration, refused."

Exception. — If such nouns are single, or form only a proper name, they are not divided: as, "Paul the apostle suffered martyrdom."

EXAMPLES.

1. That distinguished traveler, Dr. Livingston, was at the meeting of the geological society.
2. Humboldt, the great philosopher, resides at Berlin.
EXCEPTION. — Wellington the statesman died in 1851.

RULE VI. — When sentences contain correlative words, and have each a nominative and verb expressed, they are separated by a comma: as, "Better is a dinner of herbs with love, than a stalled ox and hatred with it."

Exception. — If the members in comparative sentences

are short, the comma is, in general, better omitted: as, "How much easier is it to get gold than wisdom." "Mankind act oftener from caprice than reason."

EXAMPLES.

1. As virtue is its own reward, so vice is its own punishment.
2. How much easier is it to go with the popular current, than it is to oppose public opinion.

EXCEPTION.— The child in the humble walks of life, is as richly gifted as the highest.

RULE VII.— When words are placed in opposition to each other, or have some marked relation, they require to be separated by a comma: as, "Good men, in their frail, imperfect state, are not always found in union with, but sometimes in opposition to, the views and conduct of each other."

EXAMPLES.

1. The goods of this world were given to man for his occasional refreshment, not for his chief felicity.
2. It is the province of superiors to direct, of inferiors to obey.

RULE VIII.— An important expression, or a short observation, somewhat resembling a quotation, may be properly marked, with a comma: as, "It hurts a man's pride to say, I do not know." "It may be laid down as a truth, that adversity is our best teacher."

EXAMPLES.

1. Vice is not of such a nature that we can say to it, thus far shalt thou go, and no farther.
2. We are strictly enjoined, not to follow a multitude to do evil.

RULE IX.— Relative pronouns generally admit a comma before them, except when closely connected with the antecedent: as, "There is no charm in the female sex, which can supply the place of virtue." "A man, who is of a detracting spirit, will misconstrue the most innocent words that can be put together."

EXAMPLES.

1. The gentle mind is like the still stream, which reflects every object in its just proportions and in its fairest colors.
2. He, who is good before invisible witnesses, is eminently so before the visible.

RULE X. — When an infinitive mode can, by transposition, be made the nominative case, it should be separated from the verb by a comma: as, "The most obvious remedy is, to withdraw from all associations with bad men."

EXAMPLES.

1. It ill becomes good and wise men, to oppose and degrade each other.
2. Charles's highest enjoyment was, to relieve the distressed and to do good.

RULE XI. — When a verb is understood, a comma may often be properly introduced: as, "From law arises security; from security, curiosity; from curiosity, knowledge."

EXAMPLES.

1. If spring puts forth no blossoms, in summer there will be no beauty, and in autumn, no fruit: so, if youth be trifled away, without improvement, manhood will be contemptible, and old age miserable.
2. As a companion he was severe and satirical; as a friend, captious and dangerous; in his domestic sphere, harsh and irascible.

RULE XII. — The words: *nay, so, why, again, first, secondly, formerly, now, lastly, once more, above all, on the contrary, in the next place, in short,* and all other words and phrases of the same kind, must, as a general rule, be separated from the context by a comma: as, "First, I shall state the proposition, and, secondly, I shall endeavor to prove it." "Remember thy best and first friend; formerly, the supporter of thy infancy and the guide of thy childhood; now, the guardian of thy youth and the hope of thy coming years."

EXAMPLES.

1. On the other hand, be not self-confident.
2. His high reputation, undoubtedly, contributed to his success.

RULE XIII. — A simple member of a sentence, contained within or following another, must be distinguished by a comma: as, "She may still exist in undiminished vigor, when some traveler from New-Zealand shall, in the midst of a vast solitude, take his stand on London bridge to sketch the ruins of St. Paul's."

EXAMPLE.

1. If we delay until tomorrow what ought to be done today, we overcharge the morrow with a burden which belongs not to it.

THE SEMICOLON.

The semicolon (;) is placed between the members of a sentence which are not so closely connected as those which are separated by a comma.

1. A semicolon is placed between two parts of a sentence, when these are divided, according to the preceding rules, into smaller portions: as, "At a later period, when he possessed an ample fortune, he was one of the most liberal of men; but, until his means had become equal to his wishes, his greediness was unrestrained either by justice or by shame."

2. A semicolon is placed between two clauses, one of which is explanatory of the other: as, "Evidence for the imputation there was scarcely any; unless reports, wandering from one mouth to another, and gaining credence by every transmission, may be called evidence."

3. Short sentences, slightly connected, are separated by a semicolon: as, "The advance of civilization among the Indians can be known by these sure and unmistakable signs: the entrance of the missionary; his entrance closely followed by the whisky-jug; this, by thieving; and this, by that great conservator of the public, the common jail."

EXAMPLES.

1. We can not give a distinct name to every object which we perceive, nor to every thought which passes through the mind; nor are these thoughts, or even these objects, so entirely distinct to human conception as many persons are apt to imagine. If I see a horse today, and another tomorrow, the conceptions which I form of these different objects are, indeed, dissimilar in some respects, but in others they agree.

2. Life, with a swift though insensible course, glides away; and, like the river which undermines its banks, gradually impairs our state.

3. Philosophers assert, that nature is unlimited in her operations; that she has inexhaustible treasures in reserve; that knowledge will always be progressive; and that all future generations will continue to make discoveries of which we have not the least idea.

THE COLON.

The colon (:) is used to divide a sentence into two or more parts, less connected than those separated by a semicolon, but not so independent as distinct sentences.

1. When a member of a sentence is complete in itself, but followed by some supplementary remark, or further illustration of the subject, the colon is used: as, "A brute arrives at a point of development that he can never pass: in a few years he has all the endowments he is capable of; and, were he to live ten thousand more, he would be the same thing that he is at present."

2. The colon is also used when one or more semicolons have preceded, and a pause, still greater than a semicolon, is needed to render clear the connection and distinctness of each individual portion of the complex sentence, which they together form: as, "As we perceive the shadow to have moved along the dial, but did not see it moving; and it appears the grass has grown, though nobody ever saw it grow: so the advances we make in knowledge, as they consist of such insensible steps, are perceivable only by the distance."

3. The colon is commonly used when an example, a question, or a speech is introduced: as, "He was often heard to say: 'I have done with the world, and am ready to leave it.'"

EXAMPLES.

1. For the training of goodness, the ancient reliance was on the right discipline of habit and affection: the modern is rather on the illumination of the understanding.

2. When we look forward to the year which is beginning, what do we behold there? All, my brethren, is a blank to our view: a dark unknown presents itself.

3. All our conduct, towards men, should be influenced by this important precept: "Do unto others as you would others should do unto you."

THE PERIOD.

When a sentence is complete, independent, and unconnected, in construction, with the following one, it is marked with a period (.).

1. Some sentences are independent of each other, both in their sense and construction: as, "Have charity toward all men." Others are independent only in their grammatical construction: as, "Worldly happiness ever tends to destroy itself, by corrupting the heart. It fosters the loose and the violent passions. It engenders noxious habits, and

taints the mind with false delicacy, which makes it feel a thousand unreal evils."

2. A period may sometimes be admitted between two sentences, though they are joined by a copulative or disjunctive conjunction; for the quality of the point does not always depend on the connective particle, but on the construction of the sentences: as, "Recreations, though they may be of an innocent kind, require steady government, to keep them within a due and limited province. But such as are of an irregular and vicious nature are not to be governed, but to be banished from every well-regulated mind."

3. The period should be used after every abbreviated word: as, Dec., Mr., N.B., A.D., etc.

EXAMPLES.

1. Self-control is promoted by humanity. Pride is a fruitful source of uneasiness. It keeps the mind in disquiet. Humility is the antidote to this evil.

2. Thought engenders thought. Place one idea upon your paper: another will follow it, and still another, until you have written a page. You can not fathom your mind. There is a well of thought there, which has no bottom. The more you draw from it, the more clear and fruitful it will be.

3. The key to every man is his thought. Sturdy and defying though he looks, he has a helm which he obeys: it is the idea after which all his thoughts are classified. He can be reformed only by showing him a new idea, which commands his own.

THE DASH.

1. The dash (—), though often used improperly by hasty and incoherent writers, may be introduced with propriety, where the sentence breaks off abruptly, where a a significant pause is required, or where there is an unexpected turn in the sentiment: as, "If thou art he, so much respected once — but, oh, how fallen! how degraded!" "There was to be a stern death-grapple between might and right — between the heavy arm and the ethereal thought — between that which was and that which ought to be."

2. The dash should also be used, when conversations are printed without making each question and reply a separate paragraph, so as to cut off each pair from the preceding and succeeding one: as, "Are you the man who owns this wood?" "Yes, I am." — "Well, I am the gentleman who wishes to saw it."

EXAMPLES.

1. She was great and respected, before the Saxon had set foot on Brit ain — before the Frank had passed the Rhine — when grecian eloquence still flourished at Antioch — when idols were still worshiped in the temple of Mecca.
2. "Is Mr. Frazer at home?" "No, sir, he an't."—"Where is he gone to?" "I'm sure, sir, I can't tell."—"Is his servant in the way?" "No, sir, the other gentleman's gone, too."

THE INTERROGATION.

1. A note of interrogation (?) is used at the end of an interrogative sentence; that is, when a question is asked: as, "Who will accompany me?" "Shall we always be friends?"

2. A note of interrogation should not be employed in cases where it is only stated a question has been asked, but where the words are not used as a question: as, "The Cyprians asked me why I wept." To give this sentence the interrogative form, it should be expressed thus: "The Cyprians said to me, 'Why do you weep?'"

As it is often the case that persons, in reading an interrogative sentence, do not find it to be such until they come to the point at the end, it would be far better if we could, as the spanish writers and printers do, place the point at the beginning of the interrogative sentence: as, instead of "What time is it?" to put it thus: "¿What time is it."

EXAMPLES.

1. When will you return from New-York?
2. Can our curiosity pierce through the clouds, which nature has made impenetrable to mortal eye?

THE EXCLAMATION.

The note of exclamation (!) is applied to expressions of sudden emotion, surprise, joy, grief, etc., and also to invocations or addresses: as, "My friend! this conduct amazes me!" "How are the mighty fallen!"

When the interjection *oh* is used, the point is generally placed immediately after it; but, when *O* is employed, the point is placed immediately after one or more intervening words: as, "But thou, O hope! with eyes so fair." "Oh! my offence is rank; it smells to heaven."

EXAMPLES.

1. To lie down on the pillow, after a day spent in temperance, how sweet is it!
2. Gripus has long been endeavoring to fill his chest, and, lo! it is now full.

It is difficult, in some cases, to distinguish between interrogatory and exclamatory sentences; but a sentence in which any wonder or admiration is expressed, and no answer is either expressed or implied, may be properly terminated by a note of exclamation: as, "How much vanity in the pursuits of men!" "What is more lovely than virtue!"

The interrogation and exclamation points are indeterminate as to their quantity, or time; and may be equivalent, in that respect, to a comma, a semicolon, or a period, as the sense may require. They mark an elevation of the voice.

The utility of the interrogation and exclamation points will appear, from the following examples, in which the meaning is signified as discriminated solely by the points:

EXAMPLES.

1. What do you think? I'll shave you for nothing and give you a drink!
2. What! do you think I'll shave you for nothing and give you a drink?

OTHER POINTS AND MARKS.

The parentheses ( ) are used to enclose a word or clause not essential to the sentence, but introduced to make it more explicit; and which may be omitted without injury to the meaning: as, "To gain a posthumous reputation is to save four or five letters, (for what is a name besides?) from oblivion."

The parenthesis may be accompanied by any point which the sense may require. It should terminate with the same kind of a point which the preceding member does, and it should be placed outside the parenthetic mark. If an interrogation or exclamation should be required, it must be considered an exception to this rule.

Brackets [ ] enclose a word or sentence which is to be explained in a note, or the explanation itself, or a word or sentence which is intended to supply some deficiency or rectify some mistake: as, "He [Mr. Canning] was of a different opinion."

The asterisk (*), dagger (†), double-dagger (‡), and parallel (‖) are called marks of reference; and are used in the body of printed works, to call the attention of the reader to notes, with similar marks, at the bottom of the page.

The section (§) and paragraph (¶) were used, originally, to mark where change of subject, and breaklines should occur. The paragraph is the only one now in use, and that in the bible merely, to distinguish the paragraph from the breakline at the end of each verse.

WORDS CONTAINING *EI* AND *IE*.

As the spelling of words containing *ei* and *ie*, when these diphthongs have the sound of *e* long, is a source of trouble to many compositors, the following lists have been inserted, so as to save the trouble of referring, for each word, to a dictionary:

Words containing EI.

cell	deceit	either	seignor
ceiling	deceive	neither	sein
conceit	perceive	obeisance	seize
conceive	disseize	receive	seizure

Words containing IE.

achieve	fief	lien	retrieve
aggrieve	field	mien	shield
belief	fiend	niece	shriek
believe	fierce	piece	siege
bombardier	financier	pier	thief
brief	grenadier	pierce	thieve
brevier	grieve	priest	tier
brigadier	grievous	relief	tierce
cavalier	lief	relieve	wield
chief	liege	relievo	yield

WORDS ENDING IN -*ING*, -*ED*, AND -*ER* OR -*OR*.

Monosyllables, and words accented on the last syllable, ending in a single consonant preceded by a single vowel, generally double the final consonant on taking an additional syllable beginning with a vowel: as,

abet	abetting	abetted	abettor
fret	fretting	fretted	fretter
plan	planning	planned	planner
trepan	trepanning	trepanned	trepanner

When a diphthong precedes the final letter, or when the accent is not on the last syllable, the consonant is not doubled on assuming an additional syllable: as,

seal	sealing	sealed	sealer
repeat	repeating	repeated	repeater
cool	cooling	cooled	cooler
level	leveling	leveled	leveler
travel	traveling	traveled	traveler
worship	worshiping	worshiped	worshiper
pilfer	pilfering	pilfered	pilferer

RETENTION OF *E* IN DERIVATIVES.

Words ending in -*ce* and -*ge* retain the *e* before -*able* and -*ous*, to preserve the soft sound of *c* and *g*: as,

Peaceable.. Changeable.. Outrageous.. Courageous..

PLURALS.

Nouns ending in -*y*, preceded by a consonant, and those ending in -*quy*, form their plurals by changing *y* into *i* and adding *es*, making -*ies*: as,

| fly | flies | duty | duties | city | cities |
| cry | cries | ruby | rubies | colloquy | colloquies |

Nouns ending in -*y* preceded by a vowel, generally retain the *y* in forming the plural: as,

| day | days | delay | delays | attorney | attorneys |
| valley | valleys | money | moneys | boy | boys |

A large number of foreign words retain, in the english language, the plural form they have in the languages from which they have been borrowed. The following list comprises the greater part of them:

SINGULAR.	PLURAL.	SINGULAR.	PLURAL.
antithesis	antitheses	focus	foci
appendix	appendices	genus	genera
arcanum	arcana	hypothesis	hypotheses
automaton	automata	larva	larvæ
axis	axes	madam	mesdames
basis	bases	magus	magi
beau	beaux	medium	media
calx	calces	metamorphosis	metamorphoses
crisis	crises	minutia	minutiæ
criterion	criteria	monsieur	messieurs
datum	data	stamen	stamina
effluvium	effluvia	stratum	strata
ellipsis	ellipses	parenthesis	parentheses
ephemeris	ephemerides	phenomenon	phenomena
erratum	errata	vortex	vortices

There are other words, taken from foreign languages, which have two plurals; one formed after the english manner, and the other, that which they had in the language from which they were taken: as,

SINGULAR.	ENGLISH PLURAL.	FOREIGN PLURAL.
bandit	bandits	banditti
cherub	cherubs	cherubim
dogma	dogmas	dogmata
genius	geniuses	genii
index	indexes	indices
memorandum	memorandums	memoranda
rabbi	rabbis	rabbins
seraph	seraphs	seraphim
virtuoso	virtuosos	virtuosi

When a title and a name are used together, some grammarians suggest that the title only should have the plural form: as, the *Misses Glover;* others, that both should have the plural form: as, the *Misses Glovers;* and others, that the name only need have the plural form: as, the *Miss Glovers*. The last is the correct form, if the two words are viewed as a compound term; the first, if they are viewed as in opposition; the second, if they are viewed as in classical languages. The last — namely, the *Miss Glovers* — is sanctioned by the highest authorities.

Compounds, consisting of two or more words connected by a hyphen, are generally composed of two nouns, one of which is used in the sense of an adjective: as, *man-trap*, where *man* is really an adjective; or, of a noun and adjective, as *court-martial;* or, of a noun and some expression having the force of an adjective, as *father-in-law*, where *-in-law* has the force of an adjective as much as *legal*. In all compounds of this class, the plural sign is added to that part of the word which really constitutes the noun, whether at the end or not: as,

Man-traps.. Courts-martial.. Fathers-in-law.. Cousins-german.. Queen-consorts..

In forming the possessive case, the rule is different; the sign being, in all cases, placed at the end of the compound expression: as,

SINGULAR.	PLURAL.	POSSESSIVE.
father-in-law	fathers-in-law	father-in-law's

While writing of the possessive, it may be as well to remark, that proper names, which end with an *s*, should have an additional *s* placed after the apostrophe, when the singular is to be designated; but, when the plural ought to be indicated, the apostrophe should be used without the additional letter: as,

SINGULAR.	PLURAL.
Thomas's book.	Jones' store.

If they are not distinguished by some method like this, there will be no way of ascertaining whether one or more persons are intended to be indicated.

DIVISION OF WORDS.

As a compositor who wishes to space his lines uniformly will have to make divisions, and that very often, (especially when the types are large and the measure is narrow,) the method of doing so will be made as plain as it is possible to make any subject upon which no two persons have the same opinion. In doing this, it will be seen that, dividing according to derivation, instead of sound, has been followed; because, if the latter method is adopted, the same combination of letters will have to be divided differently, according to the situation of the accent.

I. PREFIXES.

1st.—English.

When either of the prefixes: *be-, down-, ever-, for-, fore-, gain-, how-, mis-, out-, some-, un-, under-, up-,* and *with-,* commences a word, and it is necessary to make a division, it may be done after the prefix: as,

Be-speak.. Be-tween.. Down-right.. Ever-more.. For-give.. Fore-tell.. Gain-say.. How-ever.. Mis-take.. Out-leap.. Some-where.. Un-able.. Under-stand.. Up-root.. With-out..

2nd.—Latin.

When the prefixes: *ante-, circum-, contra-, co-, col-, com-, con-, cor-, de-, dis-, extra-, in-, il-, im-, inter-, intro-, ob-, per-, post-, pre-, pro-, retro-, sub-, subter-, super-,* and *trans-,* occur, it is better to divide at the end of such prefix, than at any other place: as,

Ante-cedent.. Circum-stance.. Contra-band.. Co-temporary.. Col-lect.. Com-bustion.. Con-sonant.. Cor-respond.. De-scription.. Dis-advantage.. Extra-vagance.. In-equality.. Il-legal.. Im-mortal.. Inter-fere.. Intro-duce.. Ob-struct.. Per-fect.. Post-humous.. Pre-judge.. Pro-ceed.. Retro-spect.. Sub-altern.. Subter-fluent.. Super-intendent.. Trans-marine..

The word *illness* does not belong to this class, both parts of the word being english.

3rd.—Greek.

The Greek prefixes: *ana-, amphi-, anti-, apo-, dia-, epi-, hyper-, hypo-, meta-, para-, peri-, syl-, sym-,* and *syn-,* can also be divided from the other part of the word: as,

Ana-baptist.. Amphi-bious.. Anti-dote.. Apo-gee.. Dia-metre.. Epi-logue.. Hyper-bole.. Hypo-crisy.. Meta-morphose.. Para-graph.. Peri-phrase.. Syl-logism.. Sym-pathy.. Syn-onymous..

II. TERMINATIONS.

1st.—Terminations generally.

When the terminations: *-dom, -ever, -fold, -ful, -fully, -fulness, -hood, -kind, -less, -lessness, -like, -ly, -man (-men), -ment, -ness, -out, -self (-selves), -ship, -some, -th, -teenth, -ty, -ward, -where, -wise, -woman (-women),* occur, such ending may be cut off from the rest of the word, and put at the beginning of the next line: as,

Free-dom.. What-ever.. Four-fold.. Health-ful.. Faith-fully.. Faith-fulness.. Child-hood.. Man-kind.. Friend-less.. Friend-lessness.. War-like.. Great-ly.. English-man (men).. Frag-ment.. Good-ness.. Through-out.. My-self.. Them-selves.. Friend-ship.. Tire-some. Thir-teen.. Fif-teenth.. For-ty.. Back-ward.. No-where.. Other-wise.. Gentle-woman (women)..

2nd —Termination -*ing*.

If it is necessary to divide a word ending with this termination, it can be done, provided the preceding part of the word has undergone no change on account of the addition of this syllable: as,

Concern-ing.. Meet-ing.. Know-ing..

But, if, in the formation of words of this class, the preceding consonant becomes duplicated, and it is necessary to divide at this point, one of the consonants doubled must be attached to the termination: as,

Abet-ting.. Wed-ding.. Abhor-ring.. Concur-ring..

3rd —Other Terminations.

Words terminating with -*able*, -*age*, -*ance*, -*ate*, or any other derivative or grammatical termination, may be divided at that point, provided no preceding letter has been dropped: as,

Agree-able.. Patron-age.. Import-ance.. Proportion-ate.. Refer-ence.. Teach-er.. Teach-est..

OTHER DIVISIONS.

A single consonant between two vowels must be joined to the latter syllable: as, *de-light*, *bri-dal;* except the letter *x:* as, *ex-amine*, *ex-ist*. Words which are compounded are also exceptions: as, *up-on*.

Two consonants, proper to begin a word, must not be separated: as, *fa-ble*, *sti-fle*. But, when they come between two vowels, and are such as can not commence a word, they can be divided: as, *al-most*, *un-der*, *in-sect*, *cof-fin*. Should the preceding syllable be short, the consonants may be separated: as, *cus-tard*, *pub-lic*, *gos-ling*.

When three consonants meet in the middle of a word, if they can begin a word, and the preceding vowel is pronounced long, they can not be separated: as, *de-throne*, *de-stroy*. But, when the vowel of the preceding syllable is short, one of the consonants always belongs to that syllable: as *dis-tract*, *dis-prove*.

When three or four consonants, which are not proper to begin a word, meet between two vowels, the first consonant is always attached to the first syllable, in making a division: as, *ab-stain*, *com-plete*, *em-broil*, *dap-ple*, *con-strain*.

Two vowels, when they are not pronounced together, may be divided: as, *soci-ety*, *deni-al*.

Some persons object to the division of words at all in printing, as being unnecessary, and displeasing to the eye; but then they must sacrifice all regularity of spacing, which is still worse, and has the appearance of bad workmanship. A compositor should make each give way a little to the other, always preserving such a uniformity in spacing as will prevent any glaring disproportion in contiguous lines.

Avoid dividing words in lines following each other; because two or more hyphens at the ends of lines have a bad appearance. Proper names, sums of money, series of figures, and words or matter of like character, should not be divided.

The last word on an odd page should not be divided; because, to see the remainder of the word, a person must turn over the leaf, and thereby he will often lose the connection of the subject. When it can not be conveniently avoided, a word may be divided at the bottom of an even page; but it is better not to make such divisions, as it has, to say the least, a very slovenly appearance.

COMPOUND WORDS.

1. When each of two contiguous substantives retains its original accent, they should not be compounded: as, *mas'ter build'er*. But, when the latter loses or alters its accent, the hyphen should be inserted: as, *ship-builder*.

2. When two substantives are in apposition, and either of them is separately applicable to the person or thing designated the hyphen should be omitted: as, *knight templar*.

When they are not in apposition, and only one of the two is separately applicable to the person or thing, the hyphen should be inserted: as, *horse-dealer* — one who is a dealer, but not a horse.

3. When the first substantive serves the purpose of an adjective, expressing the matter or substance of which the second consists, and may be placed after it with *of* (not denoting possession), the hyphen should be omitted: as, *silk gown* — *i. e.*, a gown of silk. When the first does not express the matter or substance of the second, and may be placed after it with *of* (denoting possession), or with *for* or *belonging to*, the hyphen should be inserted: as, *school-master, play-time, cork-screw, laundry-maid*.

4. Between an adjective and its substantive the hyphen should be omitted: as, *high sheriff, prime minister*. When an adjective and its substantive are used as a kind of compound adjective to another substantive, the hyphen should be inserted between the former two: as, *high-church doctrine, ten-gallon keg*.

5. When an adjective, or an adverb, and a participle immediately following, are used together as a compound adjective, merely expressing an inherent quality, without reference to inherent action, and (in order of syntax) preceding the substantive to which they are joined, the hyphen should be inserted: as, *yellow-covered literature, quick-sailing vessel*. But, when they imply immediate action, and (in order of syntax) follow the substantive, the hyphen should be omitted: as, "The ship *quick sailing* o'er the deep."

PHRASES AND SIGNS.

In this division will be given an extended list of Latin and French phrases; Abbreviations generally; Astronomical, Algebraical, Geometrical, and Medical signs; a complete list of Roman numerals; Commercial abbreviations; Accents, and other signs and marks; and a collection of the Elisions in general use.

LATIN AND FRENCH PHRASES.

Ab initio.	From the beginning.
Ab urbe condita.	From the building of the city.
A capite ad calcem.	From head to foot.
Accedas ad curiam.	You may approach the bench.
Ad arbitrium.	At pleasure.
Ad captandum.	To attract.
Ad captandum vulgus.	To ensnare the vulgar.
Ad eundem.	To the same.
Ad infinitum.	To infinity.
Ad interim.	In the meantime.
Ad libitum.	At pleasure.
Ad litem.	For the action (at law).
Ad ostentationem opum.	To show off his works.
Ad referendum.	For consideration.
Ad valorem.	According to value.
Affaire de cœur.	A love affair; an amour.
Afflavit Deus et dissipantur.	God has sent forth his breath and they are dispersed.
A fin.	To the end.
A fortiori.	With stronger reason.
Aide-de-camp.	Assistant to a general.
A la bonne heure.	At an early hour; in the nick of time.

A la-mode.	In the fashion.
Alias.	Otherwise.
Alibi.	Elsewhere; or, proof of having been elsewhere.
Alma mater.	Kind mother.
A mensa et thoro.	From bed and board.
Amor patriae.	The love of our country.
Anglicè.	In English.
Anno Domini.	In the year of our Lord.
Anno mundi.	In the year of the world.
Anguillam cauda tenes.	You hold an eel by the tail.
A posteriori.	From a later reason; or, from behind.
A priori.	From a prior reason.
A propos.	To the purpose; seasonably, or, by-the-by.
Arcana.	Secrets.
Arcana imperii.	State secrets.
Argumentum ad fidem.	An appeal to our faith.
Argumentum ad hominem.	Personal argument.
Argumentum ad judicium.	An appeal to the common sense of mankind.
Argumentum ad passiones.	An appeal to the passions.
Argumentum ad populum.	An appeal to the people.
Argumentum baculinum.	Argument of blows.
Arrectis auribus.	With ears pricked up.
Ars est celare artem.	It is the hight of art to conceal art.
Audi alteram partem.	Hear both sides.
Au fond.	To the bottom; or, main point.
Auri sacra fames.	The accursed thirst for gold.
Aut Caesar aut nullus.	He will be Cæsar or nobody.
Auto-da-fé.	Act of faith.
Bagatelle.	Trifle.
Beau monde.	People of fashion.
Beaux esprits.	Men of wit.
Belles lettres.	Polite literature.
Billet doux.	Love letter.
Bon gré.	With a good grace.
Bon jour.	Good day.
Bon mot.	A witty saying.

Bon ton.	Fashion; high fashion.
Bona fide.	In good faith.
Boudoir.	A small private apartment.
Cacoethes carpendi.	A rage for collecting.
Cacoethes loquendi.	A rage for speaking.
Cacoethes scribendi.	Passion for writing.
Caeteris paribus.	Other circumstances being equal.
Caput mortuum.	(The dead head). The worthless remains.
Carte blanche.	Unconditional terms.
Caveat emptor.	Let the buyer beware.
Cessio bonorum.	Yielding up of goods.
Château.	Country seat.
Chef-d'œuvre.	Master piece.
Ci-devant.	Formerly.
Comme il faut.	As it should be.
Commune bonum.	A common good.
Communibus annis.	One year with another.
Compos mentis.	Of a sound and composed mind.
Con amore.	Gladly; with love.
Concordia discors.	A discordant harmony.
Congé d'élire.	Permission to choose or elect.
Consensus facit legem.	Consent makes the law.
Contra.	Against.
Contra bonos mores.	Against good manners or morals.
Coup de grace.	Finishing stroke.
Coup de main.	Sudden enterprise.
Coup d'œil.	View, or glance.
Credat Judaeus.	A Jew may believe it (but I will not).
Cui bono?	To what good will it tend?
Cui malo?	To what evil will it tend?
Cum multis aliis.	With many others.
Cum privilegio.	With privilege.
Curia advisari vult.	Court wishes to be advised.
Currente calamo.	With a running quill.
Custos rotulorum.	Keeper of the rolls.
Datum.	Point granted.
Début.	Beginning.
De die in diem.	From day to day.

Dedimus potestatem.	We have given power.
De facto.	In fact.
Dei gratia.	By the grace or favor of God.
De jure.	By right.
De mortuis nil nisi bonum.	Of the dead let nothing be said but what is favorable.
De novo.	Anew.
Dénouement.	(Unraveling). Winding up.
Deo volente.	God willing.
Dépôt.	Store, or magazine.
Dernier ressort.	Last resort or resource.
Desideratum.	A thing desired.
Desunt caetera.	The other things are wanting.
Détour.	A circuitous route.
Dextro tempore.	At a favorable moment.
Dieu et mon droit.	God and my right.
Divide et impera.	Divide and rule.
Divitae virum faciunt.	Riches make the man.
Domine, dirige nos.	O Lord, direct us.
Double entendre.	Double meaning.
Douceur.	Present, or bribe.
Dramatis personae.	Characters of the drama.
Dum lego, assentior.	While I read, I assent.
Durante bene placito.	During pleasure.
Durante vita.	During life.
Dux foemina facti.	A woman was the leader of it.
Ecce homo.	Behold the man.
Eclaircissement.	Explanation; clearing up.
Eclat.	Splendor.
Elève.	Pupil.
Embonpoint.	Jolly; in good condition.
En masse.	In a mass; in a body.
En passant.	By the way; in passing.
Ennui.	Weariness.
Entrée.	Entrance.
Ergo.	Therefore.
Errata.	Errors.
Esto perpetua.	May it last for ever.
Et caetera.	And others.
Ex.	Late; as the ex-minister means the late minister.

Ex cathedra.	(From the chair). Instructions given from a chair of authority.
Excerpta.	Extracts.
Ex nihilo nihil fit.	Nothing can come of nothing.
Ex officio.	Officially; or, by virtue of office.
Ex parte.	On the part of; or, one side.
Experto crede.	Believe one who has experience.
Ex tempore.	Out of hand; without premeditation.
Fac simile.	Exact copy or resemblance.
Fata obstant.	The fates oppose it.
Faux pas.	Fault, or misconduct.
Felo de se.	The felon of himself.
Festina lente.	Hasten slowly.
Fête.	A feast, or entertainment.
Fiat.	Let it be done or made.
Fiat justitia, ruat coelum.	Let justice be done, though the heavens should fall.
Finis.	End.
Finis coronat opus.	The end crowns the work.
Flagrante bello.	Whilst the war is raging.
Furor loquendi.	An eagerness for speaking.
Furor scribendi.	An eagerness for writing.
Genus irritabile.	The irritable tribe of poets.
Gratis.	For nothing.
Gratia gratiam parit.	Kindness begets kindness.
Habeas corpus.	You may have the body.
Hauteur.	Haughtiness.
Hic et ubique.	Here and there and everywhere.
Honi soit qui mal y pense.	Evil to him who evil thinks.
Hora fugit.	The hour, or time, flies.
Hors de combat.	Out of condition to fight.
Humanum est errare.	To err is human.
Ibidem.	In the same place.
Ich dien.	I serve.
Id est.	That is.
Idem.	The same.

Ignis fatuus.	An illusory fire.
Ignoramus.	We are ignorant.
Imperium in imperio.	One government within another.
Imprimatur.	Let it be printed.
Imprimis.	In the first place.
Impromptu.	In readiness.
In coelo quies.	There is rest in heaven.
Incognito.	Disguised, or unknown.
In commendam.	For a time; in trust.
In duplo.	Twice as much.
In extenso.	In full.
In forma pauperis.	As a pauper, or poor person.
In hoc signo vinces.	By this sign thou shalt conquer.
In loco.	In the place.
Innuendo.	By intimation or hinting.
In petto.	In the bosom; hid, or in reserve.
In propria persona.	In his own person.
In puris naturalibus.	In a state of nature.
In statu quo.	In the same state or condition in which it was.
Inter nos.	Between ourselves.
In terrorem.	In terror; as a warning.
Inter utrumque tenet.	He holds his place between both.
In toto.	Altogether.
In transitu.	On the passage.
In vino veritas.	There is truth in wine.
Ipse dixit.	Himself said it; mere assertion.
Ipso facto.	By the mere fact.
Ipso jure.	By the law itself.
Item.	Also, or article.
Je ne sais quoi.	I know not what.
Jeu de mots.	Play upon words.
Jeu d'esprit.	Play of wit; a witticism.
Jure divino.	By divine law.
Jure humano.	By human law.
Jus gentium.	The law of nations.
Labor ipse voluptas.	Even labor itself is a pleasure.
Labor omnia vincit.	Labor overcomes every thing.
L'argent.	Money, or silver.
Latet anguis in herba.	A snake lies hidden in the grass.

Lex talionis.	The law of retaliation.
Libertas et natale solum.	Liberty and my native land.
Licentia vatum.	A poetical license.
Linguae lapsus.	A slip of the tongue.
Lis litem generat.	Contention begets contention.
Locum tenens.	A substitute, a deputy.
Magna charta.	The great charter.
Magna est veritas, et praevalebit.	Truth is powerful, and will prevail.
Mal à propos.	Unseasonable, or unseasonably.
Mala fide.	In bad faith.
Malgré.	With an ill grace.
Mandamus.	We command.
Manu forti.	With a strong hand.
Mauvaise honte.	Unbecoming bashfulness.
Medice, cura te ipsum.	Doctor, cure thyself.
Meditatione fugae.	In contemplation of flight.
Memento mori.	Be mindful of death.
Memorabilia.	Things to be remembered.
Mens conscia recti.	A mind conscious of rectitude.
Meum et tuum.	Mine and thine.
Minutiae.	Trifles.
Mirabile dictu.	Wonderful to tell.
Mirabile visu.	Wonderful to be seen.
Mittimus.	We send.
Multa docet fames.	Hunger teaches many things.
Multum in parvo.	Much in a small space.
Mutatis mutandis.	After the necessary changes.
Natio comaedia est.	The nation is but a company of comedians.
Necessitas non habet legem.	Necessity has no law.
Nec prece nec pretio.	Neither by entreaty nor bribe.
Nemine contradicente.	Nobody disagreeing.
Nemine dissentiente.	Without a dissenting voice.
Nemo me impune lacesset.	Nobody shall provoke me with impunity.
Ne plus ultra.	No farther; or, greatest extent.
Ne puero gladium.	Do not give a child a sword.
Ne quid nemis.	Too much of one thing is good for nothing.

Nervi belli argentum est.	Money forms the sinews of war.
Nihil sub sole novi.	There is nothing new under the sun.
Nisi Dominus frustra.	Unless the Lord be with us, all efforts are in vain.
Nolens volens.	Willing or unwilling.
Nom de guerre.	Assumed name.
Non compos mentis.	Not in a sound state of mind.
Non est inventus.	Not found.
Nonchalance.	Indifference.
Non semper erit aestas.	It will not always be summer.
Nota bene.	Mark well.
Nullum infortunium solum.	Misfortunes never come alone.
Nunc pro tunc.	Now for then.
Obscurum per obscurius.	To make an obscure subject more so by explanation.
Occasio facit furem.	Opportunity makes the thief.
Occupet extremum scabies.	The devil take the hindmost.
Omnia venalia nummo.	Every thing has its price.
On dit.	They say.
Onus.	Burden.
Onus probandi.	Burden of proof.
Optimum obsonium labor.	Labor gives the best relish.
Ore tenus.	From the mouth; by word of mouth.
O! tempora, O! mores.	Oh, the times! Oh, the manners!
Otium cum dignitate.	Leisure with dignity.
Otium omnia vitia parit.	Idleness produces every vice.
Otium sine dignitate.	Leisure without dignity.
Outré.	Preposterous.
Pari passu.	With an equal pace.
Particeps criminis.	A partaker in crime.
Passim.	Everywhere.
Pater patriae.	The father of his country.
Pax in bello.	Peace in war.
Peccavi.	I have sinned.
Pecuniae obediunt omnia.	Money will buy every thing.
Pendente lite.	While the action (at law) is pending.
Per curiam.	By the court.

Perdue.	Concealed.
Per fas et nefas.	By right or wrong.
Permitte divis caetera.	Leave the rest to the gods.
Per saltum.	By a jump.
Per se.	Alone; by itself.
Petit maître.	(Little master). Fop.
Peu de bien, peu de soin.	Little property, little care.
Plus sonat quam valet.	He makes more noise than his company is worth.
Posse comitatus.	The power of the county.
Post bellum auxilium.	Aid after the war.
Post tenebras lux.	Light comes after darkness.
Postulata.	Things required.
Pour autre vie.	For the life of another.
Prima facie.	On the first view.
Primum mobile.	The prime mover.
Primus inter pares.	The first among his equals.
Principiis obsta.	Resist the first innovations.
Pro aris et focis.	For our altars and our hearths.
Pro bono publico.	For the public good.
Pro et con.	For and against.
Pro forma.	For form's sake.
Pro hac vice.	For this time.
Pro loco et tempore.	For the place and time.
Pro re nata.	For the occasion.
Pro tanto.	For so much.
Pro tempore.	For the time; or, For a time.
Protégé.	A person patronized or protected.
Quamdiu se bene gesseret.	As long as he shall have acted well.
Quantum.	The due proportion.
Quantum meruit.	As much as he deserves.
Quare impedet.	Why he hinders.
Quasi dicas.	As though you should say.
Quid nunc?	What now?
Quid pro quo.	A mutual consideration.
Quis separabit?	Who shall separate us?
Quoad hoc.	As to this.
Quo animo.	The intention with which.
Quo jure?	By what right?
Quondam.	Formerly.

Re infecta.	The business not being done.
Requiescat in pace.	May he (or she) rest in peace.
Respice finem.	Look to the end.
Res publica.	The common good.
Respue quod non es.	Do not appear what you are not.
Resurgam.	I shall rise again.
Rouge.	Red, or red paint.
Ruse de guerre.	A stratagem in war.
Rus in urbe.	The country in town.

Sang froid.	Blood cold; coolness.
Sans.	Without.
Satis superque.	Enough and more than enough.
Sauve qui peut.	Let him save himself who can.
Savant.	A learned man.
Scandalum magnatum.	Scandal, or scandalous stories relating to the upper classes.

Secundo amne defluit.	He floats with the stream.
Semel et simul.	At once and together.
Semper avarus eget.	The miser is always in want.
Semper eadem.	Always the same.
Senatus consultum.	A decree of the senate.
Seriatim.	In regular order.
Sic passim.	So every where.
Sic transit gloria mundi.	Thus vanishes worldly glory.
Sicut ante.	As mentioned before.
Simplex munditiis.	Simple elegance; free from ornament.
Sine die.	Without naming any particular day.
Sine qua non.	(Without which not). Indispensable requisite.
Soi-disant.	(Self-styling). Pretended.
Specie duci.	To be caught by appearances.
Spectas et tu spectaberis.	You see and you will be seen.
Spes alit exules.	Hope supports us even in exile.
Statuae erectae stultitiae.	Living images of folly.
Status quo.	The state in which it was.
Sua cuique voluptas.	Every one has his hobby.
Sub poena.	Under the penalty.
Sui generis.	Singular; of its own kind.
Summum bonum.	Greatest good.

PHRASES AND SIGNS.

Sunt superis sua jura.	The gods themselves are bound by laws.
Supra.	Above.
Suum cuique.	Let each man have his own.
Suum cuique pulchrum.	Every man pronounces his own beautiful.

Tapis.	Carpet.
Tête à tête.	Face to face; private conversation of two persons.
Timor mortis morte pejor.	The fear of death is worse than death.
Toties quoties.	As often as.
Trait.	Feature.
Tria juncta in uno.	Three joined in one.
Tutum silentii praemium.	The reward of silence is certain.

Ultimo ratio regum.	The final appeal of kings.
Ultimus.	The last.
Una voce.	Unanimously.
Un bel esprit.	A wit; a virtuoso.
Unique.	Singular.
Usus adjuvat artem.	Habit instructs us in our trade.
Utile dulci.	Utility with pleasure.
Uti possedetis.	As you possess; or, present possession.

Vade mecum.	Constant companion.
Vale.	Farewell.
Valet-de-chambre.	A servant who assists his master in dressing.
Veluti in speculum.	As in a looking-glass.
Ventis verba fundis.	You talk to the wind.
Verbatim.	Word for word.
Versus.	Against.
Vestis virum facit.	The garment makes the man.
Veto.	I forbid.
Via.	By way of.
Vice.	In the place of.
Vice versa.	The terms being exchanged, or reversed.
Vide.	See.

Vide ut supra.	See as above.
Vi et armis.	By force and arms.
Vir sapiens forti melior.	A wise man is better than a brave one.
Vis poetica.	Poetic genius.
Viva voce.	By the living voice.
Vive la bagatelle.	Success to trifles.
Vox et praeterea nihil.	A voice and nothing more.
Vox populi.	The voice of the people.
Vulgo.	Commonly.

ABBREVIATIONS.

A.	Answer.	B.V.	Blessed Virgin.
A.A.S.	Fellow of American academy.	Bart.	Baronet.
		Bp.	Bishop.
A.B.	Bachelor of arts.	Cal.	California.
A.D.	The year of our Lord.	Cant.	Canticles.
		Capt.	Captain.
A.M.	Master of arts.	Cash.	Cashier.
A.M.	Before noon.	Chap.	Chapter.
A.M.	In the year of the world.	Chron.	Chronicles.
		Clk.	Clerk.
A.U.C.	From the year of the building of the city.	Co.	Company, County.
		Col.	Colonel.
		Com.	Commissioner.
Abp.	Archbishop.	Conn., Ct.	Connecticut.
Admr.	Administrator.	Cor.	Corinthians.
Al., Ala.	Alabama.	D.C.	District of Columbia.
Anon.	Anonymous.		
Apr.	April.	D.C.L.	Doctor of Civil law.
Atty.	Attorney.		
Aug.	August.	D.D.	Doctor of divinity.
B.A.	Bachelor of arts.		
B.C.	Before Christ.	D.F.	Dean of faculty.
B.C.	Bachelor of Civil law.	D.M.	Doctor of music.
		Dea.	Deacon.
B.D.	Bachelor of divinity.	Dec., 10^{ber}	December.
		Deg.	Degree.
B.M.	Bachelor of medicine.	Del.	Delaware.
		Dept.	Deputy.

PHRASES AND SIGNS.

D.V.	God willing.	Fig.	Figure.
Dr., D^r	Doctor.	Flor.	Florida.
Deut.	Deuteronomy.	G.B.	Great-Britain.
E.	East.	G.C.B.	Grand Cross of the Bath.
e. g.	for example.		
Eccl.	Ecclesiastes.	Ga.	Georgia.
Ed.	Edition, Editor.	Gal.	Galatians.
Eng.	English, England.	Gen.	Genesis, General.
Ep.	Epistle.	Gent.	Gentleman.
Eph.	Ephesians.	Gov.	Governor.
Esq.	Esquire.	H.B.M.	His *or* Her Britannic Majesty.
et al.	and others.		
etc.	and so forth.	H.R.H.	His *or* Her Royal Highness.
Ex.	Exodus, example.		
Exr.	Executor.	h. e.	that is, this is.
F.A.S.	Fellow of the Antiquarian society.	Heb.	Hebrews.
		Hon.	Honorable.
		I.H.S.	Jesus, the Saviour of Men.
F.A.S.S.	Fellow of the Antiquarian society of Scotland.		
		I.N.R.I.	Jesus of Nazareth, king of the Jews.
F.E.S.	Fellow of the Ethnological society.		
		i. e.	that is.
		Ia.	Iowa.
F.H.S.	Fellow of the Horticultural society.	ib., ibid.	in the same place.
		id.	the same.
		Ind.	Indiana.
F.L.S.	Fellow of the Linnæan society.	inst.	instant.
		Isa., Is.	Isaiah.
F.R.A.S.	Fellow of the Royal Astronomical society.	J.D.	Doctor of law.
		J.P.	Justice of the peace.
F.R.S.	Fellow of the Royal society.	J.V.D.	Doctor of Civil and Canon law.
F.R.S.E.	Fellow of the Royal society of Edinburgh.	Jan.	January.
		Jas.	James.
		Josh.	Joshua.
F.S.A.	Fellow of the Society of arts.	jun., J^r	junior.
		K.	King.
F.T.C.D.	Fellow of Trinity college, Dublin.	K.A.N.	Knight of Alexander Newski, of Russia.
Feb.	February.		

K.B.	Knight bachelor.	K.R.E.	Knight of the Red Eagle, of Prussia.
K.B.	Knight of the Bath.		
K.B.E.	Knight of the Black Eagle, of Prussia.	K.S.	Knight of the Sword, of Sweden.
K.C.	Knight of the Crescent, of Turkey.	K.S.L.	Knight of the Sun and Lion, of Persia.
K.C.B.	Knight Commander of the Bath.	K.T.	Knight of the Thistle.
K.C.S.	Knight of Charles III., of Spain.	K.T.S.	Knight of the Tower and Sword, of Portugal.
K.G.	Knight of the Garter.		
K.G.F.	Knight of the Golden Fleece, of Spain, or of Austria.	K.W.	Knight of William, of the Netherlands.
		Kal.	Calends.
K.G.H.	Knight of Guelph of Hanover.	Km.	Kingdom.
		Knt., Kt.	Knight.
K.G.V.	Knight of Gustavus Vasa, of Sweden.	Ky.	Kentucky.
		L.C.	Lower-Canada.
		LL.B.	Bachelor of laws.
K.H.	Knight of Hanoverian Guelphic order.	LL.D.	Doctor of laws.
		L.S.	Place of the seal.
		La., Lou.	Louisiana.
K.L.A.	Knight of Leopold of Austria.	Lat.	Latitude.
		Lev.	Leviticus.
		Lieut.	Lieutenant.
K.L.H.	Knight of the Legion of honor.	Lon.	Longitude.
		M.	Marquis.
K.M.	Knight of Malta.	M.A.	Master of arts.
K.M.T.	Knight of Maria Theresa, of Austria.	M.B.	Bachelor of medicine.
		M.B.	Bachelor of music.
K.N.S.	Knight of the Royal North Star, of Sweden.	M.D.	Doctor of medicine.
		MM.	Messieurs.
		M.R.I.A.	Member of the Royal Irish academy.
K.P.	Knight of St. Patrick.		

M.P.	Member of parliament.	Ol., Olymp.	Olympiad.
MS.	Manuscript.	P.M.	After noon.
MSS.	Manuscripts.	P.M.	Post-master.
Maj.	Major.	P.O.	Post-office.
Mass.	Massachusetts.	P.P.	Parish priest.
Mat.	Matthew.	P.S.	Postscript.
Math.	Mathematics.	p.	page.
Md.	Maryland.	Pa., Penn.	Pennsylvania.
M^{dlle}	Mademoiselle.	Parl.	Parliament.
Me.	Maine.	Pet.	Peter.
Mem.	Memorandum.	Phil.	Philippians.
Mens., Mo.	Month.	Philom.	A lover of learning.
Messrs.	Messieurs.	Pon. Max.	Supreme pontiff.
Miss.	Mississippi.	Pres., Pres^t	President.
Mme	Madame.	Prof.	Professor.
Mo.	Missouri.	pro. tem.	for a time.
Mons.	Monsieur.	prox.	approaching.
Mr., M^r	Mister.	Ps.	Psalm.
Mrs., M^{rs}	Mistress.	Q.	Question.
Mt., M^t	Mount.	Q.B.	Queen's bench.
Mus.D.	Doctor of music.	Q.E.D.	Which was to be demonstrated.
N.	North.		
N.A.	North-America.	Q.E.F.	Which was to be done.
N.B.	Mark well.		
N.C.	North-Carolina.	q. d.	as if he should say.
N.H.	New-Hampshire.		
N.J.	New-Jersey.	q. l.	as much as you please.
N.L.	North latitude.		
N.S.	New style.	q. v.	which see.
N.T.	New Testament.	R.	King or Queen.
N.Y.	New-York.	R.A.	Royal Artillery.
n.	note.	R.A.	Royal Academician.
n. l.	it appears not.		
nem. con.	without dissent.	R.E.	Royal Engineers.
No., N^o	Number.	R.I.	Rhode-Island.
Nov., 9^{ber}	November.	R.M.	Royal Marines.
O.	Ohio.	R.N.	Royal Navy.
O.S.	Old style.	R.R.	Railroad.
O.T.	Old Testament.	Reg^r	Register.
Obt., Ob^t	Obedient.	Reg^t	Regiment.
Oct., 8^{ber}	October.	Rep.	Representative.

Rev.	Revelations.	T.E.	Topographic engineers.
Rev.	Reverend.		
Rom.	Romans.	Tenn.	Tennessee.
Rt. Hon.	Right Honorable.	Thess.	Thessalonians.
S.	South.	Tim.	Timothy.
S.A.	South-America.	U.C.	Upper-Canada.
S.B.	Steamboat.	U.S.	United States.
S.C.	South-Carolina.	U.S.A.	United States Army.
S.L.	South latitude.		
S.P.Q.R.	Senate and People of Rome.	U.S.M.	United States Mail.
S.T.D.	Doctor of theology.	U.S.N.	United States Navy.
S.T.P.	Professor of theology.	ult.	the last.
		V.D.M.	Minister of God's word.
s. a.	without date.		
s. l.	without place.	v.	see.
Sam.	Samuel.	v. g.	as for example.
scil., ss.	to wit.	Va.	Virginia.
Sec.	Section.	viz.	namely.
Sec^y	Secretary.	Vol.	Volume.
Sen.	Senator.	vs.	against.
sen., S^r	senior.	W.	West.
Sept., 7^{ber}	September.	W.I.	West-Indies.
Serg^t	Sergeant.	X^t	Christ.
Servt	Servant.	X^{mas}	Christmas.
St.	Saint, street.	4to	quarto.
Supt., Sup^t	Superintendent.	8vo	octavo.
Tom.	Volume.	12mo	duodecimo.

ASTRONOMICAL SIGNS.

ZODAIC.

♈ Aries.
♉ Taurus.
♊ Gemini.
♋ Cancer.
♌ Leo.
♍ Virgo.

♎ Libra.
♏ Scorpio.
♐ Sagittarius.
♑ Capricornus.
♒ Aquarius.
♓ Pisces.

PHRASES AND SIGNS.

SUN AND PLANETS.

- ⊕ Sun.
- ☿ Mercury.
- ♀ Venus.
- ⊕ Earth.
- ♂ Mars.
- ⚳ Ceres.
- ⚴ Hebe.
- ⚴ Pallas.
- ⚵ Juno.
- ⚶ Vesta.
- ♃ Jupiter.
- ♄ Saturn.
- ♅ Uranus.
- ♆ Neptune.

MOON'S PHASES.

- ● New moon.
- ☽ First quarter.
- ○ Full moon.
- ☾ Last quarter.

ASPECTS.

- ☌ Conjunction.
- ✶ Sextile, 60°
- ◻ Quadrille, 90°
- △ Trine, 120°
- ☍ Opposition, 180°
- ☊ Ascending node.
- ☋ Descending node.

ALGEBRAICAL SIGNS.

- $+$ + plus.
- $-$ - minus.
- $=$ = equal.
- $\pm$ plus *or* minus.
- $\times$ × multiplication.
- $\sim$ difference.
- $\cong$ difference equal.
- $>$ greater than.
- $<$ less than.
- ∞ ∞ infinite.
- $\int$ sum.
- $\equiv$ equivalent.
- $\sqrt{}$ √ radicals.
- $\div$ division.
- $::::$ arithmetical proportion.
- $\div\div$ geometrical proportion.
- $\therefore$ therefore.
- $\because$ because.

GEOMETRICAL SIGNS.

‖ ≠	parallel.	⟋⟋	rhombus.
∦	not parallel.	▱	rhomboid.
⋕	equality.	°	degree.
⊥	perpendicular.	′	minute.
∠	angle.	″	second.
△	triangle.	‴	third.
∟	right angle.	⁗	fourth.
⋎	equiangular.	ǫ	foot.
⋩	sector.	ᴊ	prime *or* inch.
☐ ▫	square.	″	twelfth.
○	circle.	‴	third.
⌒	concentric.	⁗	fourth.

MEDICAL SIGNS.

♃ ℞	Take.	℈	scruple.
℔	pound.	g̈	grain.
℥	ounce.	ß	one-half.
ʒ	drachm.	āā	of each.

ROMAN NUMERALS.

NUMBER.	VALUE.	NUMBER.	VALUE.
I.	1	IX.	9
II.	2	X.	10
III.	3	XI.	11
IV.	4	XII.	12
V.	5	XIII.	13
VI.	6	XIV.	14
VII.	7	XV.	15
VIII.	8	XVI.	16

PHRASES AND SIGNS. 41

NUMBER.	VALUE.	NUMBER.	VALUE.
XVII.	17	CM.	900
XVIII.	18	C ∞.	900
XIX.	19	M.	1,000
XX.	20	CIƆ.	1,000
XXV.	25	∞.	1,000
XXX.	30	⋈.	1,000
XXXV.	35	I̅.	1,000
XL.	40	MM.	2,000
XLV.	45	CIƆCIƆ.	2,000
L.	50	IICIƆ.	2,000
LV.	55	∞ ∞.	2,000
LX.	60	MMM.	3,000
LXV.	65	CIƆCIƆCIƆ.	3,000
LXX.	70	IIICIƆ.	3,000
LXXV.	75	∞ ∞ ∞.	3,000
LXXX.	80	MMMM.	4,000
LXXXV.	85	MIƆƆ.	4,000
LXL.	90	CIƆIƆƆ.	4,000
XC.	90	∞IƆƆ.	4,000
XCV.	95	DƆ.	5,000
C.	100	IƆƆ.	5,000
CL.	150	V ∞.	5,000
CC.	200	V̅.	5,000
CCL.	250	CCIƆƆ.	10,000
CCC.	300	ƆMC.	10,000
CCCL.	350	IMI.	10,000
CCCC.	400	XM.	10,000
CD.	400	X ∞.	10,000
CDL.	450	X̅.	10,000
D.	500	DƆƆ.	50,000
IƆ.	500	IƆƆƆ.	50,000
DC.	600	L̅.	50,000
IƆC.	600	CCCIƆƆƆ.	100,000
DCC.	700	C̅.	100,000
IƆCC.	700	✋.	100,000
DCCC.	800	DƆƆƆ.	500,000
IƆCCC.	800	IƆƆƆƆ.	500,000
CCM.	800	D̅.	500,000
CC ∞.	800	CCCCIƆƆƆƆ.	1,000,000
DCCCC.	900	CCIƆƆCCIƆƆ.	1,000,000
IƆCCCC.	900	M̅.	1,000,000

"The roman signs, for numbers, have arisen from simple geometrical figures. The perpendicular line (|) is one; two lines across one another (╳) make ten; half this figure (∨) is five; the perpendicular line, with a horizontal one at the lower end, (⌊) fifty, and when another horizontal line is added, at the upper end (⌐), we have one hundred. From this sign arose the round c, which is accidentally, at the same time, the initial of *centum*. This c reversed (ɔ), which is called apostrophus, with a perpendicular line preceding it (Iɔ), or drawn together, as D, signifies five hundred. In every multiplication with ten a fresh apostrophus is added: thus, Iɔɔ = 5000, Iɔɔɔ = 50,000. When a number is to be doubled, as many c are put before the horizontal line as there are ɔ behind it: thus, cIɔ = 1000, ccIɔɔ = 10,000, etc. A thousand is expressed, in manuscripts, by CƆ, which is evidently a contraction of cIɔ. M., which is used for the same number, is the initial of *mille*." [*Zumpt.*

When a dash is drawn over any number, it shows that the number so designated is multiplied one thousand times.

The lower-case letters are sometimes used, instead of the capitals, as numerals; for instance, when quotations are made from the bible, the chapters are indicated by lower-case roman numerals and the verses by arabic figures.

They are also used for folios in the prefatory matter of books, to distinguish that part from the regular subject.

In medical works, the quantities, in the formulæ, are always set in lower-case letters, with this difference: if the number end with an *i*. a *j*. is always used in its place: as, *viij*. instead of *viii.*, *xj*. instead of *xi.*, etc.

COMMERCIAL ABBREVIATIONS.

@	to.	b^{ot}	bought.
ac., acct.	account.	brl., bbl.	barrels.
a|c	account current.	brot.	brought.
Agt., Ag^t	Agent.	bu., bush.	bushels.
&	and.	bxs., b^{xs}	boxes.
at 3 m. d^{te}	at 3 months' date.	cld., cl^d	cleared.
b^{es}	bales.	Co.	Company.

PHRASES AND SIGNS.

Cr., Cʳ	Creditor.	£ s. d.	Pound sterling, shilling, pence.
₵, ct., cts.	cent, cents.		
cwt.	hundred weight.	℔., ℔s.	pound, pounds.
d|dᵗᵉ	days' date.	M.	thousand.
Dr., Dʳ	Debtor.	mdz., mdⁱᶻᵉ	merchandize.
dft.	draft.	mkt.	market.
disg.	discharging.	mo., mos.	month, months.
$, dol., dols.	dollar, dollars.	⌗, No.	Number.
do.	ditto.	ord.	order.
doz.	dozen.	oz.	ounce.
ds.	days.	⅌	per.
d¦st.	day's sight.	pble.	payable.
dupᵉ	duplicate.	º|º, p. ct.	per cent.
exchᵉ	exchange.	pks., pᵏˢ	packages.
•|•	errors excepted.	Recᵈ	Received.
fm.	from.	Recpᵗ	Receipt.
gall.	gallon.	sld., slᵈ	sailed.
ʰ|ᵃ	his account.	ᵗ|ᵃ	their account.
hhd.	hogshead.	tᶜᵉˢ	tierces.
Int.	Interest.	wt.	weight.
ldg.	loading.	yd.	yard.

ACCENTS, ETC.

*	Asterisk.	Ñ ñ	Spanish *n*.
†	Dagger.	℣	Verse.
‡	Double-dagger.	℟	Response.
‖	Parallel.	ᵃᵇᶜᵈᵉᶠ	Superior letters.
§	Section.	¹²³⁴⁵⁶⁷⁸⁹⁰	Superior figures.
¶	Paragraph.	½ ⅓ ¼ ⅛	Diagonal fractions.
☞	Index.		
á é í ó ú	Acute accents.	½ ⅓ ¼ ⅛	Horizontal fractions.
à è ì ò ù	Grave accents.		
â ê î ô û	Circumflex accents.	²³⁴⁸₂₃₁₅	Piece fractions.
ä ë ï ö ü	Diæreses.	1̶2̶3̶4̶5̶6̶7̶8̶	Canceled figures.
ā ē ī ō ū	Long vowels.	" "	Quotation marks.
ă ĕ ĭ ŏ ŭ	Short vowels.	( )	Parentheses.
Ç ç	French *c*..	[ ]	Brackets.

ELISIONS.

altho',	although.	shouldn't,	should not.
an't,	am not, are not.	t',	to.
can't,	can not.	th',	the.
couldn't,	could not.	that's,	that is.
'd,	had, would.	there's,	there is.
d',	do.	they'd,	they had, they would.
don't,	does not, do not.		
d'ye,	do you	they're,	they are.
'em,	them.	they've,	they have.
e'en,	even.	tho',	though.
e'er,	ever.	thou'dst,	thou wouldst.
gi'me,	give me.	thou'lt,	thou wilt.
ha',	have.	thou'rt,	thou art.
hadn't,	had not.	thou'st,	thou wast.
haven't,	have not.	thro',	through.
he'd,	he had, he would.	'tis,	it is.
here's,	here is.	to't,	to it.
in't,	in it.	t'other,	the other.
I'd,	I had, I would.	t'th', t'the,	to the.
I'll,	I will.	'twas,	it was.
I'm,	I am.	'twere,	it were.
isn't,	is not.	'twill,	it will.
i'the,	in the.	upon't,	upon it.
it's,	it is.	wasn't,	was not.
I've,	I have.	was't,	was it.
let'em,	let them.	we'd,	we had, we would.
let's,	let us.	we're,	we are.
mayn't,	may not.	wer'n't,	we are not.
mightn't,	might not.	we've,	we have.
ne'er,	never.	w'ch,	which.
n't,	not.	what's,	what is.
o'er,	over.	wher's,	where is.
on't,	of it, on it.	who's,	who is.
o'th',	of the, on the.	won't,	will not.
oughtn't,	ought not.	wouldn't,	would not.
're,	are.	you'd,	you had, you would.
'rt,	art.	you're,	you are.
shan't,	shall not.	you've,	you have.
she's,	she is.	y'r,	your.

MATERIAL.

Under this heading it is proposed to treat of the Types, Rules, Leads, Quotations, Furniture, and other material belonging to the composing-room.

THE TYPES.

METAL.

The idea which some printers have, that the harder the metal is the better the types will be, is erroneous. If it be made over a certain degree of hardness, the hairlines will crumble, under the impression to which they are generally subjected at the printing-press. The metal used by the French is very little harder than that used for job-types in this country; yet the types made from it will, if well used, last as long, without being liable to these objections.

Printers, generally, put too much impression on their types, when first used, and, by this means, they become injured in such a manner that each time they are required to be used afterward, the impression must be made heavier, so that by the time fifteen or twenty jobs are done the types are not worth more than the price of old metal. And, when they are thus worn out — say, by four or five months' bad usage — the fault is laid at the door of the type-founder, when, in fact, it is caused by their own negligence or ignorance.

SIZES.

In France the sizes of types are regulated by law, pica (cicéro) being the size to which all others conform. They make 250 lines pica equal to a *metre*, (39.381 inches). The pica is divided into 12 parts, which they denominate *points;* and all the other sizes are made to correspond with a specified number of these points, as may be seen by the following table:

Diamant,	(half Nonpareil)	3	points, or	1	millimetre.
Perle,	(half Brevier)	4	" "	1½	"
Parisienne,	(half Long Primer)	5	" "	1⅔	"
Nonpareille,	(Nonpareil)	6	" "	2	"
Mignonne,	(Minion)	7	" "	2⅓	"
Petit Texte,	(Brevier)	8	" "	2⅔	"
Gaillarde,	(Bourgeois)	9	" "	3	"
Petit Romain,	(Long Primer)	10	" "	3⅓	"
Philosophie,	(Small Pica)	11	" "	3⅔	"
Cicéro,	(Pica)	12	" "	4	"
Saint-Augustin,	(English)	14	" "	4⅔	"
Gros Texte,	(2-line Brevier)	16	" "	5⅓	"
Gros Romain,	(Great Primer)	18	" "	6	"
Petit Parangon,	(Paragon)	20	" "	6⅔	"
Gros Parangon,	(2-line Small Pica)	22	" "	7⅓	"
Palestine,	(2- " Pica)	24	" "	8	"
Petit Canon,	(2- " English)	28	" "	9⅓	"
Trismégiste,	(3- " Pica)	36	" "	12	"
Gros Canon,	(4- " Small Pica)	44	" "	14⅔	"
Double Canon,	(4- " English)	56	" "	18⅔	"
Triple Canon,	(6- " Pica)	72	" "	24	"

The following list comprises the sizes of types cast in this country. It was the intention, in giving it, to place opposite to the names the number of m contained in a foot of each; but the standards of the foundries vary so much from each other that it would be of no practical utility.

Diamond,	Bourgeois,	Great Primer,	2-line Great Primer,
Pearl,	Long Primer,	Paragon,	3-line Pica,
Agate,	Small Pica,	2-line Small Pica,	Double Paragon,
Nonpareil,	Pica,	2-line Pica,	4-line Small Pica,
Minion,	English,	2-line English,	4-line Pica.
Brevier,	2-line Brevier,	4-line Brevier,	

The sizes above 4-line (canon) increase, by 1-m pica, until they reach 10-line, and by 2-m up to 20-line; after which the sizes are sometimes augmented by 4-m, at others, by 6-m, (that is, by the inch), until they reach any size which may be required.

The greater number of the above sizes are called by two names, which depend on the faces altogether, and not on a variation in the sizes of the bodies, as many printers suppose; for instance: pica and 2-line nonpareil are, generally, cast in the same mould; but the face of the former does not fill the body by the amount of space occupied by

MATERIAL.

the descending parts of the lower-case g, j, p, q, y, and the semicolon, while that of the latter fills the body, because, having no lower-case cast to it, there are no sorts which hang below the hairlines, with the exception of the Q, the semicolon, and the comma.

As a general thing, the faces of job-types are cast so as to fill the body, and, consequently, come under the class denominated two-line letters. If they were cast with the common-sized faces, the printer would have to pay fully one-fourth more than he does at present, on account of the weight of the superfluous metal.

The plain two-line letters are generally used in title-pages, and work of that character. To each size there are three faces cast: the condensed, the regular, and the extended; which no printing-office should be without, because, in work of the above description, each shape and size will, at one time or another, be found useful.

The following is a list of the names of the two-line letters, together with the sizes to which they correspond:

2-line Diamond	=	Bourgeois.
2- " Pearl	=	Long Primer.
2- " Agate	=	Small Pica.
2- " Nonpareil	=	Pica.
2- " Minion	=	English.
2- " Brevier	=	2-line Brevier.
2- " Bourgeois	=	Great Primer.
2- " Long Primer	=	Paragon.

Above paragon both lists correspond in name, with the exception of double paragon, which is called by that name when a lower-case is cast to it; but, when the face fills the body it is called 4-line long primer.

It would be a great convenience to printers were the above sizes regulated by some standard, in which each would contain a certain number of m to the foot, beside coinciding with each other at certain intervals. This would save a great amount of time and labor in the composition of mathematical, or any other description of work, which requires the justification of two or more sizes of types in the same line.

It is often found that, if a row of capitals or figures be run down by the side of a corresponding number of lines of lower-case types, a considerable variation will be found to exist between them. This is particularly fatal in tables, because it entirely prevents that accuracy so requisite to justification. Yet, there is much to be alleged in extenuation of this fault: for even were the apparatus perfect, a change of the dresser of the fount, or, if confined to one, the variation of his hand, bearing sometimes heavier or lighter on his scraping-knife, would still make a great difference in a number of lines. The variation in the density of the metal, the force with which it is thrown into the mould, and even the unequal amounts of metal in sorts of the same fount — varying, as they do, from a 6-m space to a 3-m quad — have, more or less, an effect on the types, and cause them, in cooling, to contract unequally.

PROPORTION

Of each sort in a 400-pound fount of types, in pounds and ounces:

A,	2	0	a,	0	12	a,	18	0	1,	1	8	⁋	0	8
B,	1	8	b,	0	8	b,	5	0	2,	1	8	&,	0	8
C,	2	0	c,	0	8	c,	8	0	3,	1	8	æ,	0	4
D,	1	8	d,	0	8	d,	12	0	4,	1	8	ff,	1	0
E,	2	8	e,	1	0	e,	28	0	5,	1	8	fi,	1	8
F,	1	8	f,	0	8	f,	4	0	6,	1	0	ffi,	1	0
G,	1	8	g,	0	8	g,	5	8	7,	1	0	fl,	1	0
H,	1	8	h,	0	8	h,	16	0	8,	1	0	ffl,	1	0
I,	1	8	i,	0	8	i,	12	0	9,	1	0	DASHES.		
J,	1	0	j,	0	4	j,	1	0	0,	2	0	n,	0	12
K,	1	0	k,	0	4	k,	2	0	¼,	0	4	m,	1	0
L,	1	8	l,	0	8	l,	7	0	½,	0	4	2-m,	1	0
M,	2	0	m,	0	12	m,	12	0	¾,	0	4	3-m,	1	0
N,	2	0	n,	0	12	n,	20	0	⅓,	0	3	4-m,	1	0
O,	2	0	o,	0	12	o,	18	0	⅔,	0	3	BRACES.		
P,	1	8	p,	0	8	p,	6	0	⅛,	0	3	2-m,	0	4
Q,	0	8	q,	0	4	q,	1	8	⅜,	0	3	3-m,	0	4
R,	2	0	r,	0	12	r,	14	0	⅝,	0	3	4-m,	0	4
S,	2	0	s,	0	12	s,	14	0	⅞,	0	3	⌐	0	4
T,	2	0	t,	0	12	t,	16	0	@,	0	4	⌢	0	4
U,	1	8	u,	0	8	u,	10	0	℔,	0	3	⌐	0	4
V,	1	0	v,	0	6	v,	4	0	℔,	0	3	QUADS.		
W,	2	0	w,	0	8	w,	7	0	§,	0	4	n,	8	0
X,	0	12	x,	0	4	x,	2	0	£,	0	2	m,	6	0
Y,	1	8	y,	0	8	y,	5	0	]	0	8	2-m,	16	0
Z,	0	8	z,	0	4	z,	1	0	*	0	4	3-m,	16	0
Æ,	0	4	æ,	0	4	æ,	0	4	†	0	4	SPACES.		
Œ,	0	4	œ,	0	4	œ,	0	4	‡	0	4	3-m,	24	0
,|	5	0	.	3	0	!	0	8	‖	0	4	4-m,	8	0
;	1	0	-	2	8	?	0	8	§	0	4	5-m,	4	0
:	0	12	'|	1	0		0	8	¶	0	4	6-m,	1	0

In founts of any other weight the sorts are cast in the same proportion.

FACE.

When a printer wishes to select a number of sizes of types, his first consideration should be given to the face; because there are so many different faces cast on the same size of body, that, if he be not careful in his selection, he may get two sizes of letter which will not have any perceptible difference, in face, when printed. The only way to obviate this would be, in ordering types, to make the selection out of one series. By doing this, all the sizes will bear a relative proportion to each other — faces as well as bodies — and will, when two or more sizes are used in the same work, have a far better appearance than they would have, were one of them a heavy and the other a light face.

NICKS.

In selecting types, attention should be paid to the nicks as well as to the faces; so that no two sizes next to each other would have their nicks so much alike that the difference could not be distinguished at a glance. This is a thing which is generally overlooked by proprietors, and the consequence is, that, in almost every office, the various founts are more or less mixed.

The nicks should be deep, so that the eye could catch sight of them quickly, and a single nick should not be cast on pica or any smaller size; because, when types are small the nicks are made in proportion, and, consequently, they are more liable to be turned when being put in the composing-stick.

It would save printers a great amount of trouble were the small capitals cast with a nick differing, in appearance, from that on the lower-case letters, for, if any part of the fount should happen to get pied, it would be almost impossible to separate such sorts as: o, s, v, w, x, and z, on account of their similarity in appearance.

HIGHT TO PAPER.

The hight to paper should be particularly attended to. The best mode of ascertaining whether each letter be of right hight is, to take a composing-stick and make it up so as to hold ten lower-case m endways; after which try all the sorts in the fount, and, if any material variation should be found to exist between them and the m, the sorts so varying should be recast.

LINING.

To find whether the types line or not: take a lower-case m, and see if its hairlines are even with the hairlines on the other lower-case sorts of the fount. Then see if its lower hairlines are even with the corresponding strokes on the capital M, and, if they are, ascertain whether the capitals and small capitals line, at the bottom, with the last-mentioned letter.

WEIGHT.

If persons should wish to find out, at any time, what weight of types it would require to compose a certain sized form of a newspaper or number of pages of a book, all they have to do is, to ascertain the number of square inches in the page or pages; then to divide that number by 3, and the quotient will be the number of pounds required. For instance: suppose a printer desires to find out what would be the weight of a fount necessary to compose 36 pages, 3½ inches wide and 6 inches long:

```
      6                         21
     3½                         36
     ──                        ───
     18                        126
      3                         63
     ──                       ──────
     21                        3)756
                              ───────
                              252 pounds.
```

This calculation will vary, slightly, with the weight of the fount and the size of the types: small founts, weighing less than 100 pounds, leaving more sorts in case, in proportion to their weights, than large ones; and the sizes of types under bourgeois weighing more to the square inch than those above that size.

BRASS RULE.

Brass rule is now cut, by type-founders, into combination series, in such a manner that, if a printer, when he first commences business, would get a good fount of it, he

MATERIAL. 51

could obviate the necessity of cutting rule for almost every job or table which he might have to set up thereafter.

The rules are cut to sizes, varying by nonpareil, from 1-m to 12-m pica, and above the latter size they are cut to pica sizes, up to 50-m.

With a set of rules of this description all kinds of rule-work may be done without the use of file or shears. This is of great advantage to employers; because, apart from the waste of material in such cases, there is hardly one person out of ten, working at the trade, who is capable of cutting a piece of rule correctly.

If a printer should not wish to go to the expense of getting all the sizes mentioned above, let him have his rules cut, to nonpareil m, from 1-m to 13-m pica, inclusive, and have two other sizes cut, 15-m and 20-m pica, in addition to these, and he can, by using one, two, or three pieces, as the case may require, make any length, up to 50-m pica; as may be seen by the following table:

Sizes.—4, 7, 9, 13, 15, and 20.

11	12	13	14	15	16	17	18	19	20
7 4	4 4 4	13	7 7	15	9 7	13 4	9 9	15 4	20
21	22	23	24	25	26	27	28	29	30
7 7 7	15 7	15 4 4	20 4	9 9 7	13 13	20 7	15 13	20 9	15 15
31	32	33	34	35	36	37	38	39	40
20 7 4	15 13 4	20 13	15 15 4	20 15	20 9 7	15 15 7	20 9 9	15 15 9	20 20
41	42	43	44	45	46	47	48	49	50
15 13 13	20 15 7	15 15 13	20 20 4	15 15 15	20 13 13	20 20 7	20 15 13	20 20 9	20 15 15

The plain rules, of this series, should be 6 to pica, as the No. 1 is apt to get bent by the least misusage; and, when this once happens, it can hardly ever be brought to its proper position.

The type-founders send, with their labor-saving rules, mitred corners to correspond with the double rules which are generally a part of the combination series; but as, in using them, it is always necessary to take three or more pieces to form each rule, and as one of the lines on the rule having a heavy face, the joinings will show, more or less, it would be better for the printer to get all his rules, with the exception of the single rule, of the length made at foundry, and, with the help of a mitering-machine, cut them as wanted.

Above the thickness of long primer, the rules are generally made of type-metal, and are cut with a great variety of styles of face; but, as they wear out very soon, they should not be used on jobs of which large numbers are worked; neither should they be printed in the same form with large types, on account of the extra impression which they would be subject to, thereby wearing them out by the time a few hundred copies are worked.

THE MITERING-MACHINE.

Is a semicircular plate of cast-iron, at the base of which rises a flange perpendicular to its plane. In the centre of this flange the cutter works in a groove, and is moved by a lever of sufficient power to cut rules or borders. At the centre of the circle, of which the semicircle is a part, one end of the guide is fastened, by a pin running through the plate and bolted on the lower side; the other end of it being movable, any required angle may be obtained, as will be shown hereafter.

As there are but two marks on the machine — one for trimming the rules square and the other for mitering rules so as to form a square — it will be necessary to give directions so that any other angles may be cut.

Suppose it be required to mitre the rules for a triangle: that is, to cut three rules with a bevel of 30° on both ends of each. Take a protractor — the semicircular plate, in a case of drawing-instruments, marked with degrees — and put its straight edge against the face of the cutter, the guide being at the mark for the perpendicular; move the protractor either way until 90° is over one of the edges of the guide, and, holding the protractor in this position, move the guide down until 30° coincides with the same edge; then fasten the movable stop, in the semicircular groove, so that the guide cannot be moved any further in that direction. Bring the guide again to the perpendicular, and proceed in getting 30°, on the other side, in the same manner.

If the rules be thicker than No. 2, they should be cut with a saw, somewhat longer than the measure, and then trimmed to the exact length outside the mitre. Having done this, fasten the gauge, which is movable on the guide, to the length of the rule, and proceed with the mitering: cutting the opposite ends of the rules on the corresponding sides of the guide.

Proceed, in the same manner, in getting any other angle in the following list :

3 sides,	30 deg.	8 sides,	67½ deg.	12 sides,	75 deg.
4 "	45 "	9 "	70 "	18 "	80 "
6 "	60 "	10 "	72 "	24 "	82½ "

The angles: 30°, 45°, and 67½°, are generally used for mitering rules; and the others, for mitering borders, so as to make circles of different sizes.

It is often necessary to mitre four rules, so that when they are joined, they will have the form of a lozenge. This can be easily done by bearing in mind the fact, that in a 4-sided figure, both the mitres, on each rule, must be equal to 90°. In the square they are equal, each being 45°; but, in any other 4-sided figure, one must be as many degrees above 45 as the other is below. In cutting rules for a figure of this shape it must be borne in mind that rules parallel to each other must be cut on the same side of the guide. The following will make the most useful shapes: 30° and 60°, and 22½° and 67½°.

SPACE-RULES.

In every printing-office, where any amount of table-work is done, there should be, to each size of letter below pica, a complete set of space-rules; because, in the composition of the kind of work above-mentioned, these rules will look better, in the headings, than 2-m or 3-m dashes. Beside this, they may be used, with advantage, between the columns of figures, when these columns are short, as in the table on page 51, where, if brass rules had been used, it would have taken three or four hours to cut and file them so that they would fit as correctly as the space-rules do.

All space-rules are, or should be, of the same thickness, five to pica, or, which is the same thing, half pearl; and, consequently, any desired length may be made: as, for instance, if it be found that 2-m pica is too long for a given measure, a pica and a small pica may be used; or, if it be too short, a 3-m nonpareil and a 1-m minion. In the same manner any width whatever can be made, without cutting the rules.

LEADS.

Leads are cast: 4, 5, 6, 8, and 10 to pica; but, in a printing-office where job-work is done, it would be well to have but one thickness, and that which has been found to be the most useful is, 6 to pica. If two thicknesses should be purchased, they can not be used in a job the width of both measures, and, consequently, their usefulness will be greatly diminished.

The following are the measures generally used for job-work:

Bank Post,	50 m.	Cap,	38 m.	Note,	22 m.
Post,	42 m.	Letter,	36 m.	Common Card,	19 m.

It will often be necessary to set up a job differing in width from any of the foregoing, on account of borders being used, or the person ordering such work wishing the measure made wider or narrower. For such cases, instead of cutting down regular leads to the size required, it would be better to have six lengths: 4-, 7-, 9-, 13-, 15-, and 20-m pica, cut — an equal number of each — and any measure, from 11- to 50-m pica, may be made out of them, if used in the manner recommended for the rules, in the table on page 51.

As the hight of leads is a little over four m, it would be well to have the 4-m pica leads cut square, so that it would not make any difference which way they are put into the composing-stick.

MATERIAL.

For book-work, the thickness of the leads should be in proportion to the size of the type and the width of the page: 4 to pica being that which looks best in an octavo page of long primer or small pica.

The measures most likely to be used are the following:

8vo, 22 m.   12mo, 19 m.   24mo, 16 m.

Should a printer wish to know what weight of leads would be required to interline a certain number of pages, the following figures may be of service:

```
3 pounds 6 to pica leads = 400 inches.
4   "    5 "   "    "   = 500   "
1   "    4 "   "    "   = 100   "
```

The inch being equal to six pica lines, the weight for any work can be easily ascertained. For instance, were it required to determine the weight of 6 to pica leads necessary for 32 pages, 22 m wide, and 40 leads in a page:

```
No. of leads in a page,   40
22 m pica              = 32½ inches.
                         120
                          26½
No. of inches in a page, 146½
No. of pages,             32
                         292
                         438
                          21½
Inches of leads in 32 pages, 4693½

400 : 4693 :: 3 :
            3
4|00)140|79
    35 pounds.
```

If it were required to find the weight of 5 to pica leads for the same number of lines and pages, 500 and 4 should be used instead of 400 and 3, in the above.

QUOTATIONS.

They are used, in book-work, for justifying marginal notes in their proper places at the sides of the pages, and for the blanks at the heads and ends of chapters, as well as for the blank pages. They are also used, in job-work, to justify the rules which run down the blank part of the sheet, in such jobs as bills of lading. There are three kinds cast, each of which is useful for certain purposes.

The first and most useful sort consists of six sizes: viz.,

$$1\times 4 \quad 2\times 4 \quad 3\times 4 \quad 4\times 4 \quad 6\times 4 \quad 8\times 4$$

These quotations will be found far more convenient than those heretofore furnished by the type-foundries; because, being a certain number of pica m each way, they will, if properly cast, come out even and square, in any manner in which they may be put together. This could not be done with the old quotations, because they were made to 6- or 8-line pica one way and double great primer the other.

The second kind consists of the four sizes following:

$$6\times 6 \quad 8\times 8 \quad 10\times 10 \quad 12\times 12$$

And, beside their use as quotations, they can, as the hollow parts run entirely through, and are perpendicular and circular, be used to set up such jobs as the labels on the covers of pill-boxes.

The third kind has the same number of sizes as the second; but, being longer one way than the other, the hollow parts assume the shape of ovals. The sizes are:

$$6\times 12 \quad 8\times 14 \quad 10\times 16 \quad 12\times 18$$

The hollow parts, in the second and third kinds, coming within 1-m pica of the sides, the jobs set in them will be two m shorter, each way, than the numbers given above.

METAL FURNITURE.

When leads are of a greater thickness than 4 to pica they are called reglet or metal furniture, and are cast solid, if the size be nonpareil, pica, or 2-line pica; but, above the latter size they are cast hollow, so as to obviate any unnecessary weight in the form, yet strong enough to bear any pressure to which they may be liable in locking up. In width, the hollow furniture increases, by single m, from 3- to 12-m pica.

In regular sized work: such as, books, pamphlets, and

periodicals, this furniture will be found far more convenient than the wooden furniture in use generally; because there is no possibility of its expanding or warping, as the wood does, every time the form is washed, or the types are dampened for distribution.

With this furniture the printer can, as a matter of course, make any width of margin he may desire, by putting two or more pieces together: but it is better, if the margin is not over 12-m pica, to have it all in one piece; because the more pieces there are to a set of furniture the more likely it is for parts of it to get mislaid.

WOODEN FURNITURE.

This furniture is made to every size of type under great primer, and above that size it is made to pica up to 12-m.

It is used in the larger class of jobs, instead of leads, on account of its cheapness; and, being of less weight, broadside jobs, in which it is used, can be locked up and lifted from the stone with less trouble than would be the case were metal used.

It would be a saving to the printer, were he to cut this furniture to the sizes generally required in the course of business: that is, to cut it so as to suit the paper he commonly uses for posters. He should have two sizes for the whole sheet — one for the broad and the other for the narrow way. For the half and the quarter sheet the furniture should be cut in like manner; and with these six lengths he will, at all times, be able to do a job with more expedition and less expense than he would were he obliged to get the pieces out of the drawer and saw them for every handbill which he might be called upon to print.

BEVELED FURNITURE.

This furniture is generally made a yard in length, and is cut to suit the length and width of whatever job it may be required to lock up; and, consequently, the pieces are always becoming shortened, and, as a matter of course, less useful; new pieces being continually purchased to make up the waste. This could be obviated entirely, if the suggestion made in Hansard's Typographia were adopted: viz., that bevels be cast on all the job-chases, on the two sides opposite the square corner. If this were done, the use of beveled furniture would be entirely superseded, in job- and stereotype-work, the straight furniture and quoins being all that would be necessary.

THE STONE.

The stone should be of a size large enough to take on any form which it may be necessary to lock up. Its surface should be even and smooth, and that part of the frame on which the stone rests should be in the shape of a box, so that tan-bark or saw-dust could be put into it, in which the stone should be bedded. If this were not done, the stone would rest upon three points only, and, when large and thin, would be liable to get broken. The frame should be made of strong timber, and well fitted together and braced, so that it could not be moved laterally. It should also have a drawer, divided into compartments, for furniture, quoins, and such like. The slides in which the drawer moves should be so made that it could be pulled out at either side of the stone; and, when the drawer is heavy, it should run on rollers.

STANDS.

The stands are generally made three feet seven inches high, at the side next the compositor; the inclined part, on which the lower case rests, being six inches higher at the back than at the front. If the slant be greater than this, the types will fall from the upper boxes into those below them, when the case is full; and, if it be lower, the compositor will have farther to reach, beside not being able to take hold of the types so readily, when the boxes are nearly empty. The upper-case being higher on the frame than the lower, must have a still greater inclination, yet not so much as to allow the types to become pied.

COMPOSITION.

In this section it is intended to give such information as may be necessary in reference to the Cases, Casing the letter, Distribution, Casting up the copy, Composing, and Making up the pages. In doing this, it will not be required to go into any long dissertation, like those given in other Typographias, on distributing and setting types, as this work is intended for those persons only who have a general knowledge of the trade; but to throw out such hints and directions as may be of practical utility.

THE CASES.

In the plan of a pair of cases hereafter given, the manner of arranging the types in the lower-case is the same as that generally adopted throughout the United States; the only alteration made in it is, leaving out the &, which gives room for another thin-space box.

As in the arrangement of the upper-case there is no uniform method — the capitals being sometimes laid on the left-hand side, and at others, on the right, the latter has been adopted; because, when they are on that side, the compositor can reach the boxes with more facility than if they were on the left-hand side; and his copy, being placed on the part of the case which contains the small capitals, will be directly in front of, instead of to one side and a greater distance from him.

The three upper rows of boxes not being arranged alike in any two offices, it was thought best to remodel them and place the sorts in classes, so that, being seen once or twice, the compositor would remember afterward where they were kept. The fractions, instead of being put in a single row, are placed in three, those having similar denominators being together. The æ and œ of the capitals, small capitals, and lower-case are put, one above the other, at the same side of the case and in the order named. The dashes have been placed, according to size, in one row of boxes, and the commercial marks and $ are close to each other and directly in front of the compositor.

The following are the plans of the upper- and lower-cases :

UPPER CASE.

*	†	‡	‖	§	¶	☞	—m	3m	°	´	ʺ	⅓	⅔
Œ	œ	œ	&	%	℔	£	—	⁀	‿	⅛	⅜	⅝	⅞
Æ	Æ	æ	&c	℔	@	$	n	m	2m	3m	¼	½	¾
▲	B	C	D	E	F	G	A	B	C	D	E	F	G
H	I	K	L	M	N	O	H	I	K	L	M	N	O
P	Q	R	S	T	V	W	P	Q	R	S	T	V	W
X	Y	Z	J	U	]	)	X	Y	Z	J	U	fi	ffi

LOWER CASE.

ffi	h'r sp	5 m sp	4 m sp	,	k		1	2	3	4	5	6	7	8
j	b	c		d		e	i		s		f	g	ff	9
?													fi	0
!		m		n		h	o	y		p	,	w	·quand	·quand
z														
x	v	u		t		thick space.	a		r		; .	: -	quads.
q														

CASING THE LETTER.

When the types are to be used continually, as on daily newspapers, there should be a pair of cases for every fifty pounds of types in the fount; because the capitals, figures,

COMPOSITION. 61

and sorts of like character may be required at any moment, and they should be where they could be taken and returned with the least trouble and most expedition. But, in book-offices there need not be more than one pair of cases to each hundred pounds; the extra sorts being left in paper until required.

The best and most expeditious method of casing letter is: after having opened the paper of types, on the stone, so that the face will be downward, to take a small wooden galley, such as those used by type-founders, and place it so that its three ledges will be against three sides of the page of types; then to grasp the paper firmly at the side of the galley to which there is no ledge, the opposite side being pressed upon the stone to prevent the paper from slipping; then, with the other hand at the back of the galley, to turn it over by drawing the paper upward. The letter can then be taken out of the galley in lines; and, having put in case a sufficient amount of each sort, the remainder can be tied up again and put away until required. It will be found that it is better to do this than to fill the cases to repletion, as is generally done, and putting the remainder of the sorts in papers, where they will be forgotten or mislaid; causing, when they are wanted, a loss of time in hunting them out of the corners of boxes or drawers, or any other place in which they may be kept.

DISTRIBUTING.

The only directions necessary to be given, under this heading, are: that the compositor be careful not to throw the letters into the case with the faces downward, especially large types, as the hairlines thereby become injured; neither should he distribute his cases too full, because the types will, when he is composing, fall from one box into another, causing delay in putting a part of them back, while others will escape the eye, and will not be found until the types are read over in the stick or after the proof is taken. It would be well for him, also, to bear in mind the necessity of immediately picking up every type he may drop on the floor; for, apart from the careless habit which it engenders, the types are liable to be lost or destroyed.

THE COPY.

The copy should be written on one side of the paper only, if it be intended that more than one compositor shall work on it; because, at the end of takes, the persons setting the types will have to pass the manuscript from one to the other, in order that each may commence and close at a paragraph; and, were it written on both sides, the chances are that two compositors would require the same sheet; thus, one having to wait until the other gets through his part, it would cause a delay to the work and a loss of time to the compositor.

Should the manuscript contain proper names, or any other words or phrases the meaning of which can not be made out from the context, such words or phrases should be written so that every letter could be easily determined.

CASTING UP COPY.

The best method of casting up copy is: after having made up a composing-stick to the measure proposed for the width of the work, to take an average page of the copy, and set from it until a certain number of lines of the manuscript comes out even with a number of lines of types. From this a calculation can easily be made for the whole of the work.

Suppose a manuscript of 250 pages, and 31 lines in a page, be brought into an office, and it is required to determine how many pages it will make in long primer, the page being 28 m wide and 40 lines of types in length; and it is found, by setting up a few lines, that 9 of the manuscript are equal to 7 of the types. Then:

```
250  pages manuscript.        9 : 7750 :: 7
 31  lines in a page.                7
─────                        ─────────
 250                         9)54250
  75                         ─────────
─────                        4|0)602|7 lines of types.
7750 lines manuscript.            151  pages of types.
```

The number of sheets can be ascertained, by dividing 150 by 8, 12, or 16, according to the size of the press on which the work is to be done.

COMPOSITION.

Another method, which will be found to be fully as accurate as that before given, is: to ascertain, by calculation, the number of words in the manuscript; then, as it has been found that 1000 m average 380 words (that is, 2180 letters, spaces, and quads), if the number contained in the manuscript be divided by 380, the quotient will be the number of 1000 m. Having done this, the number of pages it will make in any sized type and page can be found by ascertaining how many square inches there are in a page, and multiplying that number by the number of m in a square inch of the size of type in which it is to be set; then, by dividing the number of 1000 m in the manuscript by the number of m in a page, the number of pages will be the answer.

The following is the number of m in 100 square inches of the sizes of types from pica to agate, inclusive :

Pica,	3600	Brevier,	8836
Small Pica,	4900	Minion,	10404
Long Primer,	5625	Nonpareil,	14400
Bourgeois,	6889	Agate,	19600

The numbers given in the above list are based on the supposition that: 6-m pica, 7-m small pica, 7·5-m long primer, 8·3-m bourgeois, 9·4-m brevier, 10·2-m minion, 12-m nonpareil, and 14-m agate, are equal to an inch. This is not strictly true; but the variation is so slight that it will not make a difference of 1000 m in 100 pages of the common size.

Suppose it were required to determine, according to the above method, how many pages in small pica, 25 square inches to the page, a manuscript of 254 pages, averaging 263 words to the page, would make :

```
   254      | 38|0)6680|2(176 |   25    | 1225)176000(144
   263      |        38       |   49    |      1225
  ———       |       ———       |  ———    |      ————
   762      |       288       |   225   |      5350
  1524      |       266       |   100   |      4900
   508      |      ———        |  ————   |      ————
  ————      |       220       |  1225   |      4500
 66802      |       228       |         |      4900
```

In using either of the above modes of calculation, it must be borne in mind that such matter as tables, notes, or extracts set in types differing in size from that of the body, must be cast up separately.

COMPOSING.

POSITION.

The position, when setting types, should be such that the right side of the compositor would be in a line with the central division of the lower case; because he will be able to reach the boxes at the left-hand side with more ease than he would were he to stand directly in front of the centre of the case. The hight at which he ought to stand should be such that he could reach every part of the case with facility, yet not enough to make him liable to stoop his shoulders; in fact, his position should be erect at all times.

When setting types the compositor should be careful not to acquire a habit of making any unnecessary motions: such as, moving the body back and forth, striking the type against the edge of the box or the composing-rule, or giving it a flourish in the air while bringing it from the box to the stick. These, or any other false movements, though they give an appearance of swiftness, by filling up the time, materially retard the compositor in the performance of his work.

STICK AND RULE.

The composing-stick should be selected according to the character of the work intended to be done. For newspapers, instead of having them so that they could be altered, the sticks should be riveted, to obviate the possibility of their being changed to suit the notions of the compositors. If this be not done, the types set up by different persons will be found, very often, to vary in width, thus preventing the form being locked up evenly, and allowing the looser portions to drop out, when it is lifted from the stone; or to be drawn out by the rollers, when on the press. For book-work, the stick made after the old plan is the best; because the movable part, being held in its place by a screw, is not so liable to be shifted as if it were held by a spring. For job-work, the stick which can be altered from one measure to another in the easiest manner will be found the most convenient; and, for this reason, the one which is retained by a spring is the best.

COMPOSITION.

The sticks used in this country are so large that, when they are nearly full, it is tiresome, and, often, impossible for the left hand to follow the right, as it should, when setting types. In France, the printers use sticks which will hold, the smallest four, and the largest seven lines of pica, while the smallest size made in the United States and England will contain ten lines.

The composing-rule may, when the measure is 16-m pica or less, be make with a projection at both ends, so that it can be easily lifted by the thumb and finger; but, when the measure is wider than that stated above, there should be but one projection, that being at the end of the rule which is turned to the outer end of the line. The end on which the projection is left is generally filed slanting downward, so that it can be drawn from between the lines; but, as there is a likelihood of the comma, or any other thin type, slipping past it and binding between the end of the rule and the side of the stick, it would be better if that part were left straight and the end nearer the compositor beveled upward, to the hight of the composing-stick.

THE GUIDE.

As the guide made after the old plan is inconvenient, on account of the compositor having to take his copy down from the upper-case when setting small-capitals, and to readjust it under the guide afterward, it would be better were the guide made out of two strips of thin brass, long enough to reach across a cap page, soldered together at one end, so that the sheet of copy could be held between them: and there should be two other pieces, each about one-half or three-fourths of an inch long, and the width of the centre division of the case apart, fixed at right angles to the former, so that the guide could be put on any part of the upper- or lower-case, as circumstances might require. In taking a guide of this kind down and putting it again in its place, the line of copy will always remain at the point to which it has been drawn between the rules.

SPACING.

Evenness of spacing being the best criterion of a good workman, it should, at all times, be the endeavor of the compositor to keep up a uniform method in this respect; that is, he should make the spaces between the words bear such a relation to each other that the space between such letters as d h would appear the same, when printed, as that between letters like y w.

The spacing between the words should, also, bear a proportion to the spaces between the lines; matter which is leaded, or which has a number of heads or breaklines, admitting of wider spacing than it would if it were solid.

The way in which the spaces are laid in the lower-case in common use makes even spacing troublesome to the compositor; because, the n-quad being at one corner of the case, and the thin-spaces at the other, the hand will, when a line is being spaced, have to go over a greater distance than it would were all the space-boxes placed close to each other, and near the hand of the compositor.

z	!	?	j	ffi	k		1	2	3	4	5	6	7	8
x	b	e	d		e		i		s	f	g	ff	9	
q												fi	0	
v	1	m	n	h		o	y	p	w	,	;	:		
												.	-	
u	t	h'r sp 5 m sp	4-m sp	thick space.	'pemb n	a	r	pemb H	quads.

To obviate the inconvenience mentioned, the above plan of a lower-case is offered for the consideration of the trade. It will be seen that, in this arrangement, all the spaces which are required in justifying are directly under the hand. In any of the plans heretofore proposed the n-quad is left in the old place, or, when this is not done, the hair-space is thrown into the upper-case. In arranging the above case, the letters have been made to occupy, as nearly as possible, the position which they have in the lower-case in common use; the only type left out being the apostrophe, which can be placed in the box in the upper-case occupied by the bracket — this latter being so little used, at present, that it can be laid in some of the upper boxes usually reserved for sorts which are not ordinarily cast, such as the second-mark. When distributing the types, the lower-case on this plan will, also, be found more convenient; because, as a general thing, two spaces differing in thickness will be found together, and, were the boxes to which they belong placed far apart, the hand would have to go over a greater distance in proportion.

GALLEYS.

The galleys are of two kinds: wood, and brass. The former has ledges on two sides, and is generally used in book- and job-offices, for holding the types until the "make up" is passed to it, or containing parts of a job until it is all composed. The brass galley, having ledges on three sides, can be used for proving the types in slips, beside being used for the same purpose as those made of wood.

The wooden galleys should never have water put on them; for, beside their liability to warp, the fibre of the wood becomes loose and uneven, and, consequently, the types can not be made to stand fairly on their feet.

When the brass galleys are used for proving types, care should be taken that the side-sticks are not locked up so as to spring either of the side-ledges. If this should happen, the galley so used will be worthless; because, when types are placed upon it afterward, they can not be made to set square, which will prevent the taking of good proofs, and will cause delay, when making up, in getting the lines back into their correct position.

MAKING UP.

The proportion which the length of a page should bear to its width is found by doubling the width, and taking one-fifth of that amount off: that is, if a page be 26 m wide, twice this number will be 52, from which one-fifth, or 10, is to be taken, leaving 42 m for the number of lines of reading-matter in the page. This number, with the head-line, the blank-line under the heading, and the foot-line, will make 45 lines for the total length.

When the length of the page has been ascertained, a gauge should be accurately made. The best way to make it is: to take a piece of pica furniture, a couple of inches longer than required, and out of this to cut a part, so as to leave a projection at each end, between which the page is to be gauged. Should there be chapter-headings, or any other matter of like kind, the number of lines they are to be sunk ought to be marked on the gauge, so as to obviate the risk of having such headings higher or lower in the page than they should be.

In setting the running-title or head-line of the page, types two or three sizes smaller than that of the body of the work should be used; because, if they were as large they would appear coarse and heavy.

The folios should be in the same sized types as the body of the work; and the compositor should bear in mind that the folios of the even pages are to be justified in the commencement, and those of the odd ones at the ends, of the lines.

The signature should be within 3 or 5 m of the commencement of the bottom line. If it should be put, as it very often is, in the centre of the line, the binder will, when collating his work, lose more time by drawing the sheets farther apart than he would if they were placed near the beginning of the line.

When a part of a sheet is to be cut off and folded as an inset, like the pages from the 9th to the 16th, inclusive, in a form of 24 pages, the first page of the inset should, beside the same mark as the first page of the form, have an additional mark by which it could be known as an inset: that is, if the first page of the form be marked B, the first page of the inset should be marked B2, and, if figures be used, 2 and 2* will answer the same purpose. If the work should consist of more than one volume, the number of the volume should be placed in the same line as the signature.

Head- and foot-lines, or any other lines in which quads are used, should not be justified as tightly as the lines of types. If they should be of the same length, they will bind on the furniture, and allow some of the types to fall out on the stone, or be drawn out at press.

In tying up the page care should be taken that the turns of the twine do not overlap each other, and that it is on the centre of the shank when the page is lifted.

IMPOSING.

This division will contain all that is required to be known regarding Imposing forms, Making margin, Cutting furniture, and Locking up the form.

IMPOSING FORMS.

There is a number of ways in which a sheet of paper can be folded so that the pages will follow each other in regular order: that is, a sheet of twenty-four pages can be folded six ways; a sheet of sixteen, four; a sheet of twelve, three; and a sheet of eight, two ways — being a method for each four pages in a form.

As the imposition of irregular forms, such as 20s, 40s, and forms the hebrew way, generally occupies a large number of pages in works of this class, and are of very little practical use to the printer, they are left out, and in their stead has been inserted the different methods of imposing forms inside out, which will be gone into more fully than has been done in any preceding Typographia.

After the pages are laid on the stone, and before the twine is taken off, the folios should be examined, and if the odd and even pages which lie next to each other, on each side of the back-margin, make one more than the number of pages in a form, they are laid correctly.

In laying the pages on the stone, the compositor must be mindful of the fact, that the first page of the form should always be laid with the foot toward him, in the nearer left-hand corner of the quarter of the chase in which it may be placed.

In the forms laid according to the following plans, it must be borne in mind that the folios there represented are in the position in which they will appear in the types when on the imposing-stone.

1 SHEET OF FOLIO.

The positions in which the pages appear in these two forms of folio is that which the types will have when lying upon the stone: that is, the 1st and 4th pages being the outer and the 3d the inner form, the odd page in each must be placed on the left-hand side, with the foot toward the person imposing the form.

When a number of sheets are placed, one within another, the backs of the inner sheets must be lessened in proportion to the thickness of the paper used.

Two sheets of folio, quired, are imposed according to the following plan:

```
              OUTER       INNER
              FORM.       FORM.
First sheet,   1   8  }   7   2
Second sheet,  3   6      5   4
```

SHEET OF FOLIO. 4

Seven sheets of folio are laid as follows:

```
               OUTER       INNER
               FORM.       FORM.
First sheet,    1  28  }  27   2
Second sheet,   3  26     25   4
Third sheet,    5  24     23   6
Fourth sheet,   7  22     21   8
Fifth sheet,    9  20     19  10
Sixth sheet,   11  18     17  12
Seventh sheet, 13  16     15  14
```

Eight sheets of folio are laid as follows:

```
               OUTER       INNER
               FORM.       FORM.
First sheet,    1  32  }  31   2
Second sheet,   3  30     29   4
Third sheet,    5  28     27   6
Fourth sheet,   7  26     25   8
Fifth sheet,    9  24     23  10
Sixth sheet,   11  22     21  12
Seventh sheet, 13  20     19  14
Eighth sheet,  15  18     17  16
```

I.—SHEET OF FOLIO: INNER FORM.

SHEET OF FOLIO.

Five sheets of folio are laid as follows:

	OUTER FORM.		INNER FORM.	
First sheet,	1	20	19	2
Second sheet,	3	18	17	4
Third sheet,	5	16	15	6
Fourth sheet,	7	14	13	8
Fifth sheet,	9	12	11	10

Six sheets of folio are laid as follows:

	OUTER FORM.		INNER FORM.	
First sheet,	1	24	23	2
Second sheet,	3	22	21	4
Third sheet,	5	20	19	6
Fourth sheet,	7	18	17	8
Fifth sheet,	9	16	15	10
Sixth sheet,	11	14	13	12

SHEET OF FOLIO.

Three sheets of folio are laid as follows:

	OUTER FORM.		INNER FORM.	
First sheet,	1	12	11	2
Second sheet,	3	10	9	4
Third sheet,	5	8	7	6

Four sheets of folio are laid as follows:

	OUTER FORM.		INNER FORM.	
First sheet,	1	16	15	2
Second sheet,	3	14	13	4
Third sheet,	5	12	11	6
Fourth sheet,	7	10	9	8

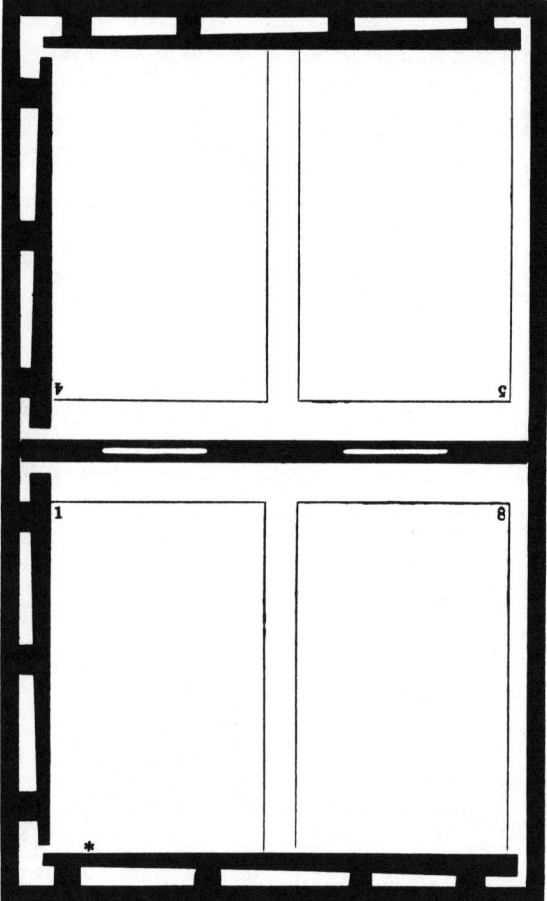

11.—SHEET OF QUARTO: OUTER FORM.

IMPOSING. 73

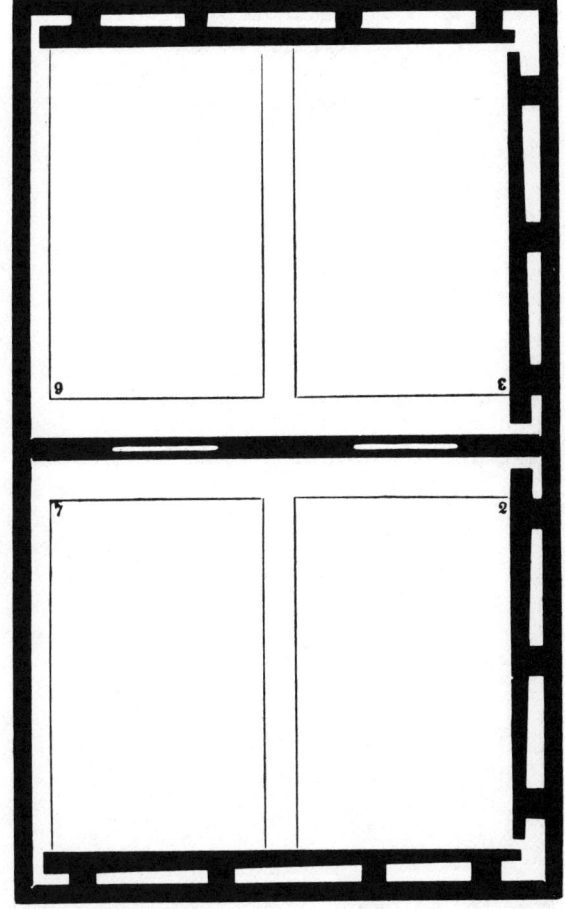

II.—SHEET OF QUARTO: INNER FORM.

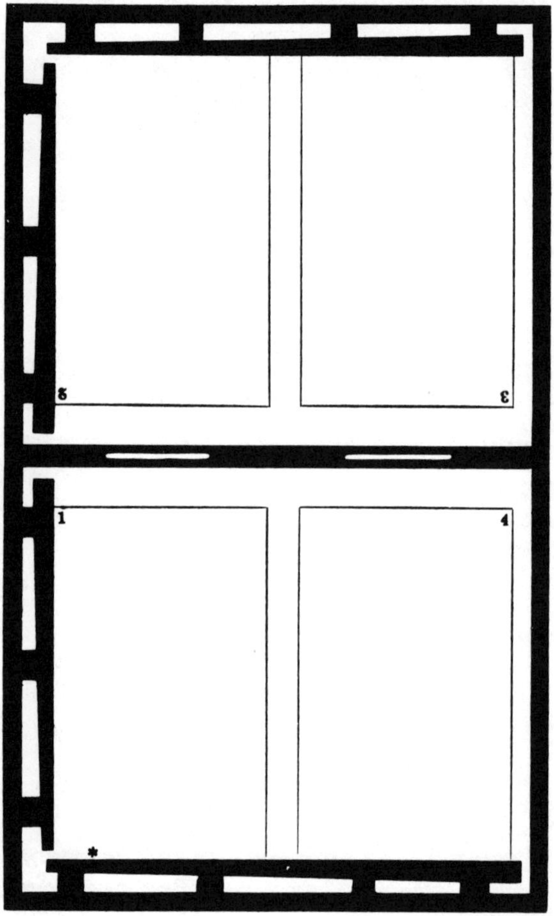

74   PRINTER'S MANUAL:

III.—HALF SHEET OF QUARTO.

IMPOSING. 75

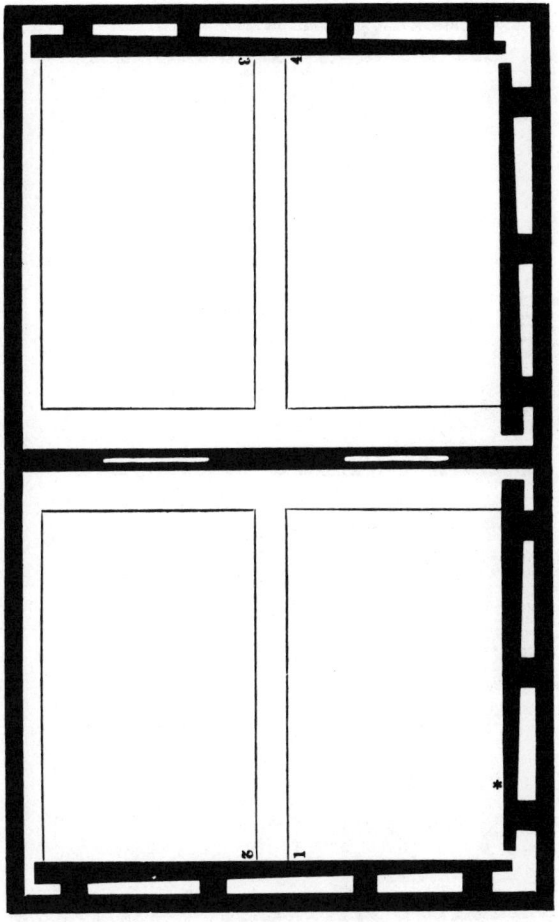

IV.—HALF SHEET OF QUARTO, OBLONG.

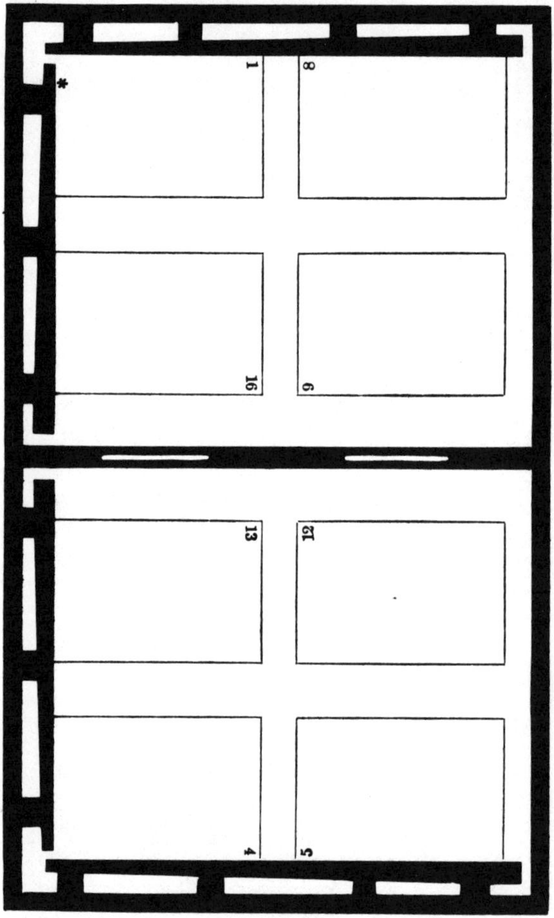

76 PRINTER'S MANUAL:

V.—SHEET OF OCTAVO: OUTER FORM.

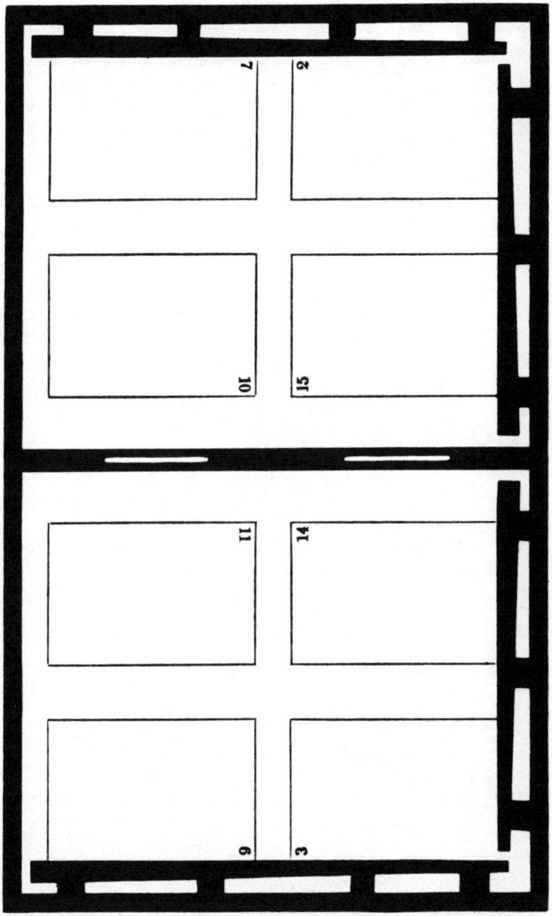

V.—SHEET OF OCTAVO: INNER FORM.

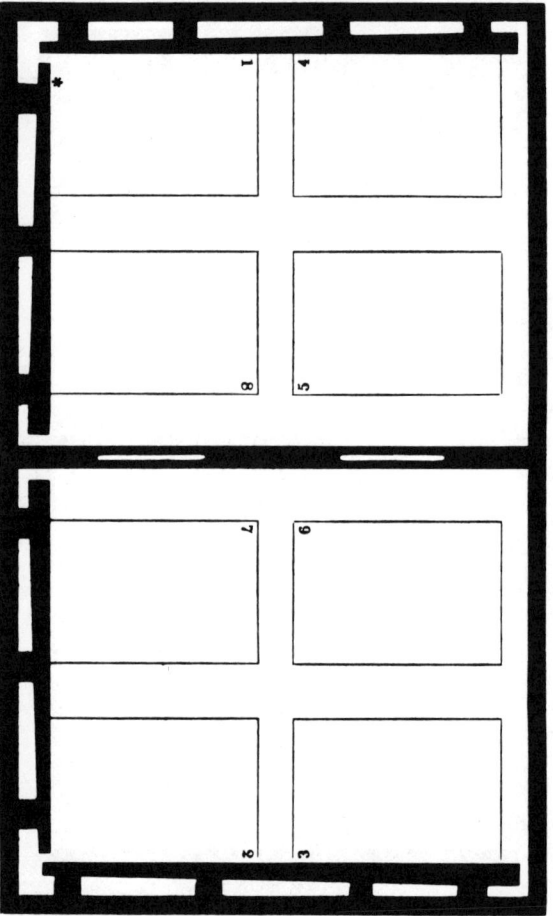

VI.—HALF SHEET OF OCTAVO.

IMPOSING. 79

VII.—HALF SHEET OF OCTAVO, INSIDE OUT.

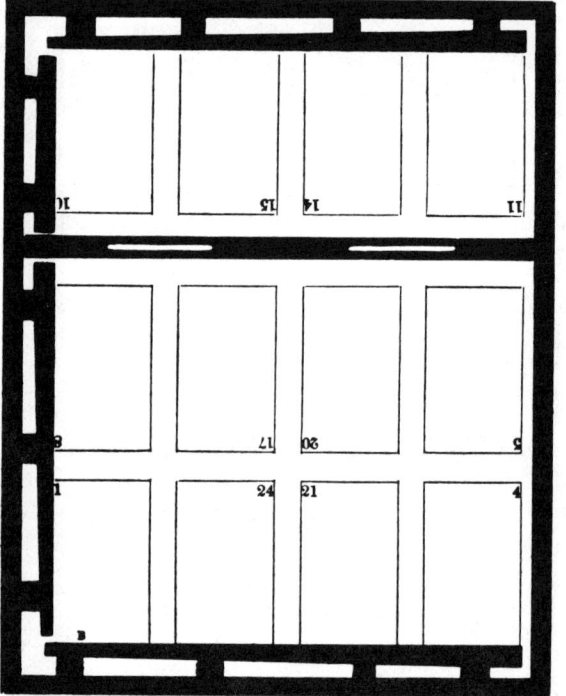

VIII.—SHEET OF TWELVES: OUTER FORM.

There are several ways of imposing a sheet of Twelves, such as: Three sheets of Fours, a sheet of Twelves to fold without cutting, and a sheet of Long Twelves; but, the most simple form only will be given, as the pressman can, in all other cases, fold a sheet of paper so that the pages of types will follow each other.

By imposing a sheet of Twelves according to the above plan, the signature of the offcut being in the inner form,

IMPOSING.   81

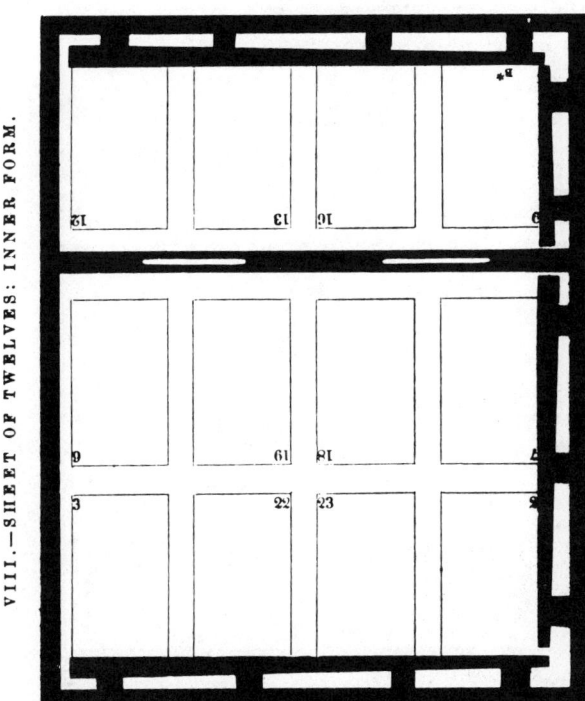

VIII.—SHEET OF TWELVES: INNER FORM.

will rise more conveniently for the binder when folding, and save him the trouble of turning the offcut over for every sheet.

As it very often happens that books printed in Twelves are injured in appearance, because there is not enough of space left at the offcut, the attention of the person who makes up the form is called to what is given, in regard to this subject, at page 125.

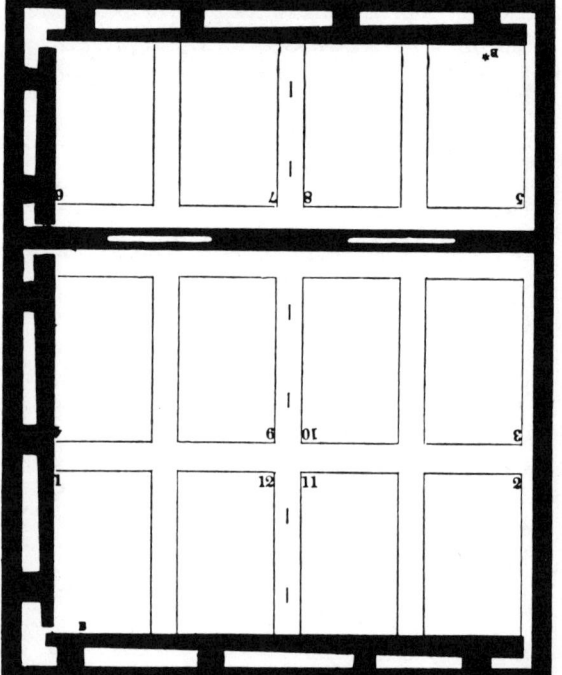

IX.—HALF SHEET OF TWELVES.

A half sheet of Twelves may be made to fold without cutting, by turning the offcut around in the chase, in the relative position which the pages hold to each other, so that the folios will be toward the outer edge of the paper. When a form is worked in this manner, the space at the offcut must be twice that of the foot-margin; and the headings must be worked to a gauge, so as to make the blank at that edge equal to half of that at the bolts.

IMPOSING. 83

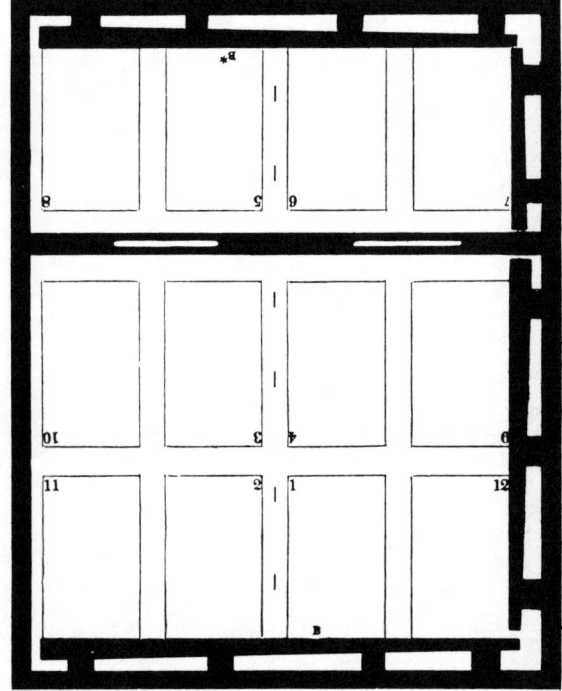

X.—HALF SHEET OF TWELVES, INSIDE OUT.

A periodical which has a large page may be worked as an outer and inner form of Sixes by making up, in separate chases, the pages which are on each side of the long-cross, in a half sheet of Twelves.

When a form is not pointed in the short-cross, there should be a couple of pieces of rule inserted at the place where the paper should be cut, to enable the folder to do so with as little trouble as possible.

84 PRINTER'S MANUAL:

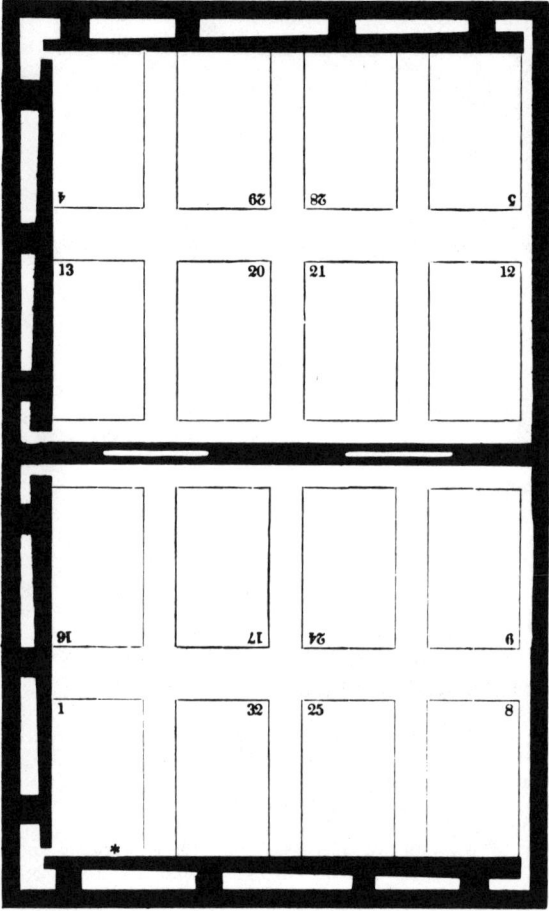

XI.—SHEET OF SIXTEENS: OUTER FORM.

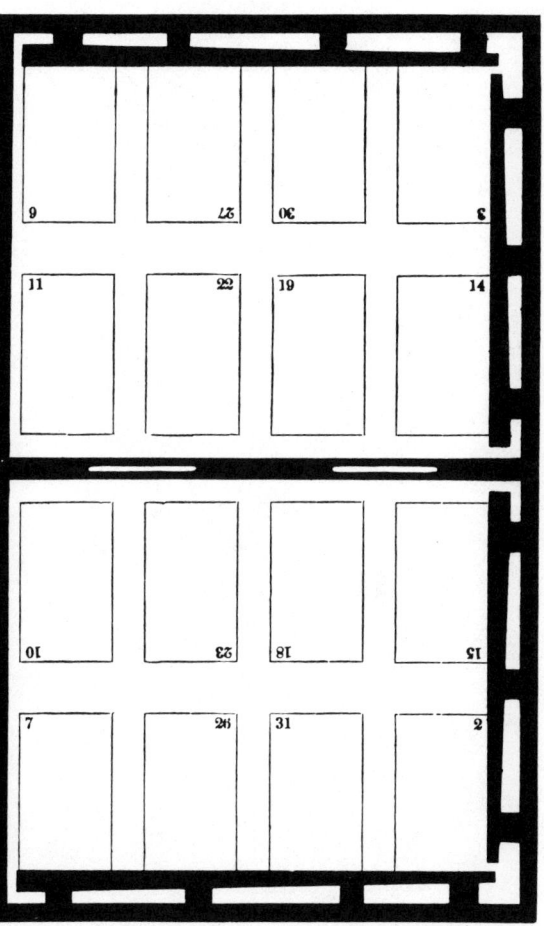

XI.—SHEET OF SIXTEENS: INNER FORM.

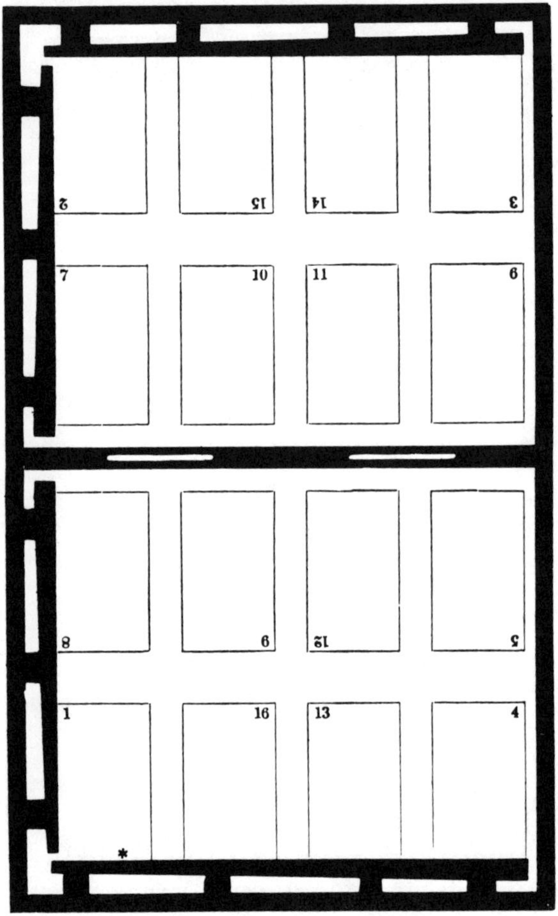

PRINTER'S MANUAL:

XII.—HALF SHEET OF SIXTEENS.

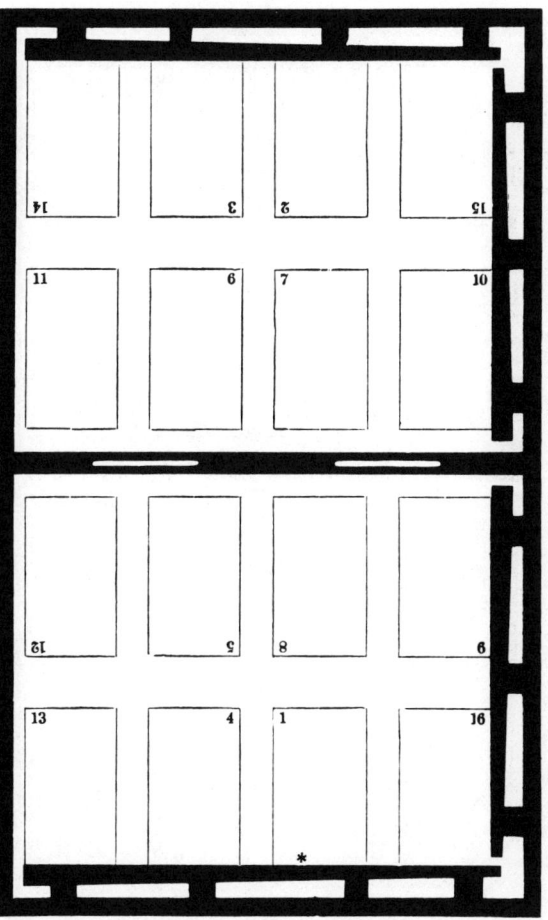

XIII.—HALF SHEET OF SIXTEENS, INSIDE OUT—No. 1.

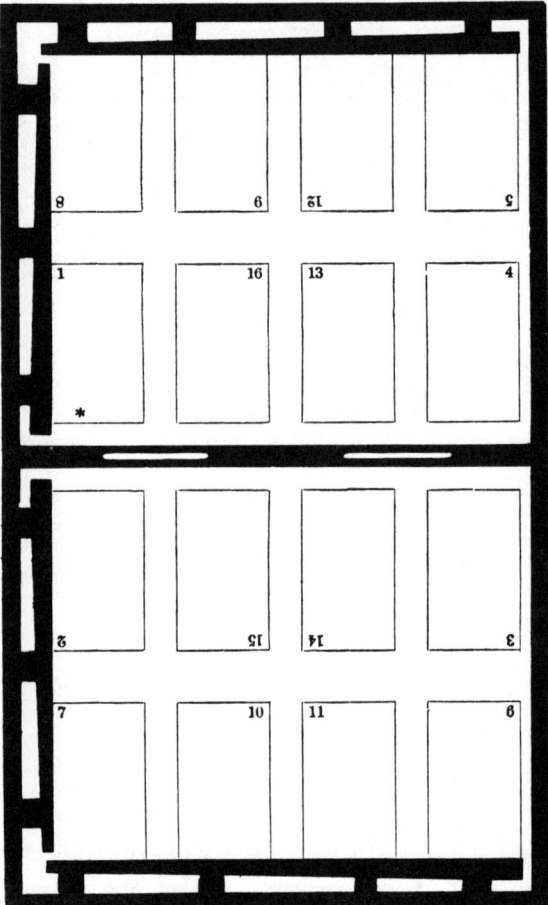

XIV.—HALF SHEET OF SIXTEENS, INSIDE OUT—No. 2.

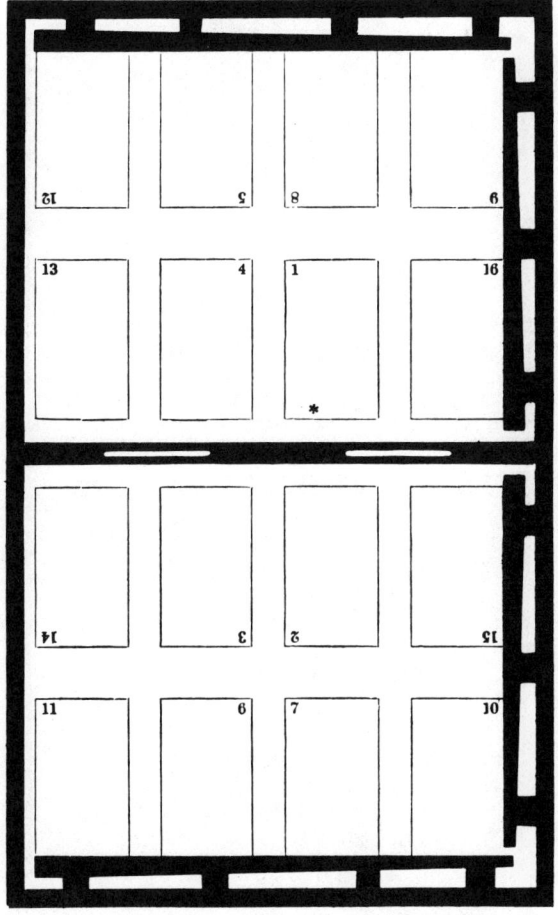

XV.—HALF SHEET OF SIXTEENS, INSIDE OUT—No. 3.

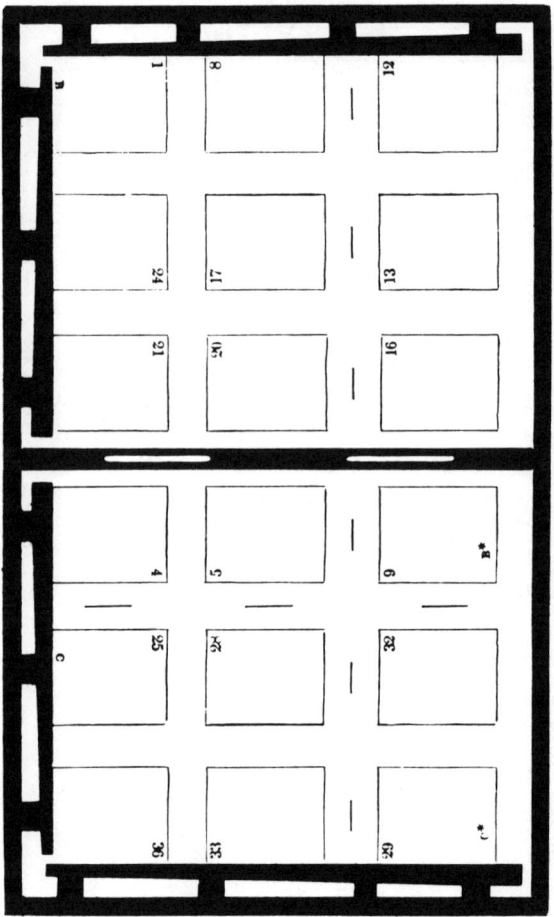

XVI.—SHEET OF EIGHTEENS: OUTER FORM—No. 1.

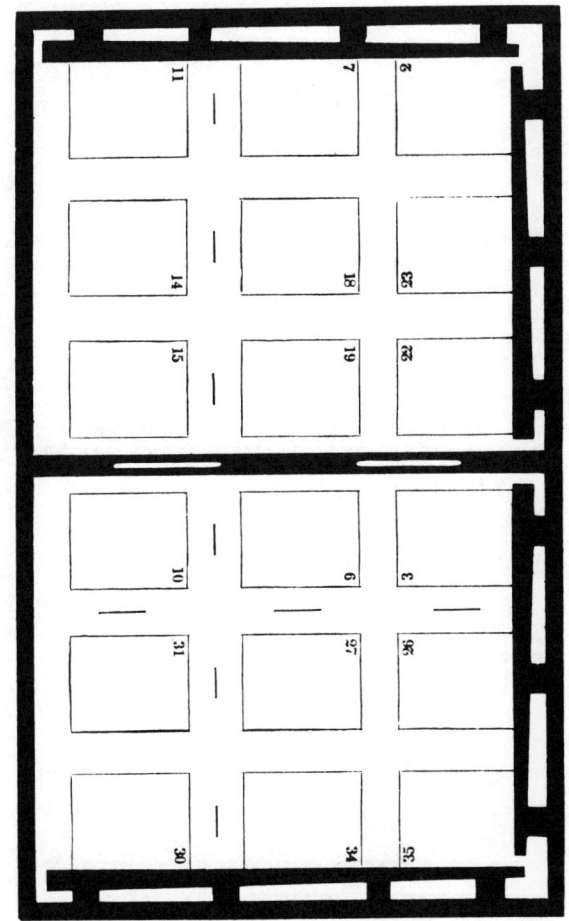

XVI.—SHEET OF EIGHTEENS: INNER FORM—No. 1.

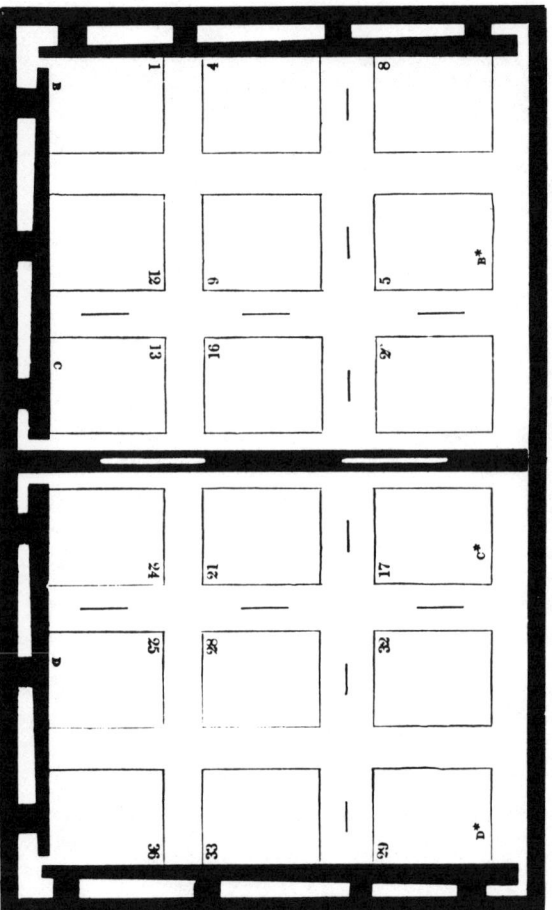

XVII.—SHEET OF EIGHTEENS: OUTER FORM—No. 2.

IMPOSING. 93

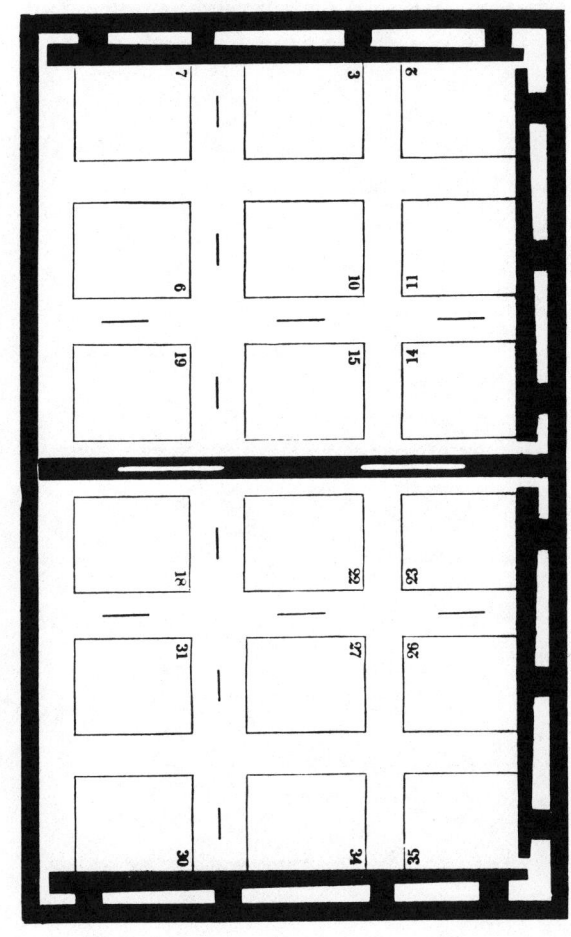

XVII.—SHEET OF EIGHTEENS: INNER FORM—No. 2.

94 PRINTER'S MANUAL:

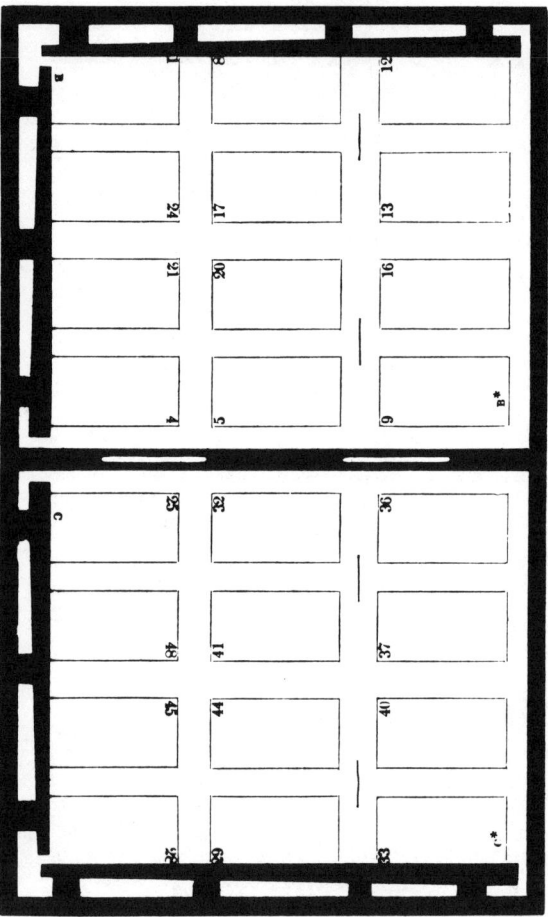

XVIII.—SHEET OF TWENTY-FOURS: OUTER FORM.

IMPOSING. 95

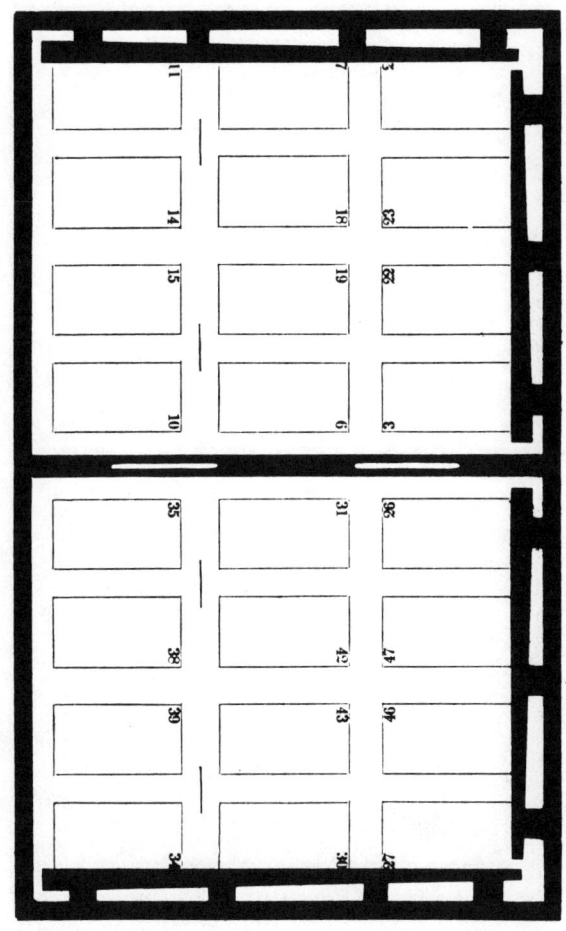

XVIII.—SHEET OF TWENTY-FOURS : INNER FORM.

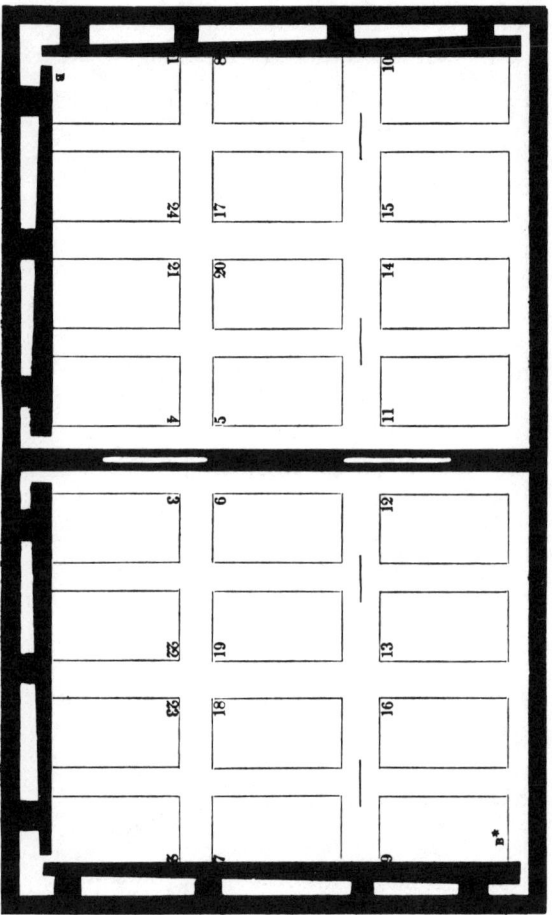

XIX.—HALF SHEET OF TWENTY-FOURS—No. 1.

IMPOSING. 97

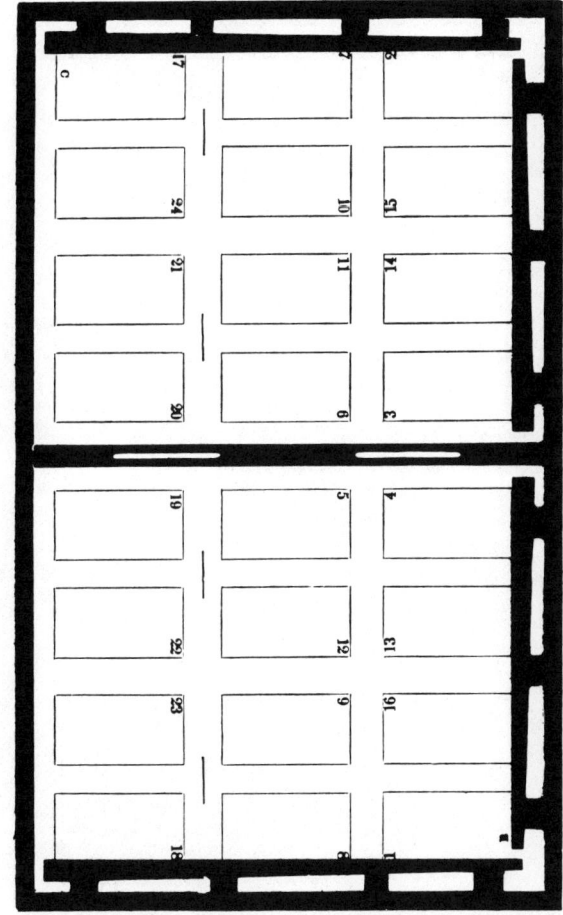

XX.—HALF SHEET OF TWENTY-FOURS—No. 2.

7

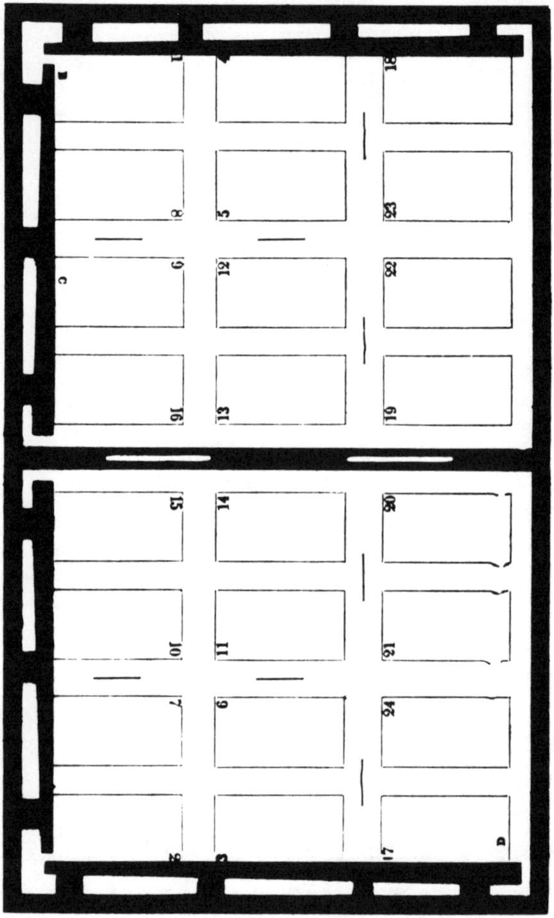

98   PRINTER'S MANUAL:

XXI.—HALF SHEET OF TWENTY-FOURS—No. 3.

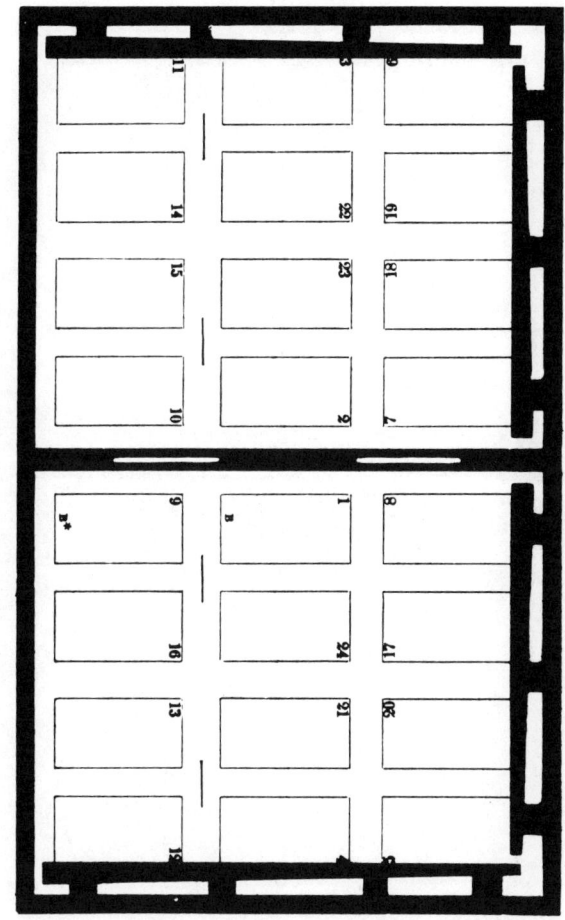

XXII.—HALF SHEET OF TWENTY-FOURS, INSIDE OUT.

100   PRINTER'S MANUAL:

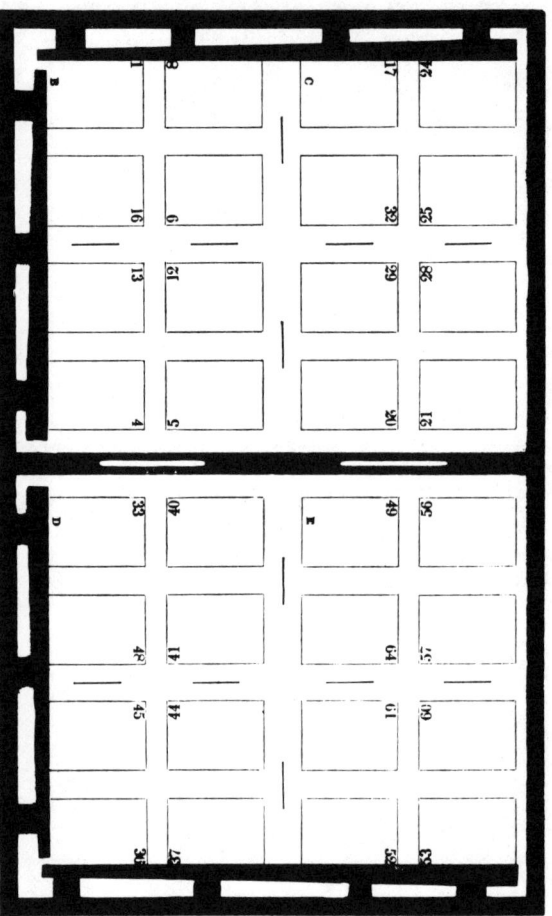

XXIII.—SHEET OF THIRTY-TWOS: OUTER FORM—No. 1.

IMPOSING. 101

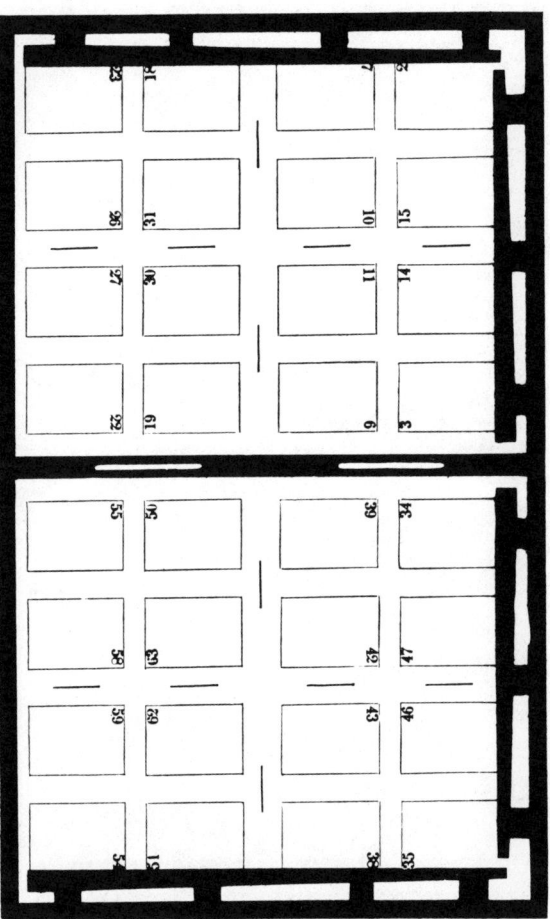

XXIII.—SHEET OF THIRTY-TWOS: INNER FORM—No. 1.

102 PRINTER'S MANUAL:

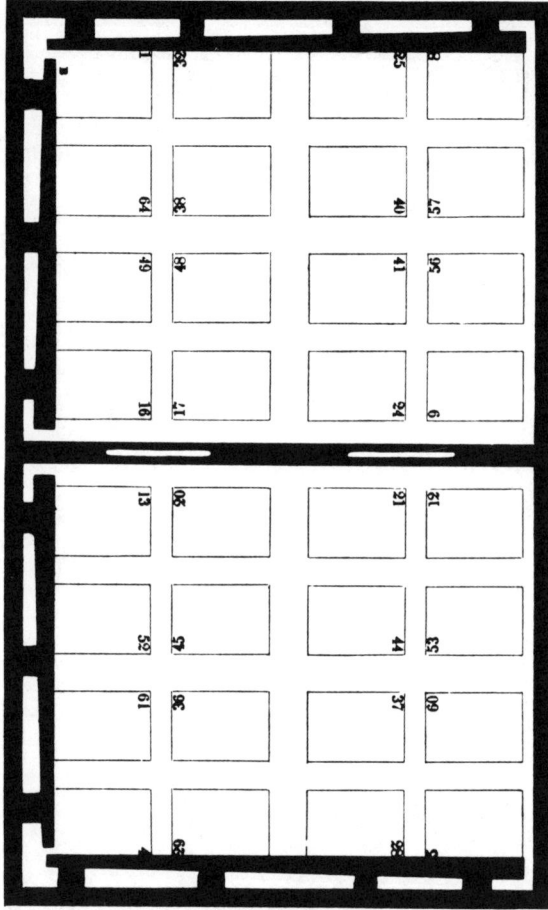

XXIV.—SHEET OF THIRTY-TWOS: OUTER FORM—No. 2.

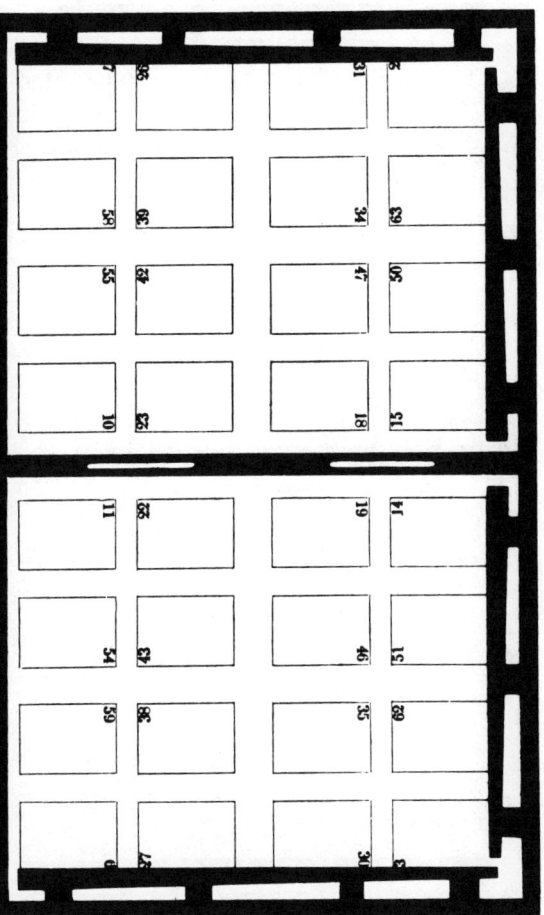

XXIV.—SHEET OF THIRTY-TWOS: INNER FORM—No. 2.

104 PRINTER'S MANUAL:

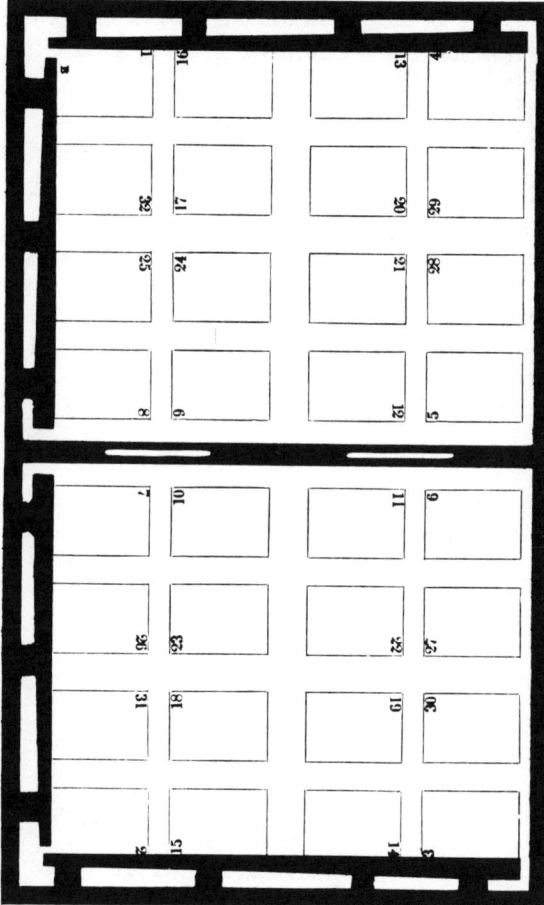

XXV.—HALF SHEET OF THIRTY-TWOS.

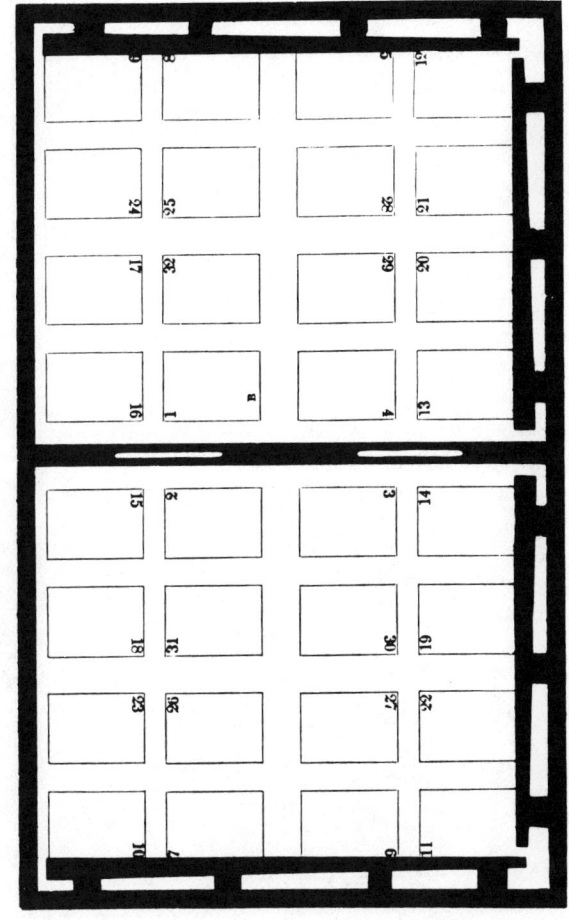

XXVI.—HALF SHEET OF THIRTY-TWOS, INSIDE OUT.

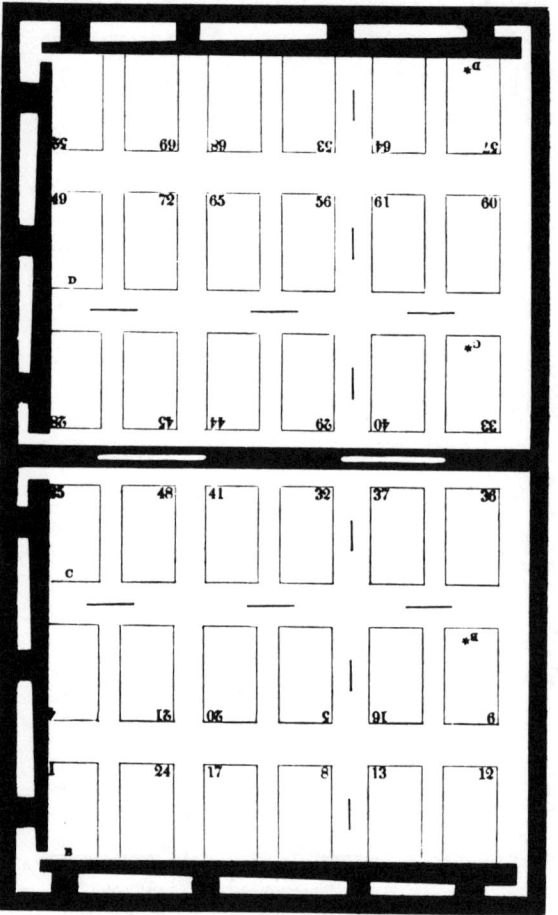

XXVII.—SHEET OF THIRTY-SIXES: OUTER FORM—No. 1.

IMPOSING. 107

XXVII.—SHEET OF THIRTY-SIXES: INNER FORM—No. 1.

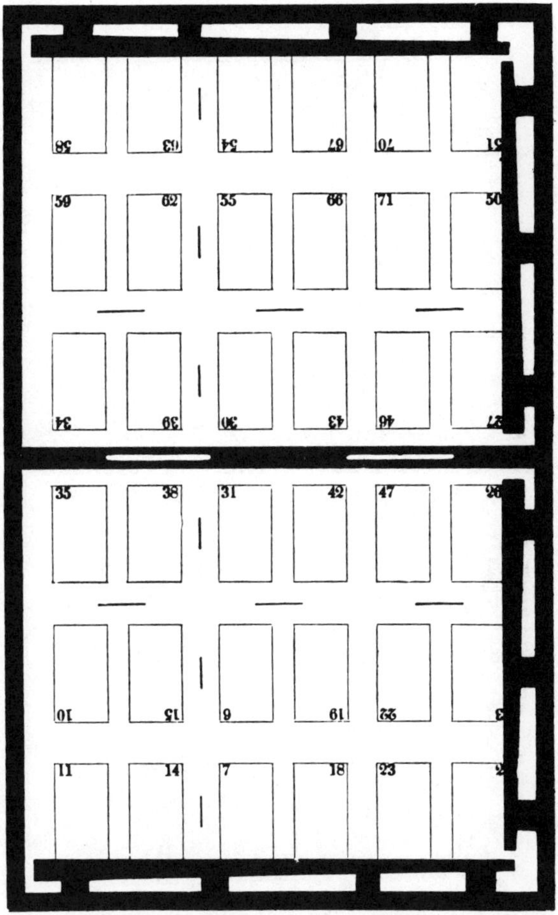

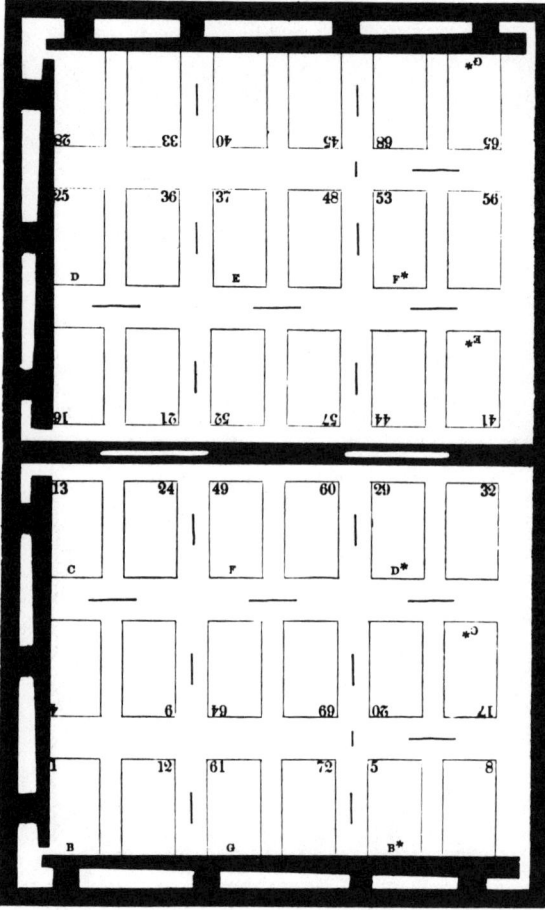

XXVIII.—SHEET OF THIRTY-SIXES: OUTER FORM—No. 2.

IMPOSING. 109

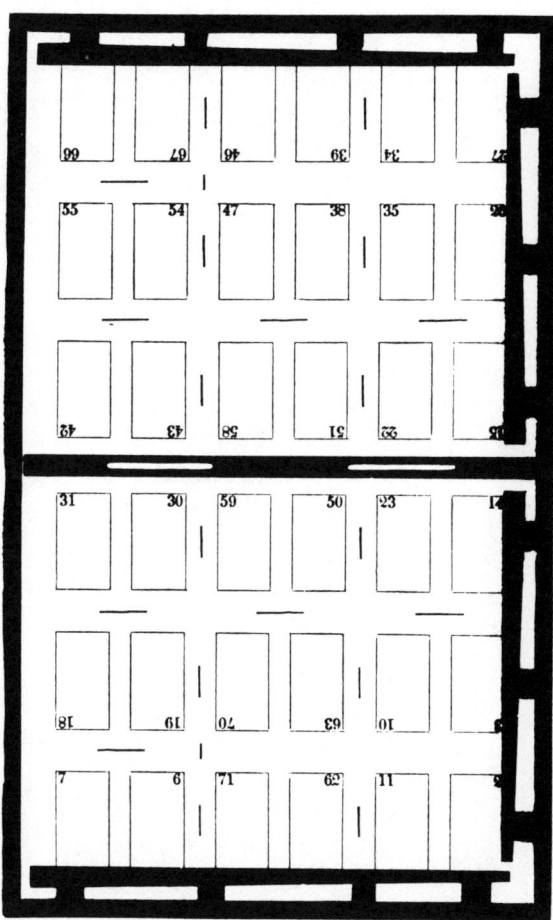

XXVIII.—SHEET OF THIRTY-SIXES: INNER FORM—No. 2.

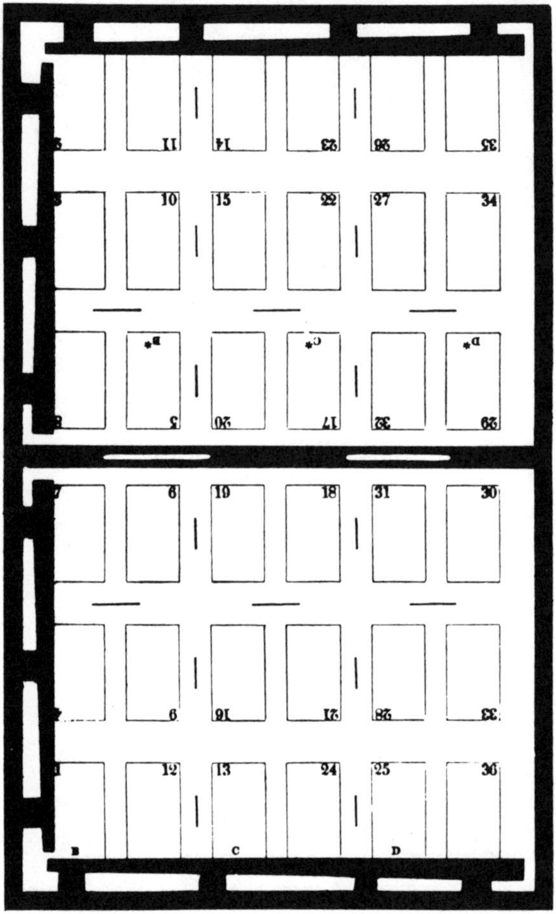

110 PRINTER'S MANUAL:

XXIX.—HALF SHEET OF THIRTY-SIXES—No. 1.

IMPOSING. 111

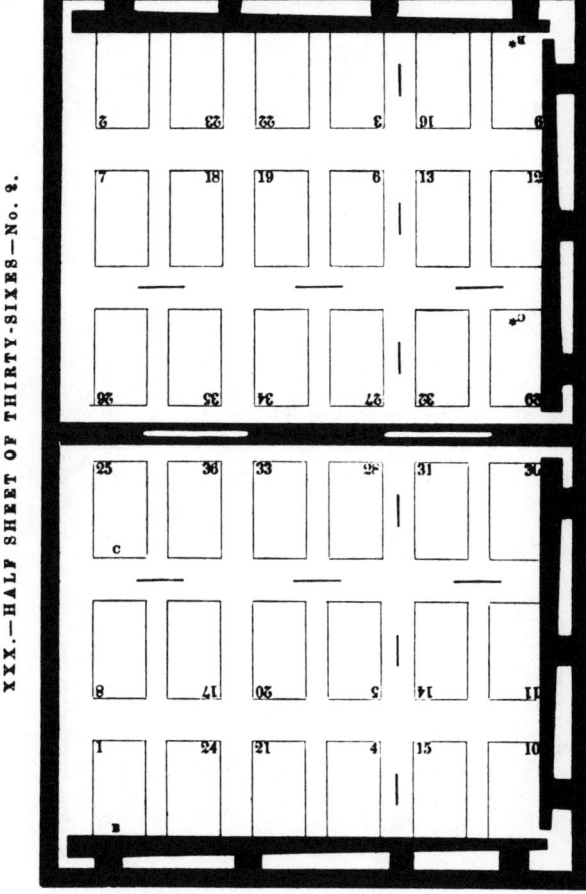

XXX.—HALF SHEET OF THIRTY-SIXES—No. 2.

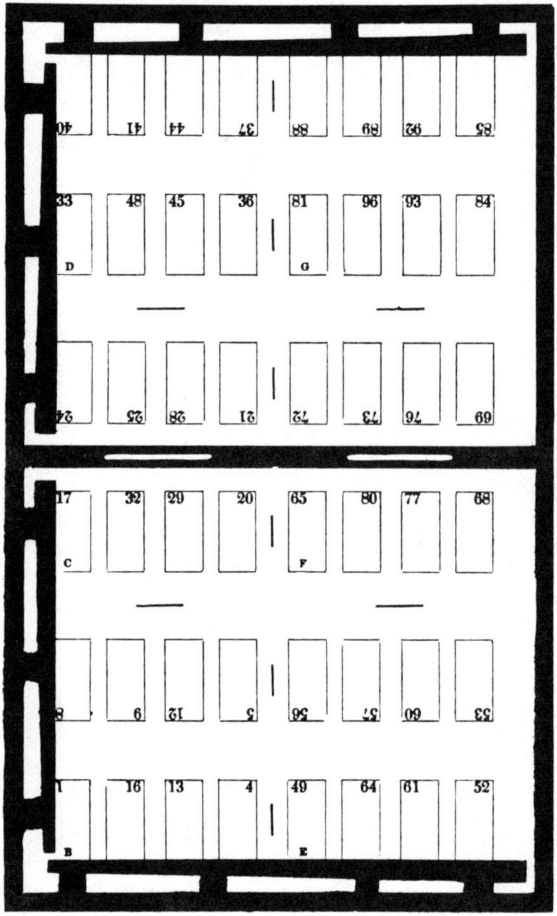

112 PRINTER'S MANUAL:

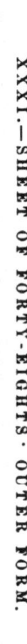

XXXI.—SHEET OF FORTY-EIGHTS. OUTER FORM.

IMPOSING. 113

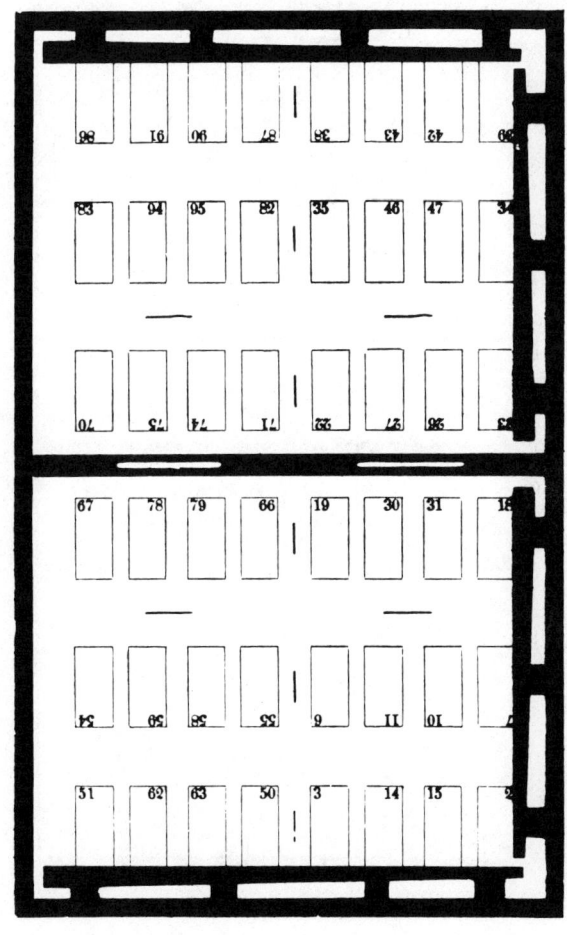

XXXI.—SHEET OF FORTY-EIGHTS: INNER FORM.

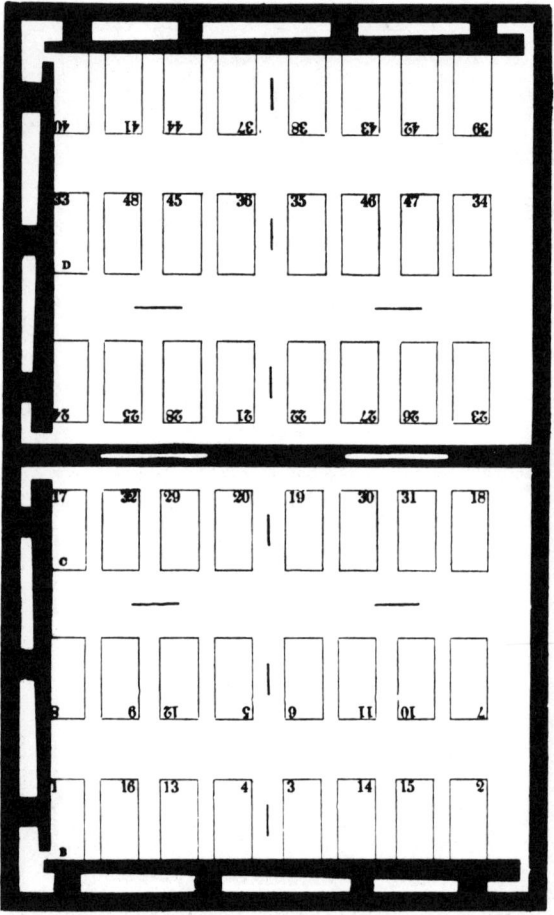

XXXII.—HALF SHEET OF FORTY-EIGHTS—No. 1.

IMPOSING. 115

XXXIII.—HALF SHEET OF FORTY-EIGHTS—No. 2.

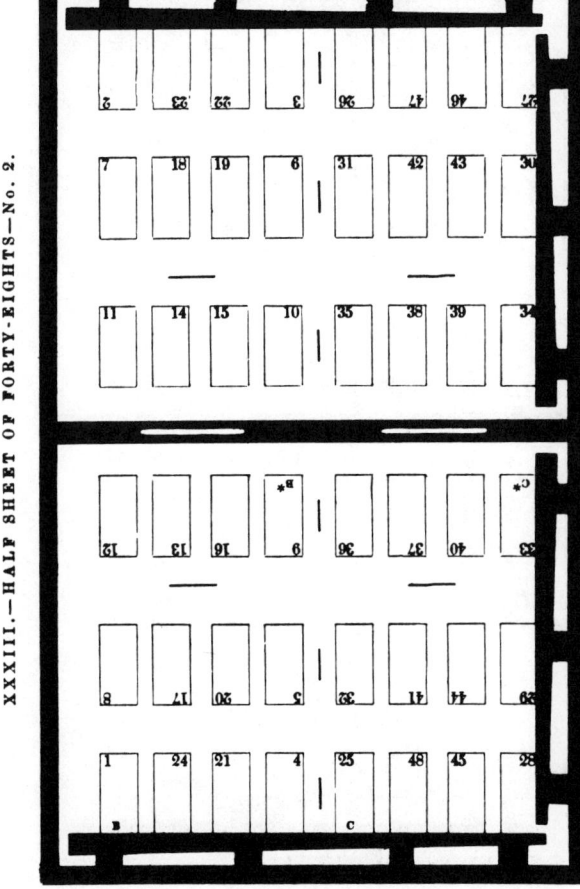

116 PRINTER'S MANUAL:

XXXIV.—HALF SHEET OF ONE HUNDRED AND TWENTY-EIGHTS.

The following is a list of the forms laid down in the preceding pages, with explanations of the purposes for which they are designed :

FOLIO.

I. — Outer and Inner Forms of a Sheet of Folio,   70, 71

> The method of laying the pages for any number of sheets under eight is given, so that they can be laid with the same ease as they would were impositions given for every sheet.

QUARTO.

II. — Outer and Inner Forms of a Sheet of Quarto,   72, 73
III. — Half Sheet of Quarto,   74
IV. — Half Sheet of Quarto, oblong,   75

OCTAVO.

V. — Outer and Inner Forms of a Sheet of Octavo,   76, 77
VI. — Half Sheet of Octavo,   78
VII. — Half Sheet of Octavo, inside out,   79

TWELVES.

VIII. — Outer and Inner Forms of a Sheet of Twelves,   80, 81
IX. — Half Sheet of Twelves,   82
X. — Half Sheet of Twelves, inside out,   83

SIXTEENS.

XI. — Outer and Inner Forms of a Sheet of Sixteens,   84, 85
XII. — Half Sheet of Sixteens,   86
XIII. — Half Sheet of Sixteens, inside out, No. 1,   87
XIV. — Half Sheet of Sixteens, inside out, No. 2,   88
XV. — Half Sheet of Sixteens, inside out, No. 3,   89

> The above modes of laying a "Half Sheet of Sixteens" are given, because that is the number generally worked in a form at present. If a cut or open work of any kind fall on any page, that page can always be laid in the centre of the form by using one of the above impositions.

EIGHTEENS.

XVI. — Outer and Inner Forms of a Sheet of Eighteens, No. 1,   90 / 91

    Two Signatures = A Sheet of Twelves, and a Half Sheet of Twelves.

XVII. — Outer and Inner Forms of a Sheet of Eighteens, No. 2,   92 / 93

    Three Signatures = Three Half Sheets of Twelves.

TWENTY-FOURS.

XVIII. — Outer and Inner Forms of a Sheet of Twenty-Fours,   94 / 95

    Two Signatures = Two Sheets of Twelves.

XIX. — Half Sheet of Twenty-Fours, No. 1,   96

    This is the usual method of laying a Half Sheet of Twenty-Fours: that is, Sixteen pages, and an inset of Eight.

XX. — Half Sheet of Twenty-Fours, No. 2,   97

    Two Signatures = The first, Sixteen, and the second, Eight pages.

XXI. — Half Sheet of Twenty-Fours, No. 3,   98

    Three Signatures, of Eight pages each.

XXII. — Half Sheet of Twenty-Fours, inside out,   99

    Sixteen pages, with an inset of Eight.

THIRTY-TWOS.

XXIII. — Outer and Inner Forms of a Sheet of Thirty-Twos, No. 1,   100 / 101

    Four Signatures, of Sixteen pages each.

XXIV. — Outer and Inner Forms of a Sheet of Thirty-Twos, No. 2,   102 / 103

    One Signature. This method of folding a Sheet of Thirty-Twos will be found convenient for such work as: almanacs, primers, tracts, and other temporary publications, as the sixty-four pages can be folded together and stitched through the back; but, for all regular book-work, No. XXIII. is better.

XXV. — Half Sheet of Thirty-Twos,   104

    One Signature.

XXVI. — Half Sheet of Thirty-Twos, inside out, 105
One Signature.

THIRTY-SIXES.

XXVII. — Outer and Inner Forms of a Sheet of Thirty-Sixes, No. 1, { 106 107 }
Three Signatures, of Twenty-Four pages each.

XXVIII. — Outer and Inner Forms of a Sheet of Thirty-Sixes, No. 2, { 108 109 }
Six Signatures, of Twelve pages each.

XXIX. — Half Sheet of Thirty-Sixes, No. 1, 110
Three Signatures, of Twelve pages each.

XXX. — Half Sheet of Thirty-Sixes, No. 2, 111
Two Signatures = A Sheet of Twenty-Fours, and a Sheet of Twelves.

FORTY-EIGHTS.

XXXI. — Outer and Inner Forms of a Sheet of Forty-Eights, { 112 113 }
Six Signature, of Sixteen pages each.

XXXII. — Half Sheet of Forty-Eights, No. 1, 114
Three Signatures, of Sixteen pages each.

XXXIII. — Half Sheet of Forty-Eights, No. 2, 115
Two Signatures, of Twenty-Four pages each.

The forms above Forty-Eights may be made up according to the manner indicated below:

Half Sheet of Sixty-Fours = Outer and Inner Forms of a Sheet of Thirty-Twos, pages 100 and 101, or 102 and 103.
Half Sheet of Seventy-Twos = Outer and Inner Forms of a Sheet of Thirty-Sixes, pages 106 and 107, or 108 and 109.
Half Sheet of Ninety-Sixes = Outer and Inner Forms of a Sheet of Forty-Eights, pages 112 and 113.

ONE HUNDRED AND TWENTY-EIGHTS.

XXXIV. — Half Sheet of One Hundred and Twenty-Eights, } 116
Eight Signatures, of Sixteen pages each.

MAKING MARGIN.

When the gutter is mentioned in the following pages, it designates the piece of furniture which separates two adjoining pages in a chase: as, in an octavo, that between pages 1 and 16; and, in a duodecimo, that between pages 1 and 24, and so on. The pieces which are put at the sides of the pages, next the cross, are called backs; and those at the tops of the pages are called heads or bolts.

Making margin is the apportioning of the proper distances between the pages of a sheet or form.

This is a most material object in book-work; for, if it be not properly done, the appearance of the book, when bound, will be injured; as the binder will be obliged either to reduce the size of the book, in order to make the edges smooth, or leave many edges untrimmed.

Convenience and custom have familiarized us to the printed page being a little higher than the middle of the leaf, and to its having a little more margin at the forepart than in the back; but the spaces between the pages should be such, that, when the book is bound and cut, the page of printing — that is, the reading-matter, without regarding the head-line — should be made to appear exactly in the middle of the page of paper.

The first of these circumstances may be accounted for, by the head, in all sizes except folio, being at the fold of the paper, which admits of the bookbinder cutting it smooth by taking off a very narrow shaving, so as to reduce the size but a mere trifle; while the bottom of the page lying toward the raw edge of the paper, which is irregular, and which often varies considerably because it is cut crookedly — machine-made paper also varies greatly in the size of the sheets, being cut up irregularly; and paper made at different times, and by different makers, which is often used in the same volume, and which likewise varies in size — all combined, render it necessary to allow a little more margin at the foot of the page and at the front than at the head and in the back: for these variations in the paper equally affect the front and the foot; but the head, the back, and the gutter, being folded, remain the same, however much the paper may vary.

It is always presumed that the backing of the book, in binding, takes up as much of the margin as is cut off the fore-edge, so as to make them both equal.

Having premised these explanatory observations, we shall proceed to describe the manner of ascertaining the proper spaces between the pages, for the different sizes of books, in the simplest manner that is known, and as it is now generally practiced; for the division of the margin by compasses is obsolete.

To facilitate the operation, it will be necessary to bear in mind the observation that, "when we arrive at a great number of pages in a sheet, they resolve themselves into the same order as quartos, octavos, and duodecimos," as a recollection of this will tend to simplify the process, and, if the person who has the imposing of the form be not experienced, it may prevent him from getting confused, by keeping him to a small portion of the form, instead of leaving him to attempt doing all at once.

After the pages have been laid upon the imposing-stone, and the chases put over them, the first thing to be done is to get a sheet of the paper of the work, wet, and to fold it as exactly as possible to the size in which the work is intended to be printed.

If the paper for the work has not been sent in, then a sheet of the same size may be taken from the paper of some other work that is in progress, which will be found to be sufficiently near, inasmuch as a lead or two in the backs and heads, more or less, will make it right; or, the first sheet may be imposed temporarily with furniture from the drawer.

It must be remembered by the compositor, or person whose turn it is to make up the form, that the furniture must never be cut until he is sure of the distance required between the pages.

To ascertain this distance, take short pieces of furniture out of the drawer, or quotations, or both, and quadrats or reglet, to fill up the interspace between two pages; then push the pages up close to them, and when you have got the right distance between the pages, you can ascertain what furniture will be of the exact width, by trying the ends of different pieces, always measuring from the edges of the types themselves, and not within the page-cords.

We will now proceed with making margin, commencing with folio, and going through the various sizes — at least through as many as may be necessary to make the subject as plain as possible:

FOLIO.

Having folded a sheet of the intended paper exactly in the middle, place the edge of the paper even with the outer-edge of the first page, and move the adjoining page toward it until the fold of the paper will lie about half an inch upon it, when the folded sheet is laid upon the face of the first page; the space between the pages on either side of the cross is then to be filled up with furniture, using one piece only on each side, where it is practicable, and where there is no reason to the contrary, in order to prevent mistakes in reïmposing. This space, with one or two leads in addition on each side of the cross, which are to assist in making register at press, will be sufficiently near for a medium-folio, where the page is of a fair dimension; but, if the page be very large, or if it be a smaller sized paper than medium, the back fold of the paper should not be allowed to lie quite so much over the adjoining page, but should be lessened in proportion to the size of the page or paper. If it be very large paper and a corresponding margin, it would be well to allow a little more in proportion; for, it is to be observed, that the more the fold of the paper lies over the edge of the adjoining page, the more margin is given at the fore-edge than in the back.

The margin for the head of a folio is arranged at the printing-press.

After the leads have been put in, the page-cords taken off, and the pages pushed up close to the furniture, you should try it again, to see that it is correct. It is a good plan to take a slip of paper, and cut it to a length equal to the width of the back, then to fold it even in the middle so as to make a distinct crease, to open it again and lay it in the back, so that the crease shall be exactly in the middle of the back; then to open out the sheet of paper, and lay it upon the form, with the crease in its middle upon the crease in the slip of paper; the margin in the back may then be compared with the margin in the fore-edge as well as if the sheet were printed, and it may be altered, if thought necessary, by putting in, or taking out, a lead.

If two jobs, that are to be cut, are worked together, it is usual to impose them so that the margin shall be equal on both sides. To effect this, fold the paper exactly in the middle, and, laying it folded on the left-hand page, with the edge of the paper even with the edge of the page of types, bring the other page toward it until the left-hand side fairly touches the fold of the paper. This is termed being out and out; and when the paper is cut evenly in two, after having been printed, the side-margins will be found to be equal.

QUARTO.

Fold a sheet of paper exactly in quarto; then lay it, thus folded, upon the first page, the fore-edge of the paper being even with the left-hand edge of the types; bring the adjoining page toward the first page until the fold in the paper lies upon the left-hand side of it, about as much as a 2-line pica body: this will make the back as nearly correct as it is possible to make it. Then place the lower-edge of the paper even with the foot of the page, and bring the heads of the pages which adjoin at that part toward each other until the fold in the paper covers the head-line, and nearly the first line of the text: this will make the head right. Then fit the furniture between the pages, and add a lead or two, if necessary. After cutting and folding slips of paper and laying them in the back and head, open out the sheet of paper, laying the folds in the paper precisely over the folds in the slips, and it will be seen how the margin corresponds with the whole of the form.

Before we proceed to octavo, it will be necessary to observe, that, in all sizes except folio and quarto, if there be not enough in the backs, the raw edge of the paper in the front-margin will project beyond the folded-margin, and this in proportion to the deficiency in the back. The same will take place in the length in duodecimo, and in smaller sizes where there are offcuts, if there be not enough at the foot of the pages whence the offcut is taken. The effect produced by these deficiencies is, that the binder will be obliged to reduce the size of the book, both in length and width, when cutting, in order to make the edges smooth.

OCTAVO.

Fold a sheet of paper in octavo, and lay it, thus folded, upon the first page, the fore-edge of the paper even with the outer-edge of the types; then bring the adjoining page toward it until the other side of the folded paper lies over the left-hand side of the page about a pica: this will give the width of the gutter. Then open the paper out a fold, into quarto, and laying it upon the two pages, bring the third page, on the right-hand, sufficiently near for the right-hand side of the paper to lie upon the left-hand side of the page about a long-primer body: this will give the width of the back. Then fold the paper up again, and laying it upon the first page, with the foot of the paper even with the direction-line, bring the head of the page above it so near that the top of the folded paper will cover the head-line, and barely, also, the first line of the matter: this will give the space at the head. Then put into all the spaces on one side of the long-cross, and into the head, small pieces of furniture from the drawer, or quotations, which are generally used where they will fit, or quadrats, making both the gutters alike, and push the pages up close. Cut the slips of paper as before, and fold them; lay them in the gutters, head, and back, and open the sheet of paper to its full size; lay it with the crease of the middle fold exactly upon that in the slip of paper in the back, and, if the margin be right, the creases between the other pages will fall upon those in the slips of paper laid in the gutters; if they do not, the space in the back must be increased or diminished until they do, when the margin will be right. The furniture may then be cut, and a lead inserted in the crosses at the backs and heads in each of the quarters.

TWELVES.

After folding a sheet exactly in duodecimo, proceed as in octavo for the gutter; but let the fold lie rather less over the adjoining page than a pica. Proceed in the same manner for the back; but it will be sufficient if the paper cover the third page only a long-primer body. The fold in the head will just cover the top line of matter in the adjoining page above it, as in octavo; and the pieces of furniture put in there are called bolts. The offcut is now to be considered: this is always imposed on the outside of the short-cross, and the back and gutters are the same as those in the other part of the sheet. For the head of the offcut, the space between the running-title, or, where there is no running-title, the head-line, and the middle of the groove in the short-cross, must be exactly half the width of the bolts; because, as register is made at this part, and the points fall into the groove and there make point-holes, the binder folds to these holes and takes off the offcut in accordance. Thus, when the sheet is folded, and the offcut inserted in its place and knocked-up, the head-lines of the offcut ought to range with the head-lines of the outer pages, and this should always be kept in view by the printer.

When duodecimo forms are printed on a power-press, they are generally pointed in the long-cross. This leaves the offcut without any mark by which the binder will be able to separate it correctly from the rest of the sheet. In all such cases it would be well to justify a couple of small pieces of single rule in the places where the points should strike.

The space between the bottom of the other pages and the middle of the groove in the short-cross should be within a pica of the outer margin at the foot of the pages, which will allow for a little variation in the size of the paper, and not affect the size of the book in cutting the edges. When the distances are thus arranged, put short pieces of furniture, quotations, etc., as before directed, between the pages, in the gutters and back in one row, and in the head and both sides of the short-cross in another, and push the pages of both these rows close up. Cut slips of paper and fold them for the gutters and the back, as also for the bolts; then open out the sheet of paper, and lay the middle crease in it exactly upon the one in the slip of paper laid in the back; and, if the side-margin is right, the creases in the sheet of paper between the other pages will fall upon those in the slips of paper in the gutters; if they do not, the space in the back must be altered until they do. Then try it the other way, by laying the crease in the sheet of paper upon the one in the slip laid in the bolt, and if the crease of the offcut fall exactly in the middle of the groove of the short-cross, it is right; if it does not, the space at the foot of the pages next the cross must be altered until it does. It being presumed that the gutters and bolts are right, the only places at which to alter are the back and the space at the foot of the pages which lie at the offcut; a lead or two, as may be required, should be put in each of the quarters next the crosses.

In duodecimo, music-way, the pages are reversed in shape, being so wide that two of them occupy the width of the sheet, and so short that six of them are equal to the length. In this case there are no backs, technically so called, but only gutters; but, as the long-cross comes between the pages, they must be treated as backs, in the same manner as in folio, and the fold of the paper must be allowed to lie more over the side of the adjoining page, as was described in making margin for folio: if the page be very wide, less than half an inch; if it be narrow, and a large margin, it may be a little more. The head-margins or bolts are three in depth, and may be ascertained in the same manner precisely as for octavo or common twelves, which being done, the foot-margins may be ascertained. These, being two, may have a pica body each less than the outer foot-margins, to allow for any inequality in the size of the paper, or in laying on the white paper at press. This can be done by folding the paper exactly in three portions the narrow way of the sheet, and extending the pages until one of these portions covers the two outer pages with the gutter, and lies over the third about a pica body. When this has been done at one end of the form, the other end may be regulated in the same way. The margin may then be tried in the manner described before, and any alteration necessary must be made in the space at the foot of the pages, care being taken that both spaces are equal.

In long duodecimo, the pages are of the same size as the preceding, only that they exchange the length for the width, and the width for the length. The manner of making margin is the same for this size as for the last; the only difference between them being, that which was the gutter in the other making the head in this, and what was the head or bolt and the foot-margin now becoming the gutter and the back. The spaces between the pages, for heads, gutters, and backs, are ascertained in the same manner as described for ordinary duodecimo.

As the number of pages increases in a sheet, so the utility of placing slips of paper, folded in the middle, in the gutters, backs, etc., becomes greater, by enabling the person whose business it is, to ascertain readily the middle of each space when he tries the whole margin with the sheet opened out. To some this may seem unnecessarily minute; but whatever method tends toward facilitating an operation, and enabling a person to perform it more accurately, is useful.

SIXTEENS.

After having described so fully the manner of folding the paper and ascertaining the spaces between the pages for the gutters, the heads, and the backs, which may be needed for folios, quartos, octavos, and duodecimos, it will be unnecessary to repeat those directions for the other sizes.

For sixteens, fold a quarter of a sheet of paper exactly in four, and proceed to find the width of the gutter, the back, and the head, in one quarter of the chase, and having made these correctly, arrange the remainder of the form in the same manner. After this is done, the whole must be tried with an entire sheet of paper opened out, and any slight alteration which is to be made must be done by increasing or lessening the space in the backs and at the foot of the pages next the short-cross.

The greater the number of pages in a sheet, the lesser in proportion does the margin become: it must therefore be evident, that the folded paper should lie proportionably less over the edges of the adjoining page, both for gutter and for back, as the number of pages increases; for, as a folio may require the page to be half an inch nearer the back than the fore-edge, a form of eighteens may not require it to be more than a long-primer; and so in proportion with respect to the size of the pages and of the margin.

EIGHTEENS.

A sheet of eighteens is the same as three half sheets of duodecimo imposed together: there are two backs and three gutters in each form. The other way of the chase it is three pages in depth, having bolts and an offcut the same as duodecimo; and the process is the same as when making margin for that size, with this difference, that the first gutter and back are ascertained by one-third of the sheet of paper the long way instead of one-half of it the narrow way. Having made the spaces between the six pages at the near side of the chase correct, make the other two rows correspond with them, and then try the whole with the sheet of paper opened out. The creases in the folds should fall exactly in the middle of the gutters and backs; but as the offcut is not imposed on the side of the short-cross with the groove in it, the crease for the offcut should be exactly one-half the width of the bolt from the running-title, or head-line, or it should fall in the middle of the long-cross.

It should be kept in mind that in making margin, the arranging of the whole form must not be attempted at once; because it is more than probable that it will be wrong and the source of additional trouble and waste of furniture. The safer plan is to get one portion right, then to make a row of pages, each way, through the form, and afterward to try them with the sheet of paper opened out, when any slight variation that may occur can be easily remedied before the furniture is cut.

TWENTY-FOURS.

The side-margin is to be ascertained in the same way as recommended for eighteens, both being the same number of pages in width; and the head- and foot-margins can be determined in the manner recommended for sixteens. The difference in the size of the pages does not affect the principle of making margin.

A form of long twenty-fours is similar to a sheet of twelves imposed in one chase, the width of the pages being the longest way of the paper: the method of making margin for it will be the same as for twelves or eighteens.

IMPOSING.

The only difference between square twenty-fours and twenty-fours is, that in the former the width occupies the sheet the longest way. The margin is made in a similar manner in both.

THIRTY-TWOS.

As one quarter of a form of thirty-twos is similar to a form of octavo, the margin may be made by folding a quarter of a sheet of paper and arranging the pages of one-fourth of the form only in the first instance. When this is done, the remaining pages should be placed in the same relative position, and the whole should be tried with the sheet of paper opened out, before cutting the furniture.

There is no variation in the principle of making the margins of the other sizes; as they are all composed of a number of octavos, twelves, or eighteens, and it would be nothing more than a repetition of the directions previously given for determining the width of the gutters, backs, heads or bolts, and of the spaces at the foot of the pages when they either cut up or fold at that point.

Whenever a half sheet is imposed, or two half sheets to be worked together, the middle margin, where the sheet is cut in two, should always be made out and out, so that both the fore-edges may be equal.

When the margin to the first sheet of a work has been made and the quoins tightened with the fingers, a gauge should be cut for the back and head, so that those spaces in the succeeding sheets may be measured whenever it is found to be necessary.

CUTTING FURNITURE.

In cutting the furniture the heads or bolts should be made so that they would fit in the composing-stick in which the work has been set; this will allow the gutters to be a line or two longer than the pages, so that they can be pushed down close to the foot-sticks, and will, at the other end, project between the head-sticks, thereby securing the insides of the pages, without there being any liability of the gutters binding, when locked up, as is likely to be the case when the head-sticks to each quarter are in one piece, and the gutters are cut to the exact length of the pages. The gutters being a little longer than the pages, may answer for other works, where the pages are of the same width but different in length.

The head-sticks and gutters being cut and put in the parts of the form to which they belong, the next thing to be done is to cut the backs. They should be made so that, when put in their places, they would reach from the cross-bar to a short distance below the foot of the page, yet not so long as to interfere with the quoin, if it should be driven up close to the cross-bar.

The side-stick should reach from the cross-bar, or from the furniture at that place, to a short distance beyond the foot of the page, but not enough to pass the end of the foot-stick, as it would be in the way of the outer quoin at the foot.

The foot-stick should be a little shorter than the width of the pages and gutter; for, as there is always a line of quads at the foot of each page, the foot-stick may be a pica shorter without the risk of any of the types falling out when the form is lifted; it also prevents the side- and foot-sticks from binding when locked up.

If the furniture be cut according to the foregoing directions, it will be perceived that all the pages are secure, and that it is impossible for the furniture to bind in any place when locked up: as the gutter is pushed down to the foot-stick and extends a short distance above the heads of the pages; the heads or bolts being cut so as to fit the composing-stick; the back is pushed up close to the cross-bar, and extends a little below the foot of the page; the foot-stick rests against the back, and, by being a little short, prevents the side-stick from binding against it; the side-stick abuts against the cross-bar or furniture, and passes the quad-line at the foot of the page.

The pieces of furniture placed at the cross-bars should not be so long as to project past the ends of the side- and foot-sticks; for, when they do, they are in the way of the shooting-stick, if a quoin has been driven up closely, when the form has to be unlocked.

When either the side- or foot-stick is so long as to project one beyond the other, it prevents the quoin from passing, and, in unlocking, occasions a great amount of trouble in getting it out; and is likely to cause the side-stick to be battered or broken, or, perhaps, a page to become squabbled. This is produced by carelessness or idleness, both of which generally create more trouble in the end than if the work had been done properly in the beginning.

If it be thought unnecessary or wasteful to cut down side- or foot-sticks for a job or pamphlet, when there are none of a proper length in the office, a piece of furniture taken out of the drawer, of the correct length and width, and placed between the side-stick and the page, will obviate the difficulty and allow the quoin to be driven with ease.

When placing the furniture around the pages, leave the ends of the page-cords out, so that they may be taken off easily, without the necessity of disturbing the furniture or pages to find the ends, which will be the case if they be hidden from view.

To prevent, as much as possible, one piece of furniture from being mistaken for another in the hurry of business, it would be well to cut all the gutters for the sheet of the same length. The same should be done with the heads and backs; but each kind should be of a different length from that of the others. If this be done, they can be easily distinguished, and the liability to make mistakes will be obviated.

When it can be done, it is preferable to have each part of the furniture in one piece, as it prevents them from being transposed and the margin from getting wrong: but sometimes pieces will be wanted of a width that is not equal to any particular size, and then two must be used.

The heads and gutters, for all regular sizes, should be made out of type-metal, which is cast from two to twelve m in width, and a foot in length. These pieces, to insure accuracy, should be cut at the foundry. The furniture at the back and short-cross should be of wood, because the spaces will often have to be altered at these places on account of the difference in the sizes of paper mentioned when treating of making margin. The side- and foot-sticks should be either wrought-iron or gun-metal, and made perfectly smooth and perpendicular on the sides which the types and the quoins rest against. If this be not done, the form will be thrown off of its feet when it is locked up.

LOCKING UP THE FORM.

The furniture being now around the pages, the person making up the form should put a few quoins between the side- and foot-stick, and the chase, not with any particular care that they fit, but merely to secure the pages, and by that means to push them up close to the heads, backs, and gutters.

After having taken a page-cord from a page, push that page up close to the furniture toward the cross-bars, by means of the side- and foot-sticks, to prevent the letters at the ends of the lines falling down, and, at the same time, tighten the quoins gently with the fingers.

The page-cords being all taken off, and the pages pushed up, it will next be necessary to examine particularly whether the margin be right; and also to put a thin lead between the furniture and the crosses. These leads enable the pressman to make register, if there be any inequality in the furniture or the crosses, by changing their situations, or taking some of them away. They also enable the compositor to make the distance between the pages in the backs and heads uniform, which should always be the case; and no form of book-work that has to be printed on both sides of the paper should be imposed without them; but they should never be used in the gutters.

The form has now to be quoined, which many compositors are in the habit of doing very carelessly, thinking that if the form lifts it is quite sufficient. This is an erroneous opinion, and frequently causes mistakes from the careless manner in which the quoining is done, by letters and even line dropping out when the form is lifted from the stone or laid on the press, and which may not get replaced correctly; and the pages are more likely to fall out of the chase, if the form be allowed to stand, without a letter-board at its back, for a day or two. As octavo is the most common size worked, whatever directions may be given will be for that size; but the principle is the same, whatever the size of the page may be. There should be two quoins at the side of each outer page. The one near the cross-bar, when in its right position, should be about three-quarters of an inch from the broad end of the side-stick, which will allow room for the shooting-stick in unlocking, and also for the form being tightened, if the furniture in the back should shrink; and the other quoin, when driven tight, should be its whole length within the other end of the page, and, if it be the one at the outer end of the side-stick, it should no more than pass the end of the foot-stick; because this end of the side-stick, being thin, will be likely to spring from the page if the quoin be driven in far, and thus leave the lines below it insecure, and in danger of falling out. There should be two quoins at the foot-stick in the same situations, and a third in the middle, to cover the end of the gutter. Each quarter, of a form of octavo, thus quoined, will be perfectly secure when the quoins are driven tight, provided the pages be made up to the same length, and the lines properly justified.

Before the quoins are tightened the pages in each quarter should be examined to see that they are of the same length, which may be done by pressing against the foot-stick, and raising it a little from the stone; if it lifts up with it equally the ends of both the pages against which it presses, they are right. The other quarters of the chase must be examined in the same way, and, if any variation in the length of the pages should be found to exist, it must be rectified. This arises generally from the carelessness of the compositor, who will not take the trouble of cutting a gauge by which to make up his pages, but does it by counting the lines, sometimes putting in a line too much, and at others leaving out one, and, again, by a having too few or too many leads in a page.

The quoins should now be pushed up with the fingers, and the form planed down gently. If any letters should happen to project above the rest, they are easily pushed down, by this mode of proceeding, without injuring the face. After this is done, the sides of the pages should be examined to see that no letters have slipped out of their places at the ends of the lines, which is frequently the case when pages which have been tied up have lain on the galley or under the frame for some time; this may also happen in taking the page-cords off, particularly if they be knotty. Having examined the pages and rectified any thing that may have been found misplaced, which is easily done in this stage of the form, the quoins should be gently tightened, with the mallet and shooting-stick, until the types are held firm and upright in their places in the form. It should then be planed down, by putting the face of the planer down evenly on the types and striking it firmly, but not violently, with the mallet. If any letters stand higher than the rest, because there is some substance underneath them, such as a space, or a letter, or a piece of page-paper, it will be better to omit planing that part down, as it will only injure the types. The quoins should now be driven up tight enough to lift the form, taking care that, after the form is locked up tight enough at the foot to retain the lines firmly in their place, the remainder must be done at the side.

The reasons for locking the pages up tighter at the sides than at the feet are these: the lines will give more in the direction of the width of a page than in that of the length; and, if the pages be first locked up tightly at the sides and the feet be driven up afterward, the lines will be bent by reason of their ends being held fast by the side-sticks and backs, while the middle parts are driven up by the pressure at the feet.

In locking up forms, some compositors finish one quarter completely before proceeding to the next. This should never be done, as it will spring the cross-bars, and thereby hinder the pressman from making register. The proper way is to lock up each quarter, a little at a time, until the form can be lifted.

One side of the form is now to be lifted from the stone, just enough to allow the compositor to see whether it will rise or not, but not so high as to let any loose letters drop out. If any thing of the kind should be found, the form should be unlocked, and the lines containing such letters, justified. Some persons, instead of doing this, will thrust a bodkin between some of the words, or tighten the quoins; but this, beside being slovenly, is not a safe way of remedying such defects, as the letters are always in danger of being drawn out at press. Sometimes parts of a page are loose on account of a letter having slipped down at the end of a line: in this case it is easily rectified, by unlocking the quarter and putting such letter in its place; when this is done, and the form will rise, take any

IMPOSING.

thing that may be under it away, lay the form on the stone again, loosen the quoins in that quarter, then plane it down, and lock it up as before directed.

The form being now locked up, the stone must be cleared of every thing: such as, the mallet and planer, quoins, page cords, and any other material which may have been used during the locking up of the form.

In imposing a sheet with the furniture of one that has been worked off, there are certain things to be attended to which are frequently neglected. The chase and furniture of one form should always be used for a similar form: that is, those for an outer form should again be use for an outer form, and those of an inner form for each succeeding one of the same kind; they should also be put around the pages in the same order in which they were placed about those of the preceding forms. For want of care or thought in these apparently trifling circumstances, a great amount of trouble, inconvenience, and loss of time, are frequently incurred; because, the register will almost certainly be wrong when this is neglected, and then the form must be unlocked and the leads changed, some of them having to be taken out or other ones inserted.

It will be a great saving of time if the compositor is methodic when taking the chase and furniture from one form and putting them around another. The quoins should be taken out and laid on the adjoining pages in regular order; then, after the chase and furniture have been put around the pages of the other form, there will be no loss of time in replacing the quoins or in finding the proper place for each of them.

The chases for a sheet should always be in pairs; for if they be of different sizes, and the rims vary in thickness, it causes the pressman to lose time, in making register, when both forms are worked at the same press, and often occasions the spoiling of several sheets of paper before that object is accomplished.

If a form should not be distributed immediately after the chase and furniture are taken off, a cord should be put around each page. This will hinder the types from getting pied: at least, it may prevent an accident and save some unnecessary trouble.

TAKING THE PROOF.

The form being ready, the next thing to be done is to pull a proof. To do this properly the form should be carried to the press; but, before it is laid down, the bed and the back of the form should be brushed off, so that no grains of dirt or other hard particles will be on either of them; then, having placed the lower edge of the chase at the farther side of the bed, to let it down gently until it rests upon the press. The form should next be unlocked, planed down, and locked up again.

The form must now be inked; in doing which care should be taken that too much be not put on, as it will collect on the finer lines of the types and give the whole form a muddy appearance when the impression is taken. The proof should not be quite as black as book-work is; because, if it be a little grey, any imperfect letters can be easily seen, which would not be the case were the faces of the types surcharged with ink.

The impression should never be taken with a blanket, as it will press the paper down around the outer edges and into the counters of the types. From four to six thicknesses of paper should be put between the tympan and drawer, in place of the blanket, and an impression pulled, just hard enough to bring the pages up distinctly.

The form is now to be lifted from the press, taken to the trough, brushed over with ley, and rinsed with clean water, then laid on the stone and unlocked for correction, or inclined against a letter-board, in some safe place.

CORRECTING.

This being in itself the cause of loss of time to the compositor, it is important that he be made acquainted with the most expeditious as well as the surest method of doing it accurately.

If the types be on a galley, they should be carried to the case and corrected there, the facilities being much greater than at the stone. Both ends of the galley should be kept so far above the ledge of the lower-case that the spaces and letters in the row of boxes next the workman could be got at without difficulty.

Whether the types be corrected on the galley or on the stone, the method of performing it will be the same. If there should be an error in a line, which would cause the least alteration in the spacing, that line must be taken out of the form or galley and justified in the composing-stick; because it is impossible to do so correctly in any other manner. In figure-work, and other jobs, in which the types taken out and put in are of the same size, the line need not be lifted. In all such cases nippers, made rough on the inside like a fine file, should be used.

One class of corrections only should be attended to at a time: that is, the literal errors must be first rectified, then the doublets and outs, if there be any; after which, the galley should be carefully revised.

In correcting at the stone, the case should be brought from the stand and placed as near the form as circumstances will allow. This will save the compositor much time, as he will not have to leave the stone while making the corrections, except it be for caps, italic, or some other sorts of the kind.

When the first proof has been corrected, a second one must be pulled, which, after being compared with the other to see that the errors marked have been rectified, must be sent to the author, by whom it is looked over; and any corrections or alterations which he may deem it necessary to make being legibly marked on the margin, it must be put into the hands of the reader again, who, after having read it over carefully, for grammatical mistakes, and errors which may not have been detected in the first proof, will give it to the compositor for final correction.

Before the form is put to press, it must be revised, in the metal, by the foreman, or some person who has no part of the form; because the compositor, on account of having set the types, will not be able to detect any oversight, in correcting, as well as another person will.

On the next page is given a specimen of a proof, with the errors generally made, and the marks of correction corresponding to them; neither of which will require any explanation, as the same matter, in a corrected state, is given on the opposite page.

Chancery-Case for Three-Pence.

Eyre and Strahan, King's printers, vs. Ogilvy and Spear. May 3, 1794.

A few days previous to the last general fast, the defendants, through ignorance of the law, sold one copy of the Form of Prayer, appointed to be used on that occasion, not printed, by authority of the king's patent.

The plaintiffs, without giving the smallest *slight* intimation to desist, filed this bill to compel the defendants to account to them for the profit from arising the said sale. Upon being served with the subpœna, defendants applied to have proceedings stayed, which the plaintiffs, after considerable hesitation, agreed to, on condition of defendants paying costs, and making affidavit to the sale, this *important cause* was this day finished, when plaintiffs received three-pence! the profit arising from the sale, and when the attorney, Edward S. Foss, of Gough-square, did not blush to receive £13 6s 9d for costs incurred.

N. B. — Andrew Strahan, one of the plaintiffs, takes a considerable sum annually, in the way of trade, from the industrious defendants, against against whom the bill was filed, who now publish this case for the purpose of cautioning the public against a similar offense, and that the *liberal* character of Mr. *stet.* Strahan may be generally known.

Perhaps this the history of law, of a bill in chancery having been filed to recover so small a sum as *three-pence*, and deserves to be recorded in the future editions of the "Curiosities of Literature" as an elucidation of the old law-adage, "*Summum jus summa injuria.*"

is the only case which has ever occurred in

CHANCERY-CASE FOR THREE-PENCE.

Eyre and Strahan, King's printers, vs. Ogilvy and Spear. May 3, 1794.

A few days previous to the last general fast, the defendants, through ignorance of the law, sold one copy of the form of prayer, appointed to be used on that occasion, not printed *by authority of the king's patent*.

The plaintiffs, without giving the slightest intimation to desist, filed this bill to compel the defendants to account to them for the profit arising from the said sale. Upon being served with the subpœna, defendants applied to have proceedings stayed, which the plaintiffs, after considerable hesitation, agreed to, on condition of defendants paying costs and making affidavit to the sale. This *important cause* was this day finished, when plaintiffs received THREE-PENCE! the profit arising from the sale; and when the attorney, Edward S. Foss, of Gough-square, did not blush to receive £13 6s 9d for costs incurred.

N. B. — Andrew Strahan, one of the plaintiffs, takes a considerable sum annually, in the way of trade, from the industrious defendants, against whom this bill was filed, who now publish this case for the purpose of cautioning the public against a similar offense, and that the *liberal* character of Mr. Strahan may be generally known.

Perhaps this is the only case which has ever occurred in the history of law, of a bill in chancery having been filed to recover so small a sum as *three-pence*, and deserves to be recorded in the future editions of the "CURIOSITIES OF LITERATURE" as an elucidation of the old law-adage: "*Summum jus summa injuria.*"

THE SCHEDULE.

In the margin is given a very convenient form of a schedule, used by compositors to keep a correct account of the number of pages composed by them, as well as by the proprietor or foreman, in order that they may ascertain, whenever it may be necessary, how far the work has been made up, as well as to rectify the bills of the compositors, if it be required.

The first column indicates the folios of the work, and the remaining columns, under the names of the compositors, are intended, the first, under each, showing to whom the page belongs, and, the other, the number of nonpareil lines, or other extra matter, if there be any, in the page.

If there be two works in progress, at the same time, the title of each should be written on the schedule which belongs to it, to obviate confusion.

At the end of each week, a line should be drawn across the schedule at the last page marked, and the date and the word "charged" written in the margin.

After the work is finished, the schedules should be put away, so that they could be referred to again, if necessary.

	LYNCH.		BARNARD.	
Folios	Pages	Nonpareil	Pages	Nonpareil
5	*			
6	*	6		
7	*	12		
8	*	11		
9	*	16		
10	*	5		
11	½	12	½	
12			*	14
13			*	13
14			*	7
15	½		½	2
16	*	23		
17	*	11		
18	*	25		
19	½	6	½	
20	½		½	20
21	*	5		
22	*			
23			*	
24			*	
25			*	
26			*	
27			*	
28			*	

JOB-WORK.

All that has been said, in the previous part of this work, has been with reference to plain book-work; but, there are other things with which the compositor should be conversant; these are the setting of: titles, tables, columns, and any other kind of composition which is not of the kind herein before described.

TITLE-PAGES.

When setting up a title-page, it must be done with reference to its appearance when printed: that is, the lines must be so proportioned to each other, that no two of them will be of the same length, and, when it can be done, the lines should be alternately a long and a short one, throughout the page, taking care, at the same time, that they do not taper off into a triangular shape.

The faces of the types used should be uniform: that is, if the largest line be set in condensed letters, the others should be of the same kind, and vice versa.

The sizes of letter used should correspond with the wording of the title and the size of page: the name of the work being in the largest types, and, if possible, a full line; the other lines being set in types bearing relative proportion to it. The catch-lines should be set in the smallest types that will print well: this will allow the other lines of the page to appear to more advantage.

The spaces between the lines should be as wide as the circumstances will admit; bearing in mind, at the same time, that those closely connected in meaning must be nearer together than those which are not. In a page in which the title consists of a number of lines, they must be a uniform distance apart, without regard to the catch-line which may be between any two of them.

TABLES OR COLUMNS.

This includes every description of rule-work, whether the spaces between the rules contain matter or not, and comprehends all that is distinguished in the trade as: rule-work, tabular, or tables. This is the most difficult kind of composition, as it requires the greatest accuracy, both in the length of the rules and the justification of the headings and columns.

There is a great difference in the methods of setting this description of work; but we will only take notice of the one which, while being as accurate as any of the others, consumes the least time. In this system all the columns are set across, instead, as is usual, of being set down in single columns, and the composing-rule is used in the ordinary manner. It is applicable to any and every description of matter, and the most complicated tables may be set up, continued on one galley, and made up like common matter. The column-rules being inserted afterward, the pages can be made up, whatever doubles there may be in each column, without the possibility of making mistakes or cutting the rules into wrong lengths.

The compositor must find out how many rules run downward, in the table, and having ascertained this, he will measure those rules with quads and spaces of the size of types in which the table is to be set, until he gets the exact number. This amount of blank is to be used, in the end of each line, until the table is composed, after which it is taken away, so that the rules can be inserted in the places to which they belong.

If the table be a number of columns of figures, with words in the beginning of the lines, it can be set up, in the stick, with one justification. The manner of doing it is as follows: Set up the word or words in the first line, and having put quads or leaders in to bring it near the point whence the figures should start; these must then be set up, and the blank corresponding to the rules being put at the end of the line, it should be spaced out by putting the required amount in between the words and the first of the figures. The second and succeeding lines can be done in the same manner.

If the table should contain words, in more than one of the columns, each of these will require a separate justification; but, instead of breaking the measure of a composing-stick for each column, it is more expeditious and less liable to error, to set them in the same manner as that recommended for figure-work. Suppose the table be four columns, each differing in width from the others: set up the first line of the first column, and then get a piece of thick lead, and cut it so that it will occupy the remainder of the measure; then, having taken out the lead, set the first line of the second column, and cut a piece of lead to fit between it and the other end of the line; proceed in the same manner with the first line of the third column; and the fourth, together with a space of the width of the three rules which are to run between the columns, will fill the remainder of the first line. The pieces of lead are to be used, in the lines of the table which follow, the longest to justify the first column against, and the others in a similar manner.

If the table be more than four columns in width, it must be left to the discretion of the workman into how many measures it should be divided. It will be found that the more equally this is done the better, both for convenience and expedition. For instance, a table of six columns would be better divided into two measures of three columns each, if they be not so wide as to make the measure inconvenient, than into three of two columns. This would be more simple, and therefore less liable to mistakes. If, however, the job consists of ten or twelve columns of matter, the whole or part of which having to be justified, and which may run over, at times, in every column, it will be necessary to divide the job into four measures, and to empty the first five or six columns on one galley and the second on another. After it is finished, both parts should be placed side by side, and the lines made to correspond with the copy, by inserting quad-lines in either galley, opposite any lines that may have run over in the other; after which the matter can be made up, either into octavo, to read across two pages, or into quarto, to read on one. The rules may now be put in, by laying the galley on the stone, and opening the places for them with the blade of a penknife.

The space at the ends of the lines being taken off, it will be found, when the rules are inserted, that the table is of the exact width of the measure which it is intended to fill, without requiring any justification.

In setting the heading of a table, it should be done, complete, with short rules, between two cross-rules of the width of the table, as in page 140. This will make it look better than it would if the rules between the columns were of the full length of the table, and the separation between the heading and the other part of the table made by using space-rule or metal-dashes, as on page 51.

If a table contain too many columns for the width of the page, and it is necessary to insert it in the direction of the length, it should be imposed so as to read from the foot of the page. The reason for this is: that, when tables are imposed in this manner, the lines and pages follow each other like ordinary matter.

STEREOTYPING.

In setting up matter which is to be stereotyped, the quads and spaces used are of the hight of the shank of the letter. A line of bearers is put above the head-line, to keep it from being battered when the back of the plate is shaved. Bearers are also put in any large blank places in the body of the matter, for the same purpose. Bevels, the hight of the insides of which is equal to that of the shoulder of the types, are run down both sides of the pages. The furniture and chases used, for locking up stereotype-forms, are lower than those used for letter-press, being only half an inch in hight.

ELECTROTYPING.

The spaces and quads are of the same hight as for stereotyping. There are no bearers used in setting up the matter; instead of which, after the bevels are placed at the sides of the pages, a solid bearer is put around each. The furniture and chases need not be lower than the kinds in common use.

NEWSPAPERS.

The following description of the method of getting out an issue of the London Times is given, because it is printed on small types, and contains more matter than any other daily paper in existence, and as a consequence requires and employs more people to prepare it for publication; beside these, it has the reputation of being the most methodic in the arrangement of its matter and the performance of the work.

"The compositors employed to compose this great mass of intelligence day by day, and every day throughout the year, Saturdays excepted, there being no publication on Sundays, are seventy-five, who are divided into two classes: viz., the night- or news-hands, and the advertisement-hands. The first class consists of thirty-nine, who are divided into full hands, fourteen; supernumeraries, ten; assistants, fifteen; to these may be added ten 'outsiders,' who fill the frames of absentees in case of sickness, or from other causes: they are not considered as belonging to the establishment, inasmuch as they hold no situation, and are consequently dependent upon the workmen. The advertisement department consists of thirty-six hands.

"As it is desirable not to have to distribute letter after copy is taken, the compositors usually put their letter in after all the composing is completed, or take the opportunity when waiting for copy, to be ready for the evening, or else they attend sooner in the afternoon than the usual hour for that purpose.

"The full hands take copy at six o'clock in the evening, precisely, and go on without regard to the old rule of first work and finish, and the day's work is considered to be completed at the expiration of eleven hours, five o'clock in the morning; if engaged after that time all hands are paid by the hour, the printer never availing himself of the choice of beginning an hour later on account of the lateness of the preceding morning. The full hands are expected to compose two galleys each per night, and all over-lines are paid for extra, even though they be composed within the time prescribed by the rules laid down for the guidance of compositors.

"The supernumeraries are expected to compose one galley each per night, and all over-lines are paid for extra, the same as with the full hands.

"The full hands have each three pairs of cases — nonpareil, minion, and bourgeois; and as the matter which is the most advantageous is generally set in the smaller type, they claim the benefit of it as an equivalent for the labor of putting the forms to the machine.

"The supernumeraries and assistants take copy at seven o'clock in the evening, and continue to work until all is composed; and should there be any standing still for want of copy, they are allowed at the rate of a quarter of a galley per hour for all time they may have lost during the night. The assistants have no stated salary, but are paid by the galley, and share the same advantages as the supernumeraries, no distinction being made in the giving out of the copy.

"The compositors in the news-department have the privilege of composing a considerable quantity of extra or 'back' matter, to enable the printer to have, at all times, a resource in case of accident. This extra copy is given out and divided into half-galley shares, and taken in rotation; thus preventing monopoly and favoritism.

"As there is an immense quantity of letter in use, the division of which for distribution would occasion loss of time, and frequent disputes, the companionship pays a man to lay up the forms, mark the letter off for each person, and distribute the useless heads. He is also answerable for the clearance of the boards.

"Each compositor has a number attached to his frame, and, when he takes copy, his number is placed on the back of the copy, so that each man's matter is identified immediately, and in case of a foul proof, or an out that will occasion much trouble, it is immediately handed to him who composed it without further inquiry, which prevents exposure and annoyance to the individual. The copy is also marked with progressive numbers, which prevents confusion by enabling the compositor to know, with certainty, whom he follows in his composing, and to empty his stick in the proper galley so as to join the preceding matter.

"As the types are composed, they are taken, a galley at a time, by the printer, and made up into columns; a proof of the column is then pulled, upon the galley, by one of the compositors, who all take it in turn; it is given to the reader; after being attentively read and corrected, it is returned to the compositors to make the corrections, who take it in turn, two and two; the column is divided into four, the first compositor takes the first and third parts, and the second takes the second and fourth parts, and he who is the last in making his corrections, pulls a second proof, which is carefully revised, and when the revise is corrected the matter is ready for the paper. It thus goes on, column after column, until the whole paper is composed, when it often occurs that the arrival of foreign intelligence increases the quantity considerably; matter of less immediate interest is, in this instance, taken away, and kept as back-matter for a future day, to make room for the latest intelligence.

"If the first compositor has six or more lines to compose, of copy that he has in hand, he must give it up, and begin to correct immediately; but if he has less than six lines of copy in hand, he finishes it before he commences correcting. This regulation is adopted to prevent any interruption or delay in the progress of getting the paper out.

"The full hands take it in turn to correct the revises, lock up the forms, and take them to the machines to be worked off.

"The advertisement-department is not regulated after the same manner as the news-department, there being no distinction of grades, nor any fixed salaries, nor is there any precise time of commencing work, the uncertainty as to the time of advertisements being received at the office rendering it an impossibility to appoint any regular hour for beginning. The compositors are paid by the galley, not according to the scale of prices fixed for morning papers, but more after the scale of evening papers. The method adopted in this part of the establishment, in taking copy, is the same as in other offices, the first out of copy taking first, and so on, and as the compositors get out of copy their numbers are placed on a slate, which prevents disputes or confusion. The compositor marks his copy by putting his initials on the back of it; so that if any gross error be committed, and remain uncorrected — a wrong number in a reference, for instance — it can immediately be ascertained who composed it; and either the reader or the compositor is held responsible for the advertisement-duty, the proof deciding which is to pay the fine for negligence.

"The salary of a full hand is £2 8s per week, but the average earnings are £3 12s 6d; the salary of a supernumerary is £1 3s per week, and the average earnings are £3. It often happens that much higher bills are written, but the above may be taken as a fair average.

"The whole establishment of the Times newspaper, including editors, reporters, compositors, readers, engineers, overseers of the machines, persons to lay on, and to take off, clerks, etc., consists of one hundred and thirty-seven persons."

In the United States, the manner of getting out daily papers is somewhat different. The compositors usually have a pair of cases of each kind of types used on the paper, and take the copy as it comes from the hook, they not being divided into advertisement- and news-hands, nor day- and night-hands.

Instead of the stands being numbered, each compositor is furnished with slugs of the width of a column of the paper, on which letters or numbers are cast, of the same hight-to-paper as the types. One of them is put into the composing-stick at the head of each take of copy which the compositor may set up during the day, so that he can see, when the galley is passed to him, which parts of the matter belongs to him. Before a compositor gives the galley to the one whose take comes next, he takes out his slugs; the whole of them being removed shows that the galley is corrected.

In daily papers published in this country the compositors have nothing to do with the taking of the proofs, it being the business of the foreman or his assistant to fill out short galleys, and, after having pulled an impression, to put them where they will be readily found when wanted.

PRESS WORK.

Having gone regularly through all the departments of composition, the next thing to be considered is press-work; under which heading: the requirements of a good press, making ready the form, the manufacture of rollers and keeping them in proper order for the performance of fine work, and other things belonging to this department, will be taken up and described in consecutive order. It will not be necessary to give any information as to the mode of printing the coarser kinds of work; because, if a man can make ready and work off a form of the first kind, it will be still easier for him to do the other.

THE PRESS.

Within the last ten years there has been an entire revolution made in the printing-business by the application of machinery to the execution of all kinds of press-work. Previous to that period every thing, with the exception of a small number of newspapers, was printed at the hand-press; because it was generally believed, by those who were supposed to be competent judges, that, for job- and book-work, the speed should not exceed a certain rate, or else the appearance of the work would not come up to the standard of good workmanship.

The ideas that seem to have been the cause of this were the known facts, that, in order to do fine work, it was necessary, when the rollers passed over the form, the motion should be slow enough to allow the ink to cover the face of the types, and when the bed and platen came together they should remain in that position long enough to allow the ink time to be transferred from the form to the sheet of paper. These were correct enough; but there are other parts of the operation which can be facilitated without having any detrimental effect: these are, the movements of the sheet before and after the impression is made, and the separation and coming together of the bed and platen after they have remained together long enough to make a slight dwell on the form.

In the smaller sizes of printing-machines, made for job-work, the bed or platen generally works on a centre; the consequence of which is, that the types strike on the side nearer to that point before, and leave it after, they do the outer side, thereby having a tendency to throw the form off its feet. In making a selection of a press of this kind, it must be borne in mind that the farther the centre of motion is from the centre of the bed or platen, the less will be the liability to this inconvenience.

The press, whatever kind used, should be in the best condition; the bed and platen being perfect planes, and all parts, such as: slides and centres, being made so that they would have no lateral motion. If they have, it will affect the register in a book-form, which will disfigure the appearance of the work; slurs and doubles are also liable to ensue. The most certain way of obviating this is, to have the journals a little larger than the boxes in which they move, so that they can be tightened, at any time, if it should be found necessary to do so.

In putting together the several parts of a printing-press, it very often happens that, if the pieces be in pairs, they get transposed: for example, the legs of a hand-press. This should never happen, because the press-maker fits each piece to its proper position, and, should they become misplaced, they will be the cause of much trouble in getting them correct. This can be avoided by observing that the parts which are intended to be placed in contact are always marked with similar figures, an equal number of points, or some other convenient symbol.

THE TYMPAN.

The material used for the tympan varies with the kind of work intended to be executed, linen being used for handbills and the common kinds of book-work, and parchment for any of which it is the intention to get an even and sharp impression. The parchment should be thin and uniform in thickness, and stretched on the frame in such a manner as not to draw it out of shape, neither should it be so loose as to hang in the frame. The way to attain this is to paste the parchment on the frame without being dampened, and, after the pasted edge is thoroughly dry, to sponge the remainder of the parchment, which will bring it to the required tension. Silk is also used for making tympans with which to print fine work, and it will be found better than any thing else, on account of its thinness, smoothness, and uniformity of texture.

Tympan-frames are sometimes made with a strip of leather fastened on the inner edge, in which eyelets are pierced, so that the tympan can be laced, in its place, with a small cord, instead of being pasted. If the tympan be put on in this manner, care must be taken that, in the running in and out of the bed, the part of the cord which runs through the iron stay across the front of the frame is not cut by the edge of the platen.

THE INK.

The color of the ink must depend on the taste or fancy of the printer. Leaving the particular shade or tone out of the question, we will state our opinion as to what the qualities of black printing-ink should be for fine work:

Intenseness of color.

Impalpability.

Covering the surface of the types or engraving perfectly.

Quitting the surface of the types or engraving, when the paper is pressed on it, and adhering to the paper.

Not smearing after it is printed.

Retaining its first appearance without any change.

Ink ought to be reduced to an impalpable smoothness, either in a mill or on a stone with a muller; and this is essentially necessary, as the process gives it the next quality: of completely covering the surface of the types, or the lines of the engraving, and that with the smallest quantity; and, with proper care in printing, presents to the eye an impression in which the edges of the lines are smooth and perfect, and the surface of the impression on the paper is completely covered with ink, without any superfluity; which constitute the perfection of press-work with types.

Another property required in ink is, that it shall not only cover the surface of the lines on the paper printed, but that it should also quit the face of the engraving or types, and leave the form quite clean when the paper is pressed on it, and attach itself to the paper, so as to give a perfect impression, without the color of the paper appearing through the ink; and that this property, of quitting the types or engraving, and becoming attached to the paper, shall continue the same through any number of impressions, without any accumulation of ink upon the surface printed from.

After having obtained these results, and when the printing is as perfect as it can be made by workmanship, still something more is required: viz., that the ink shall not smear on being slightly rubbed; and that it shall retain its color and appearance, without the oil of the ink spreading at the edges, or tinging the paper — in short, that it shall continue unchanged for any length of time, thus preserving and continuing the beauty of the work.

THE PAPER.

The quality of the paper is of great consequence in fine printing, but it is frequently overlooked; because the purchaser is more apt to pay attention to a showy appearance and a low price, than to quality.

If the fabric of the paper be cotton, and the ink is stiff, at each impression some of the fibres will be drawn out of the paper, which will get on the rollers, and become mixed with the ink. For this reason, it is always better, if the paper be not of the best quality, to use ink of a tenacity in proportion to the texture of the paper.

For the generality of book-work the paper is usually dampened before it is printed. There are two methods of doing this: dipping, and sprinkling.

Paper for various works being of different qualities, it is impossible to form a regular judgment of how many dips, in each quire, all sorts of paper need; therefore, the pressman must be cautious in examining, while wetting, whether each sort is of a soft, spongy, middling, hard, or harsh nature; he must consider, also, whether it be for a light or a heavy form, and dip each sort accordingly.

If the paper be so soft that it will be necessary to dip the quire but once, it must be taken hold of by the middle of the back with one hand, and at the fore-edge with the other, and drawn quickly through the water, the back first. It is then to be laid on a paper-board, and, after being opened, the remainder must be treated in like manner.

Should the paper need two dips to the quire, the outer half of it must only be opened when laid on the board, and the other half can then be lifted and drawn through the water again.

If the paper be flat-cap, or any larger size of writing-paper, on which the headings for blank-books are to be printed, it can not be dipped; because the water would enter between the edges of the sheets and cause the side which first entered the water to be dampened more than the other. When paper of this kind is to be dampened, it must be taken, eight, twelve, or sixteen sheets at a time, according to its quality and texture, and sprinkled, by using a fine-grained sponge, or some similar article.

After the water has become thoroughly soaked into the paper, the pile must be turned, a few sheets at a time, so that any wrinkles which may have been made can be straightened, as well as to allow the water to become more evenly distributed throughout the pile. The paper should next be put in the standing-press, with a board between every five-hundred sheets, and allowed to remain under a heavy pressure for five or six hours, when it will be ready for printing.

When paper, for book- or job-work, has a glazed surface, it should not be dampened; because the least amount of water put on the surface of such paper will destroy its appearance.

When diplomas or deeds are to be printed on parchment, the harshness of the skins must be taken out, by putting them between damp sheets of paper, care being taken, at the same time, that the parchment does not become so wet as to destroy the polish on the surface.

MAKING READY THE FORM.

This term implies: the process of laying the form on the press; fixing it in its place; putting the tympan-sheet on the tympan; placing the points to make register, when both sides of the paper are to be printed; making register; preparing the frisket; and producing an equal impression from all the pages, and from every part of each page. If an engraving is to be printed, it also denotes the manner of overlaying it, so as to produce an impression, which shall possess all the effect that the subject may require. As machine-presses vary so much in construction, directions can not be given which will apply to all; for this reason the hand-press will be the one for which the method will be described; from which it will be easy to vary so as to perform the operation for any other kind.

In common work, where dispatch is necessary, thick blankets are used in the tympan; and, when the types are much worn, they are also necessary, to bring up the face of the letter. It is too common, in good work, to put an excess of blanket into the tympan, to lessen the pull, for the purpose of easing the pressman's arm, and to enable him to be more expeditious; the consequence is, that the impression will show more than the surface of the types or engraving; and, thus, what is gained in expedition and ease, is more than counterbalanced by the imperfect and rough impression that is produced.

BOOK-WORK.

In making ready a form for book-work: lay it on the bed of the press so that it will come precisely under the centre of the platen; quoin it all round; fold the tympan-sheet according to the form laid on the press; lay it on the form so that the margin will be equal on all sides; put a little paste at each of the corners, and where the cross-bars meet; pull a slight impression on it to make it stick to the tympan; put paste on any other part of the paper which may require it, taking care that none of it is laid where any part of the form will fall, as it will become hard and make the impression uneven; screw on the points, and make them fall in the channel of the short-cross, or the spurs will be spoiled by being pressed against the flat part of the bar.

When the pressman has got thus far, the next thing to be done is to cut the frisket. As the material out of which it is generally made is the wrappers which come around the bundles of printing-paper, which are always full of hard particles, an impression should never be pulled on it, because it would injure the face of the form. To get the outline of the pages, cover the types slightly with ink, and, having fastened the frisket in its place, lay it on the form, and rub the back of the tympan gently, with the palm of the hand, until the parts which require to be cut are distinct enough. Having done this, lay the frisket on a board, and cut the marked parts out. It should not be cut close to the edge; but about a nonpareil m outside, so as to obviate any risk of the edges of the frisket striking any of the types.

In making ready, it must be evident, that when a clear, sharp impression is wanted, the pressure should be on the surface only, without penetrating into the interstices; of course, the tympan ought not to be very soft, neither should a woolen blanket be used. The most perfect impression will be obtained when fine, thick paper is used in the tympan; and even of this article there should not be many thicknesses.

After an impression is printed, the pressman examines if it be uniform throughout; if it be, which is seldom the case, he goes on with the work; if not, he proceeds to overlay, in order to produce regularity of pressure, and of color, over the whole form.

To effect this object, he takes thin, smooth paper, and wherever the impression is weak he pastes a piece of it, of the size and shape of the imperfect part, on the tympan-sheet, and proceeds, in the same manner, with every part that is imperfect; he then pulls another sheet to examine the effect of his overlays, and continues to add to them where wanted, until the pressure of the platen is the same in every part, and the impression is of a uniform shade of color.

If the impression come off too strong, in parts, or at the edges or corners of the pages, or on the head-lines, it will be necessary to cut away the tympan-sheet in those parts, and if that does not ease the pressure sufficiently, to cut away the same parts from one or more of the sheets that are within the tympan.

It is generally preferable to overlay on a sheet of stout, smooth paper, inside the tympan, and particularly where the same press does the whole or a great part of a work. This sheet is cut to fit the interior of the tympan, so as not to slip about, and has the overlays pasted on it where wanted, to bring up the impression until it is nearly equal; in all the succeeding sheets it saves the pressman a great amount of time, as he will be certain that, when he pulls a sheet of another form of the same work, it will be nearly correct, and he will only have to place thin overlays on the parts of the tympan-sheet, where they may be required, to make the impression perfect, with very little trouble. On the same principle, where this method is not adopted, preserving and using the same tympan-sheet, with its overlays, will be more expeditious than having to repeat the operation with every form.

When short pages occur in a form, the bottoms of them, and the edges of the adjoining pages, will print too hard, and not make a clear impression; it will, therefore, be necessary to have bearers to protect them, which are generally made of reglet and pasted on the frisket, so as to bear on some part of the furniture or chase.

When the form is not of the full size of the press, type-high bearers should be placed outside the chase, in such a position that the ends of the rollers will not touch them when the form is inked; because, if any of the ink should get on the bearers, it will tear the frisket and soil the tympan. The impression on the form can be regulated, when this kind of bearers are used, by putting paper or thin cards under the ends of the bearers at any side where it may be necessary.

It happens, sometimes, that the tympan causes the paper to touch the form partially, on being turned down. This may occur from the tympan being slack or the paper being thin and soft. To prevent this inconvenience, cut a piece of cork so that, when it is laid on the furniture, it will be a little higher than the face of the types; place it on the piece of furniture next the part of the matter which slurs, and, having put a little paste on its upper side, it will become attached to the frisket when the next impression is pulled. The cork will hold the paper a little above the types until the pressure of the platen comes upon it, when, on account of its elastic nature, it will give way, until the pressure is removed.

Register must be made before commencing to print the form, no matter whether it be whole- or half-sheet work. After the points have been made to strike in the centres of the grooves, pull an impression, and, if the form be an octavo, or any other form which is printed in a similar manner, turn the sheet over, so that the edge which was at the top of the tympan will be at the bottom; then put the spurs of the points into the holes in the sheet of paper, and pull another impression. If the points be in their places, the pages and lines will back each other, and the work can be proceeded with; but, if they do not, one or the other, or both of them, must be moved up or down, as circumstances may require. If the sheet does not register, after the second side is pulled, leave it on the tympan and observe in which direction it is out — the first or under impression being the one on which the direction of the movement of the points will depend. Suppose it be found that the lower corner next the pressman is out of register, a pica m, the first impression being the lowest; the point at that side must be moved upward a nonpareil m, or half the distance, which will bring it to its proper position. Print another sheet, on both sides, and examine as before, and, if the register be correct, the pressman can go on with the work.

When octavo forms, or any other that turn in like manner, are worked at the hand-press, the points need not be of equal lengths, as they must be when the sheet turns as in duodecimo; in fact, it will be better to have the farther point three or four inches longer than the other, as it will save a great amount of reaching, in the course of a day, beside obviating the risk of printing any of the paper wrong, which sometimes happens, because it is laid up incorrectly for the second side.

In working the first side of the paper, pins are often stuck into the tympan to keep the sheets from slipping. This should not be done, because, in a short time, it will wear holes in the tympan, and render it useless. Instead of doing this, a piece of a card should be cut, in the shape of a duck's bill, and pasted at the foot of the tympan-sheet so that the tongue will project in front of it, and keep the sheet of paper from slipping, during the act of turning the frisket and tympan down on the form.

In proceeding with the work, the rollers should be kept perfectly clean from dirt, particles of paper, or other extraneous matter.

The ink ought to be rubbed out thin and regular, on the block, so that, when first put on, it shall be diffused tolerably smooth on the surface of the rollers; this being more likely to produce good impressions. It is advisable, also, to keep rubbing the ink out on the block with the brayer, and to distribute the rollers as much as possible; because constant friction generates a slight amount of warmth, which is of advantage, especially when the weather is cold.

In taking ink, it should be put on the back roller; because it can be distributed faster, and with more ease, than if it were laid on the front roller and had to traverse the circumference of the cylinder before coming in contact with the other.

As uniformity of color is requisite for beauty in printing, the pressman should take ink for every impression, where the form is large; this may be thought troublesome, but there is no other way of keeping up the regularity of color which should pervade good work. There is nothing which looks worse, than to see two pages that face each other, the one of a full black, rather surcharged with ink, and the other deficient in quantity and of a gray color; yet this must happen, when, as is frequently the case, three or four sheets are printed between each time of taking ink.

Rolling, for fine work, should not by any means be slighted. The form ought to be gone over three or four times, when a pair of rollers are used. The motion should be slow and uniform; for, if they be made to go over one part of a form more quickly than another, that portion will receive less ink, and, consequently, the impression from it will be paler than that from the part which has been rolled more slowly.

The cylinder should be of cast-iron, or some other material upon which water would have no effect; for, if it be made of wood, its surface will, in a short time, become rough and uneven, on account of the water getting into its pores, when being washed.

In the more particular kinds of work, where the paper is heavy and the types are large, set-off sheets are used to interleave the whole impression, while working, and are continued in it until the printed paper is taken down from the poles, and put in the standing-press. These set-off sheets are put in when the white paper is working, and moved from one heap to the other during the printing of the second side. They prevent the ink setting off from one sheet to another, while they are newly printed, which it would be likely to do, on account of the weight of the paper, and also, because fine printing is usually worked of a full color.

It will thus be perceived that, to produce press-work of a highly superior character, great expense and much time is required; and that it is necessary to have a good press; to have new types, or types the faces of which are not rounded by wear; to have the rollers in the best condition; the ink should be strong, of a full black color, the oil well burned, to prevent it separating from the coloring-matter and tinging the paper, and it should be ground so fine as to be impalpable; the paper should be of the best quality, made of linen rags, and not bleached by means of an acid which has a tendency to decompose the ink; the rolling should be carefully and well done, not in a hurried manner, the face of the types should be completely covered, without any superfluity, so as to produce a full color; and the pull should be so regulated as to have a slow and hard pressure, and to pause at its maximum in order to fix the ink firmly upon the paper. These particulars observed, with paper only in the tympan, perfectly sharp impressions of the face of the types will be obtained.

After the form has been worked and lifted from the press, the ink on its surface should be loosened with ley, and thoroughly rinsed off with water. The brush used for this purpose should have the hair about two inches in length, and they should be set closely together.

ENGRAVINGS.

When the workman puts the block on the press, he ought to be very gentle in the pull of the first impression, to prevent an accident, which has frequently occurred from thoughtlessness in this particular, by making the pull too hard, and crushing some of the lines; by avoiding this he will be safe, and can proportion the impression to the subject. The only correct manner of doing this is, to knock all the impression off, after which it should be put on, a little at a time, until the lightest part of the cut comes up with a proper degree of sharpness; then the heavier portions can be overlaid until the requisite amount of pressure is produced.

The pressman should examine, previous to pulling, that there be nothing, such as gauges or the like, on the tympan, which would strike on the block. Accidents of this kind sometimes happen, which either destroy the cut or else cause great trouble to the engraver, as well as loss of time and disappointment; beside these it entails a character of carelessness on the printer.

In imposing a single block, where the press is large at which it is to be worked, it will be in danger of springing out of the chase while being rolled, on account of the quantity of furniture placed about it. It is a good remedy to impose it in a job-chase, and to impose this chase again in a larger one: this will cause the block to remain flat and firm on the press when the roller passes over it; as the small chase can be locked up tightly in the large one, without having too much furniture, and the outer one can be secured firmly on the press by quoins.

Neither the pressure nor the impression in an engraving should be uniformly equal: if they be, the effect that is intended to be produced by the artist will fail; and instead of light, middle-tint, and shade, an impression will be produced that possesses none of them in perfection; some parts will be too hard and black, and other parts have neither pressure nor color enough, with obscurity and roughness, and without any of the mildness of the middle-tint, which ought to pervade every part of an engraving, on which the eye reposes after viewing the strong lights and the deep shades.

To produce the desired effect, great patience and nicety are required in the pressman. A single thickness of india-paper, which is the best paper for overlaying engravings, is frequently required over very small parts, with the edges of it scraped down, for it is advisable that the overlay should never be cut at the edges, but, even where great delicacy of shape is not required, that it should be torn into the form wanted, which reduces the thickness of the edges, and causes the additional pressure to blend with the surrounding parts.

Some portions of the impression will frequently come up much too strong, and others too weak: it will then be necessary to take out from between the tympans a thickness of paper, and add an additional tympan-sheet, cutting away those parts that come off too hard, and scraping down the edges. Scraping away half the thickness of a tympan-sheet in small parts that require to be a little lightened will improve the impression.

The light parts require little pressure, but the deep shades should be brought up so as to produce a full and firm impression.

If a block be too low, it is advisable to underlay it, for the purpose of bringing it to the proper hight, in preference to making use of overlays; for they act, in some measure, as blankets, being pressed into the blank places, and rendering the lines broader than they are in the engraving.

It will be necessary, sometimes, when the surface of the block is very uneven, to tear away parts of the paper in the tympan, to equalize the impression where it is too hard.

The pressman will find it convenient to pull a few impressions, while he is making ready, on india-paper; for out of these he can cut overlays to the precise shape and size that is wanted, as he will find it frequently necessary to do in instances where great accuracy is required in overlaying particular portions; and in these instances he can not do well without a sharp penknife and a pair of good small scissors.

Engravings that are in the vignette form require great attention, to keep the edges light and clear, and in general it is necessary to scrape away one or two thicknesses of paper, in order to lighten the impression and keep it clean; for, the edges being irregular, and parts, such as small branches of trees, leaves, etc., straggling, for the purpose of giving freedom to the design, they may come off too hard, and are liable to picks, which give great trouble, and are difficult to be avoided.

Type-high bearers should be used, when printing an engraving or any other light job, to keep the impression from bearing harder on the edges than on the centre. They should be placed in such a position as not to be liable to get any ink on them during the time the form is being worked. If they can not be used, pieces of reglet or cork, pasted on the frisket, and taking a bearing on the furniture, must be substituted; but the high bearers are to be preferred, when they can be adopted, because they equalize the pressure on the surface of the engraving, and protect the edges from the severity of the pull, which is always injurious to the delicacy of the external lines. They also render the subject more manageable, by enabling the pressman to add to, or take from, the pressure on particular parts, so as to produce the desired effect.

When great delicacy of impression is demanded in a vignette, it will be found beneficial, after the engraving has been rolled, to take the superfluous ink from the extremities, by using a small piece of composition on which there is no ink. This will give the edges lightness and softness, particularly where distances are represented.

If the extremities be engraved much lighter than the central parts, underlays should be pasted on the middle of the block, which will give a firmer impression to those central parts of the subject. It would save trouble to cause the block to be a little rounded on the face, as it would give facility in obtaining a good impression.

When highly-finished engravings are worked separately, cloth, or any other soft substance, should never be used for blankets, as the impression will sink into it; two or three thicknesses of smooth hard paper, or even a piece glazed pasteboard, placed in the tympan, is better.

The silk or parchment, which is next the engraving, should be stretched tightly, and it should be thin and of uniform texture, so as to enable the pressman to obtain an impression from the surface of the engraving only.

The rollers should be in the best condition for this kind of work; and the pressman should be very particular, in taking ink, that but little be put on at a time, and that it be thoroughly distributed before the rolling is done, or else he will not obtain a clear and uniform impression.

Should a wood-cut be left on the bed of the press or on the stone, for any length of time, it is apt to become warped. When this happens, a very good method of restoring it to its original shape is, to lay it, face downward, upon the imposing-stone, with a few thicknesses of damp paper under it, and to place a flat weight of some kind upon it; and, in the course of an hour or two, the block will be restored to its former position. This method is preferable to wetting the block with water, which is often practiced; for the latter swells the fine lines of the engraving, and consequently affects the impression. To retain the appearance, as it comes from the hand of the artist, the block should never be wet with water; and, for this reason, when wood-cuts and types are worked together, the engravings should be taken out before the form is washed.

When a few proofs only are wanted from an engraving, good impressions may be obtained, with very little trouble, by taking the tympan off, and using three or four thicknesses of paper between the face of the engraving and the platen.

Ley should never be used to clean a wood-engraving. It will be found, in practice, that spirits of turpentine take off the ink quicker, and affect the wood less, than any other article used; and the facility with which the block is again brought into a working state more than compensates for the trifling expense incurred, as nothing more is required than to wipe the surface dry, and to pull two or three impressions on waste paper.

The pressman will find it a great advantage, if it be necessary to do full justice to an engraving, to have a good impression from the engraver, and place it before him as a pattern, and then arrange the overlays, etc., until he produces a facsimile in effect; but it would be more desirable to have the artist at the side of the press, to give directions in regard to the overlaying, and the pressman should, by no means, become impatient on account of the tediousness of the operation, as he will obtain more information as to the best manner of producing a fine impression by this than by any other means. It will also instruct him how to meet the wishes of the draftsman and the engraver, with regard to effect, in a way superior to any other; and will, with attention and care, ultimately lead him to excellence in the printing of engravings.

Stereotype- and electrotype-cuts can be treated in the same way as wood-engravings, as far as making ready and overlaying is concerned; but as a stereotype copy is never equal to the original, it is not worth the trouble to overlay a cut of this kind. On the other hand, an electrotype, when correctly made, being an exact facsimile, it should be worked with the same care as if it were a wood-cut.

On account of the cheapness and durability of electrotypes, they should always be used in preference to the originals; because, if an accident should occur, the plate can be renewed at a small expense, and it obviates the necessity of keeping water from the cut, as it can be washed in the same manner as ordinary types.

JOB-WORK.

The generality of printers, to save time, in making jobs ready for working, use thin cloth or india-rubber in the tympan, which enables them to dispense with a little overlaying; and, again, the proprietors often order such materials to be used, because they think it will keep the types from wearing. With any soft article of this kind a fine impression can never be obtained, and, it must be evident to any one who gives the subject a moment's consideration, that they wear the types more than hard tympans; as the india-rubber or cloth will, at each impression, sink into the counters of the letters, and draw the paper with it, thereby causing a slight lateral motion, which will wear the types more than any amount of direct pressure which can be put on their faces.

Paper should be used for tympans, in printing every description of job-work, the number of thicknesses varying according to the character of the work. The impression should be put on just enough to bring up the types which are of the greatest hight-to-paper, and then the indistinct lines must be underlaid, until the outline of each letter is perfect.

If a form be made ready in this manner, there will be no danger of the types being destroyed by too hard a pressure; because, there is no more impression put on than is required to bring up the highest types. The only danger, in this method of making ready, is, that the pressman generally finishes one job and makes the first impression on another without altering the force with which the platen comes against the form. To obviate this, the impression should be taken off directly after the printing of one job, when it can be regulated, by degrees, until there is a sufficient amount put on for the next.

The paper on which fine jobs are printed should never be dampened; for, as the water, however sparingly used, has a deleterious effect on its surface, it will injure the appearance of the printing.

When very large cards are printed, it will be found necessary, in order to ease the impression, to soften the backs of the cards. The correct method of doing this is, to place two cards face-to-face, and lay them in damp paper, as recommended for parchment, on page 153.

WASHING THE FORM.

Although this has been mentioned two or three times, in the previous part of the work, yet, as this is the proper place in which any precaution or information that may be necessary should be given, it will be done in a clear and concise manner.

The ley used for the purpose of cleaning a form is, a solution of alkali in water; it ought to be made of the best pearlash. The usual proportion is, one pound of pearlash to a gallon of soft water; it should be stirred until the alkali is dissolved, which will soon take place. It is generally contained in a large jar, which should be kept covered, to prevent dirt and dust getting into the ley.

If hard water be used, it will require a greater amount of pearlash; as the acid in the water will combine with some of the alkali, to neutralize it; which, of course, will have the effect of making the ley weaker than if soft water, with which there is no such chemical combination, had been used.

Some printers use potash for cleaning the types; but, as it has a tendency to make the letters stick together, it should not be employed.

The brush should be nine or ten inches long, by three inches broad; and the hair should be at least two inches in length, of a soft texture, and set as closely together as possible. By not having a good brush, more types are destroyed, on account of its careless use in washing, than by almost any other process through which they are liable to be put. The reason for this is, that the washing is generally entrusted to boys, who scrub the faces of the types, instead of rubbing them just enough to leave the ink in such a condition that it could be separated from them by rinsing the form with water.

When a form is small, it may be rinsed by standing it on its edge in the trough and throwing water against the faces of the types; but, if it be over half a medium sheet, it should be laid flat in the trough. In either case, plenty of water should be used; for, a little care in this particular will always keep the types free from dirt.

Sometimes the counters of the letters become filled with ink before the working of the form is finished. In such cases, ley and water should not be used, as much time would be lost in drying the types. Spirits of turpentine and a soft brush will be found to take off the ink quickly, and the work can be proceeded with in a few minutes. When this article has been used, a few impressions must be made on waste paper, to remove the oil which remains on the types after the turpentine has evaporated; though, if alcohol be at hand, it will remove the oil more effectually.

PRESSING THE SHEETS.

The paper being all printed, it must be exposed to the atmosphere a sufficient length of time to let the ink set firmly in the paper, before it is put in the standing-press.

The poles, upon which the sheets are placed to dry, should be two and a half inches wide, and made of one-inch white-pine. They should be placed across the room, about fourteen inches from the ceiling and nine or ten inches apart, resting at each end on a piece of wood fastened to the walls of the room, in notches to retain them in their situations. They should be kept clean, and, if they have not had paper hung on them for some time, the dust must be brushed off before they are again used. As the weight of the paper would have a tendency to bend the poles, they should be turned over, as occasion may require, to keep them straight.

The number of sheets put, in one place, on the poles, must be regulated by circumstances. If the work be in a hurry, or the poles be not in a favorable situation for drying, or the weather be rainy and the air charged with moisture, no more than three or four should be hung in a place; but, if the situation be favorable for drying, and the weather be warm, eight or ten sheets may be put in each place.

If the sheets be allowed to remain on the poles ten or twelve hours, it will, in most cases, be found sufficient, for the purpose of setting the ink or drying the paper.

They are now ready to be put in the standing-press. This is done by laying up a press-board, and putting on a paste-board and one of the sheets of the work to be pressed, alternately, until all the sheets of paper are in the paste-boards. The pile must then be taken, fifty at a time, and placed in the centre of the standing-press, with a press-board between each lift. The press must next be screwed down tightly, and suffered to remain in that condition ten or twelve hours; when it will be found that the sheets are as smooth as they were before being run through the press.

When highly-glazed paper is printed, the ink is liable to be transferred from the sheets to the paste-boards. In such cases sheets of common printing-paper should be put between them.

If it be wished to give the surface of the print a glossy appearance, instead of proceeding according to the above method, each sheet of paper should be put between two sheets of zinc, to the number of twenty-five, and run forward and back, three or four times, between iron rollers similar to those of a copper-plate press. This will be found to give jobs done in gold and silver a brilliancy which can not be obtained by the former mode of pressing.

Still another way is, to put the sheets of printed paper between sheet-iron pressing-boards, which have been heated previously; and then the whole is subjected to the power of a hydraulic press.

Although the last method mentioned is the best, it can not come into general use, on account of the expense and tediousness of the process. When, therefore, work is to be pressed in a manner superior to that which can be done by the common standing-press, the sheets of zinc and roller-press can be used with advantage.

MAKING ROLLERS.

By the introduction of composition instead of the pelts, used formerly, there has been an entire revolution effected in the performance of press-work. But for this article, machine-printing would never have been accomplished, as all the first attempts were made with rollers coated with skins, and all failed, owing to the inability of making them without leaving a seam where the skin was joined.

Almost every printer has his opinion in reference to making rollers; but it will be found that if the following directions are attended to, the rollers will be better and last longer than if made by any other method:

THE KETTLE.

This must be a double vessel like a glue-kettle, so that the composition in the interior may be melted by the heat of the boiling water in the exterior. The vessels should be so proportioned in size that the one which contains the composition would have two inches of water between it and the fire. This can be accomplished by having a collar on the outer vessel and a flange on the inner one, which will fit together and hold the inside kettle at the correct distance from the other. For convenience in lifting, both of the kettles should have handles on each side, and the inner one should have a large lip, to facilitate the pouring of the composition into the mould. Both of the vessels should be made of copper, as it will last longer than tin.

PREPARING THE COMPOSITION.

The glue from which rollers are made should be of the best quality — thin, transparent, and brittle; it should, also, be free from any extraneous matter.

The molasses should, also, be of the best quality: that is, it should be free from any watery ingredient, and not liable to granulate. In the first case, the water will evaporate and leave a hard skin on the surface of the rollers; and, in the second, the sugar will crystallize and make the composition rotten.

It will be found that the above articles, without any admixture, such as: chloride of lime, sal-ammoniac, tar, paris-white, or any other material, will make good rollers, the only thing necessary being, that care is taken in the manufacture.

Before the glue is put into the kettle to be melted it is usual to soak it in water, so that the heat will dissolve it sooner than it would if it were in the dry state. But care must be taken, in doing this, that too much water is not left in the glue, as it will evaporate, in a short time, and leave a hard skin on the surface of the roller, which will make it unfit for any kind of work.

The usual method of dissolving the glue is, to put it in a bucket, or some other convenient vessel, and cover it completely. The glue is to be watched until the water has soaked half-way through, which can be ascertained by breaking a piece and examining the edges. When the water has remained on the glue a sufficient time, it is to be poured off, and the glue is to be spread out evenly on a board which is slightly inclined, so as to let any superfluous water run off. After being left in this position until the water has gone entirely through, it is in a proper condition for melting.

If a roller be made with no more water in it than will remain in the glue after being treated in the above manner, it may still be found that, in a short time, the surface has become hardened. This can be still farther obviated by dividing the glue into four equal parts, and soaking one of these portions in common beer, in the manner above indicated. This part of the glue must then be put into the melting-kettle, and placed over the fire. It is then to be dissolved by a steady heat, stirring it frequently, at the same time having a care that the water in the outer vessel does not become reduced by evaporation; because, if this should happen, the glue will become burned in parts, generally causing those lumps and hard portions often found in rollers, which are always attributed to the quality of the glue, instead of carelessness in this particular. After this portion is thoroughly melted, the other parts are put in, one at a time, until the whole becomes of a uniform consistence, when it is allowed to boil slowly for an hour, before the molasses is added. This must be poured in gradually, while the mass should be constantly stirred until the glue and molasses become uniformly mixed. This being done, the composition should remain over a moderate fire for an hour, stirring it every ten minutes. The composition must now be lifted from the fire and the surface skimmed, to get rid of the frothy portion, and after remaining in the kettle until air-bubbles cease to rise, it is in a proper condition to be poured into the roller-mould.

The proportions of glue and molasses necessary to make good rollers will vary according to the time of the year. The following are the correct quantities of each:

```
Summer,              2 parts glue and 1 part molasses.
Winter,              1 part    "    "  2 parts    "
Spring and Fall,     1  "      "    "  1 part     "
```

These proportions are intended for hand-press rollers. When it is required to make them for machine-presses the quantity of molasses should be one-third less.

Five pounds of glue and five pints of molasses will make a pair of medium rollers, the composition on each being twenty-eight inches in length and half an inch in thickness. From this it will be easy for the pressman to calculate the quantity of composition necessary for rollers of any other length, as it will be seen that a pound of glue and a pint of molasses make between ten and eleven inches of a roller of the ordinary diameter.

PREPARING THE CORE.

Strip off the composition with a knife, and scrape the core. Keep water away from it, and do not touch it while the hands are covered with grease or sweat. As the composition often becomes loose from the core at the ends, it would be of advantage to sponge a couple of inches at both ends, with lime-water or spirits of wine, which will effectually prevent this.

THE MOULD AND CASTING.

The mould should be of cast-iron, ground perfectly smooth on the inside, and of such thickness that the heat of the composition would not be liable to make it expand. When thin copper moulds are used, the heat becomes transferred from the composition to the mould, on account of its high conducting power, and, as the cooling takes place, the mould contracts and holds the roller so tightly that it requires a great amount of force to get it out, and sometimes causes the core to start before the composition, which leaves the roller worthless.

The mould must be carefully cleaned and oiled, after which the core is to be inserted, taking care that it is not allowed to touch the sides, as it would be likely to get some of the oil upon it. The mould being placed upright, and the centre-pieces in their proper places, the core must be fastened, to keep it from floating. This is done by placing the end of a piece of furniture on the upper centre-piece, the other end, which reaches above the top of the mould, being tied down with a piece of twine.

When the composition has been from the fire long enough for the air-bubbles to cease rising, which may be known by its surface assuming a smooth, dark appearance, it is in the proper condition to be poured into the mould. In doing this, the composition must be poured in slowly and steadily, taking care that none of it is allowed to run down the side of the mould, as it will make that side of the roller rough, on account of the oil on that part being removed by the heat. It should be poured on the centre of the core and allowed to run down so gradually that it would fill the mould without confining any air in it.

DRAWING AND FINISHING THE ROLLER.

When the composition and mould become cold, the roller can be pushed out by pressing steadily against the piece of furniture which was put in to keep the core from floating while the composition was warm.

Trim the ends with a sharp knife, beveled toward the core, so that the composition will not be likely to start at that place. Dip the ends in warm water long enough to obliterate the marks of the knife. This will prevent water, ley, or oil getting in between the composition and the core, and making it peel at the ends.

RECASTING ROLLERS.

Before recasting old rollers, take great care to wash them well with ley, in order to remove the ink with which they are coated. If the rollers be dry, they must be scraped with a knife, to get rid of the grease, which would injure the composition. Afterward cut the roller all over with a knife, and it can be easily taken from the wood. If it be new, it will not need cutting so as to make it dissolve readily; but, if it be old, it should be cut into small pieces, and, when it is put into the kettle, a small quantity of spirits of wine may be added, which will give it a tendency to dissolve sooner and better than it would by the application of heat alone.

If the materials used in the composition be of the best quality, the rollers will be better after being recast than when first made; because they are more elastic and less liable to be affected by slight changes of temperature.

If the composition be soft, or the weather changing from cold to warm, there will be no necessity of adding molasses, when recasting a roller; but, if the composition be hard, or the weather getting cold, a pint of molasses should be added to each four pounds.

There should always be two full sets of rollers cast for each press, so that while one pair is being used the other can be washed and laid in the roller-box, where they will be kept in good condition for working until it is found necessary to put them in the press, on account of the first pair not working well, or of a change of form.

PRESERVING ROLLERS.

The washing of the rollers is an operation very little attended to, by pressmen; though their preservation and good condition depend, almost entirely, on the care with which it is done. This, like the washing of forms, is usually entrusted to boys, who, if there be a number of rollers to be cleaned, frequently wash the whole with ley before any of them are rinsed with water and dried. This should never be done; because, if a roller be kept for a short time with either water or ley on its surface, the molasses will become dissolved, and the roller will lose its adhesiveness.

When it is necessary to wash a roller, it should be done as quickly as possible, by first loosening the ink with ley and a sponge, after which clean water must be thrown upon it till all the ink is removed. This being done, and the ley being rinsed out of the sponge, which should be squeezed as dry as possible, it should be rubbed over the surface and ends of the roller, so that it will absorb any water that may have been left on those parts.

When rollers are new, they should not be cleaned with ley, as it will have an injurious effect on them, although the utmost care may be taken in its application. The best method of proceeding, in such cases, is, to use either spirits of turpentine or coal oil to remove the ink; but, if neither of the above articles be at hand, new rollers may be cleaned by running them back and forth, a few times, over a dusty part of the floor which has previously been swept clear of all hard and large particles: the ink becoming absorbed by the dust, both of them can be removed, by using a sponge which has been slightly dampened.

The best method of keeping rollers in good condition is, to cover them at night, and when they are not likely to be wanted for some time, with a thick coating of common printing-ink; this keeps the air from coming in contact with the surface. When the roller is required for use, the superfluous ink may be taken off, by means of sized waste-paper, and the remainder can be washed off with ley and water.

If a roller become too hard, and the surface is clean, dampening it with clean water will restore it to a proper condition for working; but, instead of doing this, it is preferable to put it in a damp situation, where it will gradually absorb moisture. It will often be found that sponging a roller, while it is being used, will make it work as well as it would if it were washed. When this is done, the roller must be kept in constant motion, on the cylinder or stone, until all the particles of water are absorbed.

When a roller gets too soft, it should be placed where a current of dry air would act on its surface. This will evaporate the superabundant moisture which it contains, and cool the composition, if the room has been too warm. But a more expeditious and effective method is, to sponge it with spirits of turpentine, which will restore it to a proper condition sooner than any thing else.

When rollers are not in use, they should be kept in an air-tight box, so made that water could be put in or taken out of it, as occasion might require. With a box of this description, the rollers can always be kept in good order, by attending to the following directions : If the atmosphere be very damp, there should be no water left in the box, and the cover should be put down closely, so as to exclude the air; and, if the atmosphere be very dry, water should be put in the bottom of the box, the cover being as before; in the intermediate states of the atmosphere, the cover may be left more or less open, as circumstances require.

Rollers should not be allowed to rest on the cylinder or stone for any length of time, as they will thereby become flattened, which will render them unfit for the uniform distribution of the ink; neither should they be exposed to the action of the rays of the sun, in summer, nor to the direct heat of a stove, in winter, as either will soften the composition so much as to cause it to run, and thus spoil the rollers.

Although rollers can generally be kept in good order, by attending to the foregoing directions, yet it will sometimes be found that, no matter what care be taken, the rollers will work badly. This can, generally, be obviated by allowing them to rest for an hour or two.

PRINTING-INKS.

The Manufacture of Printing-inks will be the next subject that will receive consideration. In doing this, the writer will quote all the recipes which are of any importance, that are given in Mr. Savage's work, interspersed with whatever remarks it may be deemed necessary to make, both in regard to the manufacture of the inks, and the making ready and printing of the form.

The recipes for making black inks are given, because that is the part of his work in which the making of the varnish is described; and it being necessary to go fully into the one, it was thought that the other might be inserted, both on account of the high price and of the scarcity of the volume from which they were extracted.

It will be found, by the printer who has but a small amount of colored work to do, that it will be cheaper for him to keep a can or two of varnish on hand, and make whatever shade and quantity of ink he may require, than to buy them from the manufacturer, as is generally done; because he will mix no more, at any particular time, than is required for the job in hand, instead of going to the expense of fifteen or twenty dollars in procuring cans of different colors, when an ounce of each is not required.

MATERIAL AND IMPLEMENTS.

"Printing-ink is a composition, formed of two articles: namely, varnish and coloring matter.

"The varnish may be either in its natural state, as the vegetable balsams; or a compound, as generally used, formed of oil, rosin, and soap.

"The coloring matter varies in black ink, according to the quality of the ink; and, in colored inks, according to the tint required."

LINSEED-OIL.

"Linseed-oil is so generally used as the basis of the varnish, and answers so well for general purposes, when properly prepared, that it does not appear necessary to speculate on the properties of other oils for this purpose. It is generally allowed that the older it is the better, for making varnish."

ROSIN.

"The rosin that is used in making varnish for printing-ink is either black rosin or amber rosin; but amber rosin is the most generally employed, as being more common in the market than the other.

"It is an important article in the composition of good ink, as by melting it in the oil, when that ingredient is sufficiently boiled and burnt, the two articles combine and form a compound approximating to a natural balsam, which, perhaps, is the best varnish for printing-ink that can be used. It prevents the oil separating from the coloring-matter and staining the paper, and gives a binding quality to the ink which prevents its smearing; and this tenacious quality may be qualified to any degree, as will be observed under the next article."

SOAP.

"This is a most important article in the preparation of printing-ink, and, what is surprising, it is not noticed in any of the old recipes that have been published.

"Its properties are: to cause the ink to adhere uniformly to the face of the type, and to give it a complete coating with the smallest quantity; to cause the ink to leave the face of the type clean, and attach itself to the damp paper by the action of pressure, and during the process of printing to continue to do this through any number of impressions; also to cause the ink to wash easily off the type; and to prevent the ink skinning over, however long it may be kept.

"For black or dark-colored inks, the best yellow or turpentine-soap may be used; but it should be well dried. For light and delicate-colored inks, curd-soap is preferable, which is white, and does not affect their tints.

"If too great a proportion be used, it has a tendency to render the color unequal where a large surface is printed; to spread over the edges of the types, so as to give them a rough appearance; and to prevent the ink drying quickly, and to set off when pressed. The proper proportion is, when the ink will work clean, without any accumulation or clogging on the surface of the type or engraving, and then the impression will be clear; if the proportion be greater, the effect just described will be produced. It thus corrects, to any extent required, the binding quality of the rosin in the varnish."

Although soap has the qualities above stated, it can not be used, with advantage, when printing most light colors, on account of the alkali, which is one of its components, having a tendency to alter their shades.

LAMP-BLACK.

"This article varies very much in quality, and equally so in the proportion that is required for any given quantity of ink; so that any directions must be fallacious which do not specify the kind of lamp-black to be used.

"There are two kinds: mineral lamp-black and vegetable lamp-black.

"Mineral lamp-black is much the heavier, and it requires a much larger proportion of it, by weight, to make an ink of the same consistency, than it does of vegetable lamp-black, and is not suited for ink of a fine quality; but, I have found, in practice, that it answers very well in certain proportions for inferior ink. It looks blacker in the powder than the vegetable black, but it is not so when mixed with the varnish. It is in general foul, having extraneous matter in it, owing, I suppose, to the material from which it is made, and to the process, and also to the lowness of the price not allowing the manufacturer to be at the trouble of cleaning it.

"Vegetable lamp-black is much lighter than the mineral, and that which is the lightest is estimated as the best. This article varies much in the proportions that are requisite to make ink of the same strength; I have found that that which is sold in firkins takes far the most varnish, and it is said to be the best that is made as an article of commerce. The price of this sort will allow it to be used only for fine inks. There are still higher-priced lamp-blacks, which, of course, would be restricted to very select inks.

"If more than a just proportion of lamp-black be used, it will cause the ink to smear, however long it may have been printed, and also set off under the bookbinder's hammer; and this effect must of consequence take place if the quantity be more than the varnish can bind: this fact shows that the thickest inks are not always the best."

IVORY-BLACK.

"Ivory-black is too heavy to be used alone as the coloring-matter for black printing-ink, but it may be used with great advantage, in a certain proportion, which may be ascertained by adding it after the ink is made, and grinding it on the stone, taking care not to use too much at first, for select purposes; for instance, if an engraving on wood is required to be printed in a very superior manner with black ink, so as to produce the best effect that is possible, then ivory-black, with the other ingredients necessary for the composition of fine ink, will be found valuable. A difficulty, however, arises, of how it is to be procured, for the ivory-black of commerce is not of sufficient blackness to produce this effect; and the printer will not be able to purchase an article that will answer the purpose.

"The process by which this article, of the most intense blackness, may be made, (and I have made it from this recipe, when it was as superior to the very best that could be bought as that very best was to the common ivory-black of commerce), I shall now describe:

"Provide a crucible, of a size proportioned to the quantity of black that may be required, and fill it with small pieces of ivory, which may be procured at a table-knife cutler's, and are sold by the pound; the finest-grained ivory, I have observed, makes the best black; close the top of the crucible with a cover that fits closely, and that will bear a strong heat; or, in lieu of such a cover, close it with well-tempered clay; then place it in the middle of a hot fire, where every part of the crucible may be exposed to as equal a heat as possible, and let it remain until it is burned to a charcoal to the centre; it should then be taken out of the fire and suffered to cool gradually. When the ivory is taken out of the crucible, it will be found that the outside of those pieces next to the sides will be burned too much, and will be white, but the inside of them, and that in the middle of the crucible, will be of the most intense blackness. As the different pieces may vary in the intensity of the blackness, the most perfect should be picked out, any whiteness or discolorization on the outside be scraped off, and the part selected reduced to a powder, when an article the most perfectly black that perhaps it is possible to make will be produced.

"If it should happen to be wanted in a situation where a crucible could not conveniently be procured, enveloping the pieces of ivory with clay, and burning it as above described, will produce the same effect."

PRUSSIAN-BLUE.

"This article, used sparingly, greatly improves printing-ink, by giving it a greater depth of color; but, if the due proportion be exceeded, it gives the ink a coldish appearance. The best will be found to be the cheapest, as it goes farther and produces a better tone than the common. It does not affect the working of black ink, either in the smoothness or clearness of the impression, but it requires a great deal of grinding to make it fine."

INDIGO.

"This article produces the same effect as prussian-blue, and may be substituted for it; or, equal quantities of both may be used, which mixture, I think, produces a blacker ink than when used separately. I am aware of the evils arising occasionally from the mixture of colors, but I have not perceived any bad effects from these two colors being used together in printing-ink. I have not observed that indigo, any more than prussian-blue, affects the ink in its quality of working well."

INDIAN-RED.

"To give a rich tone to black printing-ink, and to take away the cold appearance of the black when indigo and prussian-blue are used, some additional coloring-matter is necessary; and I have found that indian-red has suited the purpose remarkably well: it possesses a depth of color of a purplish reddish-brown, which, with prussian-blue or indigo, adds considerably to the intensity and richness of appearance of the ink. It works free and clean, and the price of it is moderate.

"Carmine or lake might, perhaps, produce a superior effect, but their high price precludes their use; and, beside, the lake of commerce does not possess sufficient depth of color to give a richness of appearance to an intensely black ink. This I shall notice when I come to treat of colored printing-inks, and give a recipe for making a lake of greater intensity of color."

BALSAM OF COPAIVA.

"This is a most valuable article, without any preparation, as a varnish for printing-ink; but then it must be old and pure. With this balsam, a due proportion of soap and coloring-matter, and a stone and muller, any printer may, at the moment, make ink of the most superior quality without any risk, and with very little trouble; the knowledge of which he may find of great service when he has anything to print in a very superior manner."

"This natural balsam possessing such valuable properties as a varnish in the preparation of printing-ink, appears to point out to us, that the next best composition for a varnish for this purpose is, that which approaches the nearest to it in quality; and our present varnish, when properly prepared, seems to approximate sufficiently near to answer every necessary purpose."

It will often avoid disappointment if the printer will remember that the article sold by the druggists as balsam of copaiva is generally so much adulterated that it is of no value as a varnish for making printing-ink — being thin and weak, when it should be strong and viscid.

CANADA-BALSAM.

"This is also a natural balsam, and may be useful, to a certain extent, in the preparation of printing-inks, but not so generally as balsam of copaiva, as its properties are a little varied. It is much thicker, and dries sooner, than that balsam, which properties would prevent it being adopted alone as a varnish; but, for a strong ink, a small portion may, perhaps, be mixed with balsam of copaiva to advantage, and also with the regular varnish."

"These natural balsams have so little color that they do not affect the inks whose tints are light and delicate; and they also dry slowly, on which account there is no danger of the ink made with them skimming over. This property, whatever opinions may be held to the contrary, is an advantage; for, smearing is not attributable to this cause, but to too great a quantity of ink being used, and that ink containing too great a portion of coloring-matter, and also not being impressed on the paper with a power sufficient to fix it firmly on the surface, and this want of power obliging the workman to use a greater quantity to produce the desired color: but, when the materials are duly proportioned, it requires only a small portion of ink to coat the surface of the type, and when that ink is firmly impressed on the paper by means of sufficient power exerted by the press or machine, the impression will not smear when it is just printed, in the ordinary method of handling it. Master-printers are anxious, at the present day, to procure an ink that will dry immediately; but, if this property were given to it, they would be disappointed again, for the ink would work foul, and the workmen would neither be able to produce good work, nor to proceed with dispatch, as the form would require to be washed often, as was the case before soap was used — in short, I hold that it is impossible to produce an ink that will dry very quickly and also work clean to enable the pressman to proceed with his usual quickness.

"I use the word machine, as implying cylindrical printing, with steam as the moving-power generally, in contradistinction to a press which is worked altogether by manual labor."

IMPLEMENTS.

"It is necessary to have an iron boiler, of a capacity to hold at least double the quantity of oil that is intended to be boiled; as I would never venture to make varnish with the boiler more than half full of oil, on account of the risk incurred, of its rising and boiling over the top; in fact, one-third full would be safer, and cause the oil to be more manageable in case of an accident.

"The iron boiler must have three feet, and may be set on three bricks, to raise the boiler from the ground, so as to enable the fire to burn, and surrounded by a circle of bricks, to keep the fuel from spreading about, and to confine the fire under the boiler; it should also have two lugs, either to suspend it over the fire by means of a bow, or to lift it off the fire by means of iron hooks, when set on bricks, when it is necessary. It may be suspended over the fire by a bow with a hook at the end of a chain fixed to a triangle.

"The boiler should have a cover made to fit closely, but not tightly, so that it may be put on and taken off with facility. It should have a handle at the top, by which it may be taken off with a stick; for, after remaining on the boiler some time, for the purpose of putting out the flame, it will be found too hot for the hand.

"An iron spatula should be provided, to stir up the oil during the process, as well as to take out a few drops, from time to time, when it is necessary to try its consistence, and to stir it up when the rosin and soap are added; as well as to mix the coloring-matter with the varnish.

"It will also be necessary to have an iron ladle, large in proportion to the quantity of oil boiled at one time, with a long handle, to take out a portion of the oil, should it rise and be in danger of running over, from having too brisk a fire, as I shall describe in treating of boiling the oil; and it will also be requisite to lade the varnish out of the boiler, when it is complete.

"A stick, about a yard long, with a cleft in one end, will be found useful, when the oil is in a state to burn, as by putting a piece of paper in the cleft the oil may be set on fire without any risk of burning the hands or face."

BLACK INK FOR GENERAL PURPOSES.

"Having previously described the materials, and the apparatus necessary for boiling the oil, I shall now proceed to the process of making the varnish, and afterward to preparing the ink; taking the proportions for a small quantity, that would be easily managed, and would be convenient to printers in general.

"A boiler having been placed on three bricks, and surrounded by a circle of bricks, to confine the fire, placed a little apart from each other, to admit a current of air to the fuel, put into it six quarts of linseed-oil, then light a coal fire, using plenty of wood in order to make it burn briskly, and keeping it up lively and steady, but not very violent. After the oil has been some time on the fire, it begins to simmer, and small bubbles arise; it soon after has the appearance of boiling, and the bubbles increase in number; but, as the oil gets hotter, this appearance ceases, the bubbles disappear, and the surface becomes smooth and unruffled. After this, it begins to emit smoke, and begins to boil and smell very strong; and, if the boiling be prolonged, a scum arises. It should now be carefully attended to, and frequently tried with a piece of lighted paper, to see if it will take fire, which it will not do in this state, unless the flame of the paper be carried down to the surface of the oil.

"It is a considerable time before it will take fire; but, after the smoke begins to rise, it should be tried often, as it is more manageable when taken as soon as it will burn. When the vapor begins to be inflammable, it takes fire with a few flashes, which may be distinctly heard, though not seen, and these flashes immediately clear away the smoke. In a little time these flashes become stronger, may be seen, and continue flashing a short time: I would now advise that it be taken off the fire and placed on the ground, set on fire and kept stirring with a spatula, which exposes fresh surfaces to the atmosphere, and keeps the flame in. This burning increases the heat of the oil, and also increases the flame, so that it will be necessary to cover it occasionally, for the purpose of extinguishing the flame, and trying its consistence. The latter may be done by dipping the spatula into the oil, and dropping a little on an earthen plate, which will soon cool. If it do not draw out in strings, on touching it with the finger, set fire to it again, and keep repeatedly trying it, and continually stirring it with the spatula. When it will draw into strings about half an inch long, on touching it with the finger and withdrawing it from the plate, it is burned enough for an ink sufficiently good for book-work generally; the cover should then be placed on the boiler, and the flame extinguished.

"If the oil be pushed to a violent boiling-heat, in the first instance, without trying if it will take fire, the probability is that it will froth so much and rise up in the pot, as to take fire spontaneously by contact with the atmosphere, and become unmanageable, and baffle all attempts to extinguish it, endangering the safety of the building, if within one, and the adjacent ones, and the wasting of the oil. Under these circumstances, when they occur, a large sized ladle will be found particularly serviceable, as a large portion of the oil may be taken out into the cool ladle, and by taking some out and pouring it into the pot again repeatedly it will rapidly cool, and the oil may thus be saved; and if a few pieces of soap can safely be introduced without making the oil run over the top of the boiler, it will cause the rising to subside, and thus prevent loss and danger.

"When the cover is taken off again, there is a great quantity of smoke, that has a powerfully disagreeable smell, and a deal of froth. When this froth has subsided by stirring it well together, six pounds weight of amber-rosin, or black-rosin, should be gradually put into the oil and stirred up. If it were put in at once, the effervescence would be so great that the oil would run over the top of the boiler.

"When this is done, and the rosin dissolved, which the heat of the oil will do, there should be added one pound and three-quarters of dry brown or turpentine-soap, of the best quality, cut into slices. This also should be put in gradually and with caution, for it causes a violent ebullition, and as the soap dissolves it is thrown up to the top, and forms a kind of froth to a great extent. When all the soap is put in, and the ebullition has ceased, it may be replaced over the fire until it boils, which it will soon do, and the varnish will be completed.

"While the rosin is being put in, it is advisable to keep stirring the oil with the spatula; the same when the soap is put in, and also when over the fire for the last time, that the whole may be intimately and uniformly incorporated.

"Then take five ounces of the best prussian-blue or indigo, or equal parts of each to the same amount, ground to a powder, and put it into an earthen pot or tub, large enough to contain the whole quantity of ink when all the ingredients are mixed together.

"Into this vessel also put four pounds of the best mineral lamp-black and three and a half pounds of good vegetable lamp-black, then add the varnish, little by little, while warm, and keep stirring it well together, until the whole of the varnish is put in. The stirring of the ingredients together should be continued until they are well mixed and no lumps remain. It should then be submitted to the levigating-mill, or to the stone and muller, and ground to an impalpable fineness, and the printing-ink will be fit for use.

"It will be found that, if the varnish be cold when the lamp-black is added, a great deal of trouble and loss of time will be occasioned by the difficulty of mixing them; but, if the varnish be warm, or tolerably hot, they may be mixed much more readily and with very little trouble."

A FINE INK, WITHOUT OIL OR ROSIN.

"After persevering in making experiments for a series of years, I at last accomplished the object which I long had in view, of making printing-ink of the most superior character, without any oil in its composition; thus getting clear of the imperfections of inferior or adulterated oil; of over-boiling or under-boiling; of inaccurate proportions of rosin; and of the trouble and danger of boiling the oil.

"The ink, which the following recipe is for producing, is a fine and intense black, and works as freely and clean, looking at it as a strong ink, as can well be wished for. It surpasses any ink that I have ever seen manufactured for sale, lying smoothly on the surface of the paper — not sinking through the paper, nor tinging it in any way — not spreading at the edges — and retaining its intense color; for I have some before me that has been printed fifteen years which is unchanged, and has the same appearance precisely as when first issued from the press.

PROPORTIONS FOR ONE POUND.

"Balsam of copaiva, 9 oz.
Lamp-black 3 oz.
Indigo, or prussian-blue, or equal quantities of both 1¼ oz.
Indian-red ¼ oz.
Turpentine-soap, dry ⅜ oz.

"To be ground upon a stone with a muller, to an impalpable fineness, when it will be fit for use.

"This recipe for making a printing-ink of a very superior quality, without either oil or rosin in its composition, will, I believe, be found important to every printer who executes fine work, or highly-finished engravings on wood, as he may prepare it himself without the least risk, and with no more trouble than would be equal to grinding a little oil-paint, and thus keep a small quantity in a tin can, ready for use at any time; or, in case of emergency, it can be prepared in half an hour."

The objectionable smell which balsam of copaiva has may be entirely removed by putting three or four drops of kreosote in the above quantity of ink.

The writer of this work has been informed by a person who did most of the press-work on Savage's "Decorative Printing," that the black ink used in printing the part before page 53 was made according to the above recipe; and, upon examination, he finds that the outlines of the types are more definite and the surface blacker, in that portion, than in the remainder of the volume.

A SUPERIOR INK, MADE WITH OIL.

"Balsam of copaiva having a peculiar smell, which the ink made with it will retain for years, and becoming more powerful when held near the fire, some persons may prefer a fine strong ink without any peculiar scent; in which case it will be necessary to boil and fire the oil to a higher degree than I have described for an ink intended for general book-work, so as to make a stronger varnish, to prevent any fear whatever of the oil separating from the coloring-matter and staining the paper. This varnish will, of course, require a small proportion more of soap to make it work well and clean. Substituting this varnish for the balsam of copaiva, the recipe will stand, with regard to the articles and their quantities, precisely the same as the last.

"There are various reasons why strong varnish is used in fine ink for superior work: the oil being well boiled acquires a tenacity that, when combined with rosin, prevents its spreading and staining the paper; the form must be well rolled, that the face of the type or engraving may be completely coated, which it will thus be with the least possible quantity of ink; the surface only is thus coated, and no superfluous quantity is present to squeeze or run over the edges and disfigure the work; and an impression is obtained of the surface only of a full, rich color, which should always be the object in fine work. It acts also as a preservative of the color of the ink, and thus continues unimpaired the beauty of the press-work."

COLORED PRINTING-INKS.

"I would advise printers to have in readiness a small marble slab and a small muller, with some good printing-ink varnish; they may thus immediately prepare a colored printing-ink, when wanted, with but little inconvenience or trouble, and of any color or tint that is required, by reference to the following list; and if they find any ink accumulating on the face of the type so as to clog it up and prevent it working clean, a little soap rubbed into the ink with the muller, on the stone, will remedy the defect immediately.

"When a light washy tint is required, I would strongly impress on the printer not to reduce the color by the admixture of any white with it, which will take away all its liveliness, and produce dulness, but to thin it with varnish to the point required; to roll the subject with very little ink; and to apply a very strong pressure, by which means any tint may be produced that the color is capable of, still retaining all its spirit.

"I have found in practice, that, whatever varnish may be used, some colors sink through the paper and stain the back of it more than others; this is owing to the solubility of the coloring-matter in the varnish, which thus penetrates through the paper. It is therefore advisable, in imitating drawings, to avoid such colors as much as possible, and where it is not possible, to print on india-paper, and mount them; for where it happens it disfigures them greatly, whether they are bound in a book or preserved in a portfolio. It is a curious fact, that this action does not take place in thin white india-paper, the back remaining unaffected.

"It will be found that different colors will require different proportions of soap ground up with them, to cause them to work free and clean; and the utility and absolute necessity of this article in printing-ink having been kept a profound secret by the few persons who manufactured the ink for sale, and were interested in keeping the secret, prevented any great competition; and also prevented many ingenious printers from ornamenting their productions with colors, as the varnish which is sold was found not to be sufficient of itself to make even vermilion, the color most commonly used, to work clean, and beyond this there was no resource; for self-interest locked up closely the only known remedy."

Although Mr. Savage recommends the use of soap in the preparation of printing-inks, still it must be evident to any person who gives the subject a moment's consideration, that its application to this purpose will have a bad effect, on account of the non-drying oil which it always contains, it being absurd to burn the oil to get rid of its greasy principle, and afterward to add the same thing in a far worse form. The way to obviate this is simple: to add the alkali, in its pure state, to the varnish, using bicarbonate of ammonia for the light and bicarbonate of soda for the deeper colors. The quantity of either article used, should be about one-tenth of the amount of soap recommended for a given amount of ink.

During the manufacture and printing of light-colored inks, care should be taken that no metal, which is easily oxidized, such as iron or copper, comes in contact with them, because it will deaden the appearance of the color. For this reason a metal spatula should not be used while the ink is on the stone; neither should type-metal nor copper be employed to make an impression from. As an illustration of this, let the pressman take an electrotype-plate and pull an impression of it with the finest red ink he can make or procure, and he will find that the color will be nearer to a brown than to a red. The best thing to do in such a case is, to use a wooden block on which the design has been engraved. Type-metal may be used for the ordinary kinds of work, as it is less liable than copper to affect the color; but, if it should be necessary, at any time, to use the latter metal, a thin coating of silver should be deposited on it by the galvanic process, as the red or any other light color is less affected by this than by the inferior metals.

The following is a list of the pigments best adapted for the manufacture of colored printing-inks:

RED.

"Carmine.— This is a more brilliant color than lake, and possesses more depth; it is readily ground into a fine ink. I should strongly recommend balsam of copaiva to be used as a varnish, when carmine is employed as a printing-ink, on account of its paleness, as I should be afraid of the deeper shade of printing-ink varnish injuring its brightness. Carmine is too expensive to be used as a printing-ink, except for very particular purposes."

The carmine which is sold by the druggists is generally adulterated, so as to realize a greater profit than could be made by vending the pure article, as well as to have an article which could be sold at various prices. If a printer should, at any time, desire to obtain the pure coloring-matter of carmine, let him take any amount of the color and digest it in liquid ammonia, at a temperature of $60°$. The ammonia seizes the coloring-matter and dissolves it, leaving only a residuum of a pale red earthy appearance. The color can now be deposited from the alkaline tincture, by adding concentrated acetic acid, by degrees, until the ammonia is completely saturated, when a precipitate will be formed. The extreme fineness of this color requires the addition of a little alcohol to the liquid, in order to diminish its density. This addition causes the color to deposit, which then shows itself in all its brilliancy. Decant the colorless liquid; after which the deposit must be washed with alcohol and dried in a saucer or some other shallow non-metalic vessel.

"Lake.— There are two sorts of lake in commerce— crimson lake and purple lake: the crimson lake is the richer color, and is to be preferred, for a purplish tinge may easily be given to it when required, but the crimson tone could not be given to the purple lake. It is easily reduced to a fine ink with the muller; it works clean, and does not require more soap than varnish contains. It is a color that does not possess much depth.

"As it may be necessary sometime to use this color of deeper tone than that possessed by the lake of commerce, I think I shall be doing a service by giving a recipe, which has not, to my knowledge, been published before, for making a very superior lake, of a much more brilliant color than can be purchased.

"Take one ounce of the best cochineal, powder it, and boil it in one quart of water, until the coloring-matter is extracted; then let the cochineal subside, and pour the liquid into another vessel; when cold, pour gradually into this decoction some muriate of tin, and keep stirring it; the muriate of tin immediately changes the decoction into a most beautiful color. Be cautious, in the first instance, of not putting in too much of the muriate of tin. Let it subside, and if the supernatant liquor be nearly colorless, there is a sufficient quantity of muriate of tin; if it still retain any considerable portion of coloring-matter, a small quantity more must be added; but I would not advise so much as to precipitate every portion of the color in the supernatant liquor. When this is done, add a little powdered alum, and assist its dissolution by occasional stirring. Let it subside; then pour off the greater portion of the liquor, and wash the color well in three or four waters; this is done by adding a considerable portion of the purest water you can obtain, stirring it up well each time, and, when the color has subsided, pouring as much water off as you can without disturbing the color. As the color subsides, keep pouring off the water; by this process the color is divested of the acid in the muriate of tin; then dry the precipitate gradually, with as little heat and dust as possible, and a lake will be produced far deeper in color and superior to any that can be purchased in the market — in fact it may be termed a fine carmine.

"During the process of making it the addition of salt of tartar will give it a purple tinge.

"Vermilion. — This color is generally employed as the coloring-matter for red ink that is used for jobs of a neater appearance than common, and for title-lines in books. Its properties and appearance vary in different specimens. Chinese vermilion is estimated to be the best; and it is the brightest. It requires a large proportion of soap ground up with it to make it work clean, and this kind requires more than the vermilion of commerce; but the exact proportion can only be ascertained at the press-side when using it, as different specimens require different proportions: if it do not leave the type clean after a few impressions, but begins to accumulate and clog the face, a little more soap should be rubbed in; if the surface of the type be left clean, but the ink spreads over the edges, there is too much soap in it, and a little more color and varnish should be added. By paying attention to these suggestions, red ink, manufactured from vermilion, may be made to work as clean and well as black ink, as I have often experienced in my own practice.

"Preceding writers on this subject have recommended the addition of lake to vermilion, for the purpose of producing a brighter color than vermilion alone would produce; but, I have invariably found that, instead of brightening, it injured both the colors, and produced a brick-dust dull effect. A much brighter red will be produced, by taking chinese vermilion and adding a small portion of chromate of lead. But the greatest improver of color is a good contrast. This color is apt to turn black by exposure to the atmosphere.

"Red-Lead. — This article is inferior to vermilion, but is much used in posting-bills, where cheapness is required. It may, also, be found useful where a variety is wanted of a paler color. It requires a greater proportion of soap than is in the varnish, to cause it to work clean. It soon changes color, and turns black.

"Indian-Red.— This color is of a deep reddish brown with a purplish cast; it is tedious to grind it smooth, being hard and refractory under the muller, but, when ground to the proper fineness, it makes a good ink of a rich tone, and works well. It is valuable in its combinations with other colors, both in mixture and contrast, as well as in its unadulterated state. It is capable of much intensity, and would, in my opinion, be superior in many instances to vermilion for effect, and would prove a good variety for jobs, titles, head-lines, etc. The color is permanent.

"Venetian-Red.— This color is easily ground into a smooth ink, and does not require much more soap than varnish generally contains. It makes a red ink not of much intensity, but not without its value, as affording a variety of color at but little expense.

"Rose-Pink.— This is a very cheap color, and this may induce some printers to try it where economy is requisite; but, except they succeed better than I was ever able to do, they will lose the color, the varnish, and their time: for I have tried it in every way that I could think of, and I never could make it work clean, nor even make decent work with it. The result is, that I pronounce it to be a worthless color for printing-ink. It is, also, a very fleeting color. I only mention this as a caution, because it will prevent disappointment."

ORANGE.

"Orange Chromate of Lead.— This variety makes decidedly the best orange-colored ink. It can be ground smooth with very little trouble, and forms a good working ink of a brilliant hue, and capable of producing a most showy effect, judiciously contrasted with other colors.

"Orange-Lead.— This is a paler but warmer color than red-lead, and may be useful in large bills, where economy in the price of the ink is necessary. It requires an additional quantity of soap to what is contained in the varnish. It is not a permanent color. None of the preparations of lead are to be relied on, as they all change.

"Burnt Terra-di-Sienna. — This is a useful color where a warm yellow tint is required, or to shade yellows with. It works clear and clean, but requires an additional portion of soap. It is a permanent color and makes a smooth ink; but, it must be remembered that, as this is a transparent color rather than a body-color, its use is more appropriate in imitation of drawings or ornamental productions than to print lines of types."

YELLOW.

"Chromate of Lead. — This is the brightest yellow as a body-color that is yet known. It is easily ground into a fine printing-ink, and it works freely and well, and requires little or no additional soap beyond what is contained in the varnish. There are different shades of this article, from a pale yellow to an orange color.

"Indian-Yellow. — It is a transparent color, and will be useful in glazing, and where a rich mellow tone is required, in imitating a colored drawing of a landscape.

"Gall-Stone. — It is a transparent yellow of a warm tint, and it will be found useful in glazing rich mellow tones in landscapes. It is a concretion taken from the gall-bladder of cattle that are slaughtered. It is apt to fly.

"Gamboge. — Although a bright yellow as a water-color, yet gamboge used as a printing-ink possesses no merit, except in imitating drawings, when it may be used as a light washy tint where much effect is not wanted; but for a full yellow it will not answer. The color stands very well.

"King's-Yellow. — This is by no means a bright color, and it has, beside, a disagreeable smell; yet it was the only article used where a yellow printing-ink was required until I introduced chromate of lead as a coloring-matter, which is so much superior that king's-yellow is entirely superseded. It does not stand.

"Patent-Yellow. — This is a color that will not be of much use as a printing-ink, possessing little body and that of a dull hue. Where bright tints are required it is worthless.

"Roman-Ochre. — It possesses a deeper tone than yellow-ochre, with which it may be used as a shade in representing stone buildings, and in foregrounds of landscapes. It is dearer than yellow-ochre, but the latter may be easily brought up to the same shade by burning.

"Yellow-Ochre.— In representing stone buildings, yellow ochre will be found a useful color. It is easily ground into a fine ink. It is dull, but stands well."

GREEN.

"Verdigris.— This article makes an ink of a bright green color with a slight bluish tinge, which may be of use for large bills, where variety, show, and effect are required for temporary purposes; but care should be taken that the verdigris be of a good quality. It does not form a good working ink; in fact it would be almost impossible to produce an even surface, though when seen at a distance it produces a dashing effect. It is a very fleeting color; and on these accounts unfit for general purposes.

"Green.— Green ink may be made by an admixture of blue and yellow, and the choice of the materials must depend on the shade and tint of green that is wanted; and thus greens of every hue may be formed with different blues and different yellows. It is necessary to observe that the purest yellow chromate of lead must be selected if a bright green be required; for that which is of an orange or reddish tint will invariably produce a dull green color. The color of any green ink may be deadened by the addition of a little lake."

BLUE.

"Indigo.— This substance is a deep blue, but does not possess much brightness; it is a powerful color, and may be used as a shade to prussian-blue; for, when it is printed upon that color, it appears like a deep blue-black. It requires a great deal of grinding to make it a smooth ink. It is a cold but permanent color.

"Prussian-Blue.— This is a deep bright color, and makes a good ink for large bills where variety is wanted for the sake of effect, and also to form deep greens. It requires a great deal of grinding to make a fine ink, and an addition of soap to the varnish to make it work well and clean. This blue is far superior to either indigo or antwerp-blue, (being free from their greenish tint), in the composition of the various shades of peach, violet. and plum colors, and purple.

Prussian-blue being of a hard gritty character, is not easily dissolved by the varnish; but, if it be steeped in urine, until it ceases to be acted upon, which will happen in between three and five minutes' time, it can be ground into a printing-ink as easily as chrome-yellow or any other color of that kind.

"Light Prussian-Blue.— When this article can be procured of a good quality, it forms an ink of a bright blue, and of a lighter tint than prussian-blue, as its name implies. It makes a good ink, as a variety, in large bills; and for other purposes, where the color is suitable. It may be distinguished from antwerp-blue by not having the green tinge which always identifies that color.

"Antwerp-Blue.— This is a bright light blue color, with a slight tinge of green. It forms a good ink, works clean and well, and is easily ground to a proper degree of fineness, and makes a good contrast where a lively appearance is required.

"Cobalt-Blue.— In the powder this is a beautiful and rich blue; but, when made into an ink, it loses all its brilliancy under the platen, and produces a dull color that is of little worth."

Ultramarine.— Since Mr. Savage's work was published, the above-named color has been manufactured by chemical means, and the price has become nominal to what it was formerly; consequently it is now much used as the coloring-matter when a fine light blue ink is wanted. It is one of the hardest colors known, under the muller; and, for this reason, no pains should be spared in grinding it to an impalpable fineness. It is a permanent color.

PURPLE.

"Purple.— Purple inks of different shades and tints may be made by grinding together carmine, or lake, (purple lake is the best for this purpose), with prussian-blue. Indigo or antwerp-blue produces a far inferior color."

BLACK.

"Indian-Ink.— For the imitation of a drawing in indian-ink it may be used, but for the greater depths an ink can not be made with it of sufficient blackness; for them it will be necessary to use good black printing-ink. Upon the whole, it will not be found particularly useful.

"Lamp-Black.— For general purposes good black ink is the best article to use when black is required; but, in imitating drawings, the colors that are used in black ink to give it intenseness may produce an undesired change in those in the picture: in this case lamp-black is preferable. Light shades of lamp-black are better than diluted black printing-ink, as the latter becomes neutral when weakened with varnish.

"Ivory-Black.— When an intense black is required, free from the admixture of other colors, a small portion of ivory-black, prepared according to the directions given in another page, mixed with the best lamp-black, will produce the desired effect. It is a cold color."

BROWN.

"Bistre.— This color forms a useful brown, in the ground, in trunks of trees, and in shades. It is a very obstinate color under the muller, and requires a great deal of grinding to make a smooth ink. It is prepared from the soot of chimneys in which wood has been burned, and well washed. It stands well.

"Raw-Umber.— This is not so warm a color as burnt-umber, but is more of an earthy color; and is useful in the foreground of pictures and as a shade, and in many other cases. It stands well.

"Burnt-Umber.— This is browner than either bistre or raw-umber, and is useful by itself as well as to mix with other colors where a lively tone is not required. It works well, has more intensity of color than bistre, and is permanent.

"Sepia.— This is a color that is much used in water-color drawings in preference to indian-ink; possessing more richness and depth than that article. This brown has a tint peculiarly its own, which can not be imitated by any compound color. It makes a good-working ink, and may be used with advantage and effect, both in the imitation of drawings, and as a variety where black is not required.

"Prussiate of Copper.— This is a rich brown in oil-painting, but the pressure of the platen destroys all its richness; and, as a printing-ink, it becomes a dull brown.

"Brown.— In addition to bistre, raw-umber, burnt-umber, and venetian-red, deep and rich browns may be made of other colors far superior to any of these. Vermilion and black printing-ink make a very good brown, which can be varied to any tint that may be required; lake and burnt-umber make a peculiarly rich brown; but the richest that I have ever seen in a printing-ink, (and I am not aware that any person but myself has formed it), may be made of lake, prepared according to the recipe given under the article Lake, indian-red, a small proportion of indigo, it being a powerful color, and a little chromate of lead. For finely-executed engravings on wood I think this brown ink, when the different articles are well proportioned, produces a superior effect to the best black ink, for richness and delicacy."

It will be seen, by an examination of the paragraphs quoted from Mr. Savage, in this chapter, that he is not in favor of using white to lighten the color, when it is necessary to print a tint-block or any work of that kind. The reason he assigns is, that white-lead, the article used generally, would become darkened by exposure to the air, and spoil the color of the tint. But, if the coloring-matter be mixed with varnish until the required shade is attained, there is a likelihood of the varnish spreading, if it should be thin, or remaining on the surface of the paper without drying, and being liable to become smutted by handling, if too thick. When it is required to make an ink of this kind, it would be better, instead of thinning the color with varnish, as he recommends, to use oxide of zinc, which, when pure, is as permanent as any color used in making printing-inks. This article, like the other colors, is often adulterated, which can be easily ascertained if any work in which it has been used be exposed a few minutes to a stream of sulphuretted-hydrogen, when, should the color not be pure, it will become dull and darkened.

CHANGEABLE PRINTING-INK.

The two recipes following may be found useful, if it should be desired, at any time, to print such jobs as checks or notes so that the inks would change color on the application of an acid. The light-colored ink can be used for printing a ground or tint on which the wording can afterward be printed with the changeable black ink:

BLACK.

Make a strong decoction of the best nut-galls in water, having previously broken them into small pieces; when well boiled strain the decoction from the galls, and mix with it about an equal quantity of a strong decoction of logwood, strained free from the chips and other extraneous matter. Add some sulphate of iron, which will precipitate a black powder by combining with the gallic acid; at the same time add some powdered alum, which will precipitate the purple coloring-matter of the logwood, which gives richness and intensity of color to the black precipitate of the galls and copperas; stir the liquid mixture until the alum and copperas are dissolved, then let it subside, and as the liquor becomes clear pour it off; after which dry the precipitate slowly, and there will remain an intensely black powder. Then take two parts of balsam of copaiva and one part spirits of turpentine, and to these articles add as much of the black powder as will make the mass of a proper consistence for a printing-ink; after the ingredients are incorporated grind them to an impalpable fineness, and the ink will be fit for use. On the application of oxalic acid to any lines printed with this ink they will change color in the same time and manner as the parts which are filled up with the ordinary writing-ink.

CRIMSON.

Lake of commerce ground with varnish will make an ink with which the tint-block or ground can be printed. It works free and clean, and changes color immediately on the application of an acid.

These are not the only colors which can be used for this purpose. A variety of tints may be obtained from brazil-wood, fustic, galls, logwood, madder, oak-wood, and other vegetable substances that are used in dyeing, by means of different articles to precipitate and change the colors produced from them.

INDELIBLE PRINTING-INK.

As it may occasionally be required to print names and the like on linen or cotton, or any similar fabric, in such a manner that it would not become obliterated by washing, all that is necessary to be done is to procure a quantity of coal-tar, sufficient for the purpose, and to thin it with naptha, to the consistence of ordinary printing-ink.

PRIMARY COLORS AND COMPOUNDS.

Although there are seven colors usually enumerated by artists, and those who write on the subject, yet it has been agreed to designate only three of these colors as primary, namely: red, yellow, and blue; because, with the pigments representing these, the others can be formed, as far as the materials will allow. Thus, red and yellow mixed make orange; yellow and blue, green; and red and blue, purple. But red, yellow, or blue can not be obtained by any mixture of the other colors; hence, they may be considered, in an artistic sense, as strictly primitive.

To these three primary colors may be added white and black: white as the representative of pure light; and black as that of darkness, or the absence of light. The three primaries may be regarded as gradual transitions from one extreme to the other, both in color and luminosity, thus: we may pass from white, or positive light, to yellow, the color most nearly allied to it; thence to red, the mean and most important color; then to blue, the representative of coldness; and, finally, to the neutral black.

With regard to the pigments employed in mixing the colored printing-inks, we have by no means a free choice, but are limited to the use of those natural or artificial bodies, which, beside being powerful in their production of color, may be mixed, more or less, with each other, without being subjected to much alteration or decay, and also with the varnish, without mutual chemical action or injury to either the one or the other.

The following diagram is given, in order to facilitate the understanding of the manner in which the secondary and tertiary colors are formed out of the primary ones:

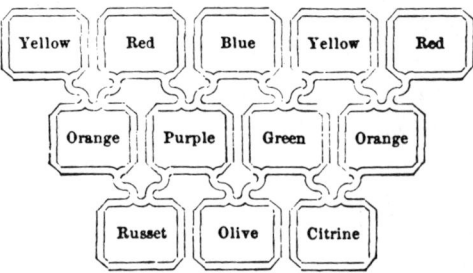

It will be hardly necessary to mention, that the reason for duplicating the yellow and the red, in the above figure, was to obviate the formation of three separate diagrams.

PRIMARY COLORS.

Red.— This, the most powerful and distinct color of the three, excites and stimulates the eye, predominating in all warm colors. It occupies a mean or middle position in the scale of color, for yellow approaches nearer to light, and blue to darkness, while both tend to produce a coolness of effect, as compared with red. Green is the color which is complementary or accidental to it.

Yellow.— This, in an artistic view, is the primary color most closely allied to undecomposed light, by the diffusing influence of which it is frequently mingled with all the other hues. Its complementary color is purple.

Blue.— This color being related to shade or darkness, is consequently retiring in its character, imparting the same quality to all the hues in which it predominates. Its complementary or accidental color is orange.

SECONDARY COLORS.

Orange (Yellow and Red).— Orange, being the most luminous, is, on that account, the most striking and prominent of the secondaries. It is the connecting-link, or harmonizing-color, between yellow and red, and it is the complementary color of blue. A small quantity of black mixed with orange makes a good brown ink.

Green (Yellow and Blue).— Green is generally considered as the mean between the other two secondary colors, taking an intermediate position between light and shade. Its complementary color is red. Chrome-yellow mixed with indigo makes a beautiful deep green; with prussian-blue, a brighter, but less intense color; and, with antwerp-blue, a brilliant green: all of them working well.

Purple (Red and Blue).— Purple is the coolest and darkest of the secondary colors. It possesses, in a high degree, the modest retiring qualities of the primary blue, with which it is most closely connected; and, as the eye delights to dwell on those colors which least fatigue it, perhaps purple may rank next to green in the pleasure it affords. Yellow is its complementary color. Purple printing-inks of any hue may be made by mixing carmine and the various blues in different proportions.

TERTIARY COLORS.

Citrine (Orange and Green).— A mixture of the two secondary colors, orange and green, is called citrine, or citron, from its likeness to the color of that fruit. It is a dark, subdued, yellowish green. It is more nearly allied to yellow than to blue or red, being composed of yellow and red, and yellow and blue (see diagram). This color is pleasant and cheerful, and, on account of the predominance of yellow in its composition, approximates nearer to light than the other two tertiary colors.

Russet (Orange and Purple).— The next tertiary color is russet, in which red predominates. It will be seen, by reference to the diagram, to be a mixture of red and yellow, with red and blue. As red occurs twice in its composition, russet inclines more to that color than to either of the other primaries.

Olive (Purple and Green). — Olive, formed from purple and green, is the last of the tertiary colors, and is more nearly connected with blue than the two former; it therefore makes the nearest approach to shade and darkness, and is the most retiring of all the colors.

The term: complementary color, in the foregoing pages, has reference to the one which, when printed in juxtaposition with another, forms the best contrast with it; for instance, if one of the colors be pure, its accidental or complementary color will be a combination of the two other primary colors, in proportions varying according to the hue of the former, as may be seen by the following list:

Orange-yellow	is complementary	to	Indigo.
Orange	"	"	Blue.
Yellow	"	"	Purple.
Indigo	"	"	Orange-yellow.
Blue	"	"	Orange.
Green	"	"	Red.
Purple	"	"	Yellow.
Red	"	"	Green.
Violet	"	"	Greenish-yellow.

PRECAUTION.

When printing a form in more than two colors, with points, two pair should be used, so that when working one color fresh point-holes would be made to carry the next. If the pressman should use the same point-holes for the third color with which he has registered the first and second, he will find that they have become too large, the consequence of which will be that the lines will not fall in their proper places.

A roller which has been used for a dark color should never be employed in printing delicate colors; because, no matter how well the surface may be washed, there will be some of the ink left in the pores of the roller, which gradually oozing out, will become mixed with the other and darken it so that it will not appear like the color which was originally intended to be printed.

DRY COLORS.

This division will contain directions for printing jobs in: Metal-leaf, Bronzes, Smalts, Flock, and Dry colors; and, the manner of executing such kinds of work as Hat-tips by the hot method, Chromotype-printing, and other matter which may be thought interesting and useful to the trade.

METAL-LEAF AND BRONZES.

When either of the above articles is to be used in printing a job, the form must be made ready on the press in the usual manner, and, an impression pulled with size, instead of printing-ink.

If leaf should be used, it must be laid on by means of a piece of cat-skin or some other substance which will exert a slightly attractive influence over it, while being transferred from the place where the leaves are cut to its proper place on the sized impression. After the leaf has been laid in its proper place, it should be beat gently with a cotton pounce covered with velvet, so as to make the leaf and the size come in perfect contact. The job should be allowed to remain from thirty-six to forty-eight hours, so that the size will have become thoroughly dried before the superfluous gold is brushed off.

The method of proceeding with the form is the same for bronzes as for leaf. In putting bronzes on a job printed with size, if the lettering be large, the most expeditious method of applying them would be to use a hat-brush; but, if the job be small it will be better to use a piece of cotton-batting, which can be rolled up to the desired shape. Bronzes, like leaf, should be allowed to remain until the size become set before cleaning the job. This operation is best done by rubbing the surface gently with clean raw cotton until all the loose bronze is wiped off.

SMALTS AND DRY COLORS.

The directions given for the putting on of bronzes will hold good with regard to these colors; the only difference being, that smalts are more liable than the bronzes to get rubbed off; because, their particles are larger, and, on this account, project farther above the surface of the paper. For this reason, the sizing by which they are held on the paper or card must be far more tenacious than that used in the printing of leaf or bronzes.

The size should be made according to the directions given, at page 183, for making printing-ink varnish, the only difference being that the linseed-oil should be burned until it would be so glutinous as to draw out into strings two-and-one-half or three inches in length. As it would be impossible to use the size in this state, because it could not be distributed on the surface of the roller, some other substance should be mixed with it, at the time of using, which would thin it to the proper consistence, and, at the same time, evaporate quickly without having a detrimental effect on the quality of the size. It will be found that either spirits of turpentine or copal varnish is the best article to use for this purpose.

As some of the smalts are transparent, the size made according to the above directions can be seen through them, on account of the oil having become darkened in appearance by the action of the fire. For this reason, the burned oil must be clarified before the rosin is dissolved in it, by proceeding according to the following method :

To the required quantity of oil add one-twentieth of its weight of caustic potash or soda, or one-twelfth of its weight of the carbonate or chloride of either of these articles, dissolved in a quantity of boiling water equal in bulk to the oil to be bleached, and stir the mixture until it is perfectly uniform. Then take chloride of lime of commerce equal to one-fourth of the weight of the oil, and, having dissolved it in cold water in the proportion of one pound of chloride of lime to six gallons of water, draw off the clear solution from the residuum, and allow this cold liquid to drop quite slowly into the mixture of oil and alkali, while it is still sufficiently warm to be in a liquid state, at the same time carefully stirring the whole mass. When this is done, the bleaching-action immediately commences, and proceeds gradually during the addition of the cold solution of the chloride of lime, and for some time afterward, until the color is sufficiently discharged. Put it into an iron boiler lined with lead, and boil it in dilute sulphuric acid, in the proportion of twenty parts water to one part sulphuric acid of $120°$ strength, until it is free from the lime or alkaline substance that may have combined with it during the bleaching-process, and floats quite clear upon the top of the acid liquor, after which draw it off into clear water, to free it from any adhering acid or other impurities, and it is then ready for use.

The article denominated flock, is made from the cuttings of woollen goods, and is of various colors. The size, by which it is held on the card, should be somewhat stronger than that used in the printing of smalts; and, as the particles of which flock is composed are somewhat larger, the method of applying it to the surface will be different. This is done by spreading the material on a flat surface and pressing the printed job upon it, face downward, when it will be found that a sufficient quantity of the flock has been transferred from the loose layer to all parts of the card which have received the size.

When flock and bronze are to be worked on the same card, the bronze must be printed and allowed to become thoroughly set before the flock is used; because, if the process be reversed, the bronze will be retained, more or less, between the particles of the flock.

Beside the articles before-mentioned, there are many other coloring-materials which can be used in the dry state: ultramarine, cobalt-blue, paris-green, and, in fact, any color which can be brought in contact with the glazed surface of a card without soiling it, may be employed.

It will be obvious that the roller employed for printing jobs with size, must have a harder surface than if used for the printing-ink of ordinary tenacity; because, a soft roller will stick too much, and probably become torn when being distributed on the stone or cylinder.

The form must be cleaned with spirits of turpentine and a soft brush, the turpentine being afterward removed by using alcohol.

PRINTING BY THE HOT METHOD.

The form must be harder than type-metal, on account of the heat and extra amount of pressure which it will have to undergo. For this reason, work such as hat-tips, must be set up with brass types, or the lettering must be engraved, or, which is far cheaper, set up with ordinary types and electrotyped.

When a large amount of work of this kind is done, in an office, presses are built for the purpose, which are heated by steam, gas, or by the insertion of hot iron bars into cavities made for the purpose in the plate to which the form is attached; but, if there be not work enough of this kind to justify the printer in the purchase of such a press, the job may be done at the ordinary hand-press, by making the plate, on which the lettering is, about the thickness of a stereotype-plate, which must be raised to the hight of type by an iron plate instead of a wooden block. The iron plate can be heated, to the required degree, by placing it on the top of a hot stove or over a charcoal-fire, after which it must be transferred to the bed of the press, when the other plate must be laid upon it, and it will be ready for use.

There can be no directions given in reference to the amount of heat which the form should receive, in order to melt the article used to hold the gold on the surface of the material which is to be printed upon. This can only be ascertained by experience. A deviation from the correct amount of heat may be known by the gold looking dead and ragged, if the form be too hot; or bright, but imperfect, if too cold.

The article by which the gold-leaf is made to adhere will vary according to the material which is to be printed. When it is required to prepare hat-tips for the reception of the leaf, transparent shellac must be dissolved in spirits of wine; then saturate a sponge with the solution, and dampen the part of each of them which is to receive the impression. The spirits of wine will evaporate in a short time, and leave sufficient of the shellac on the tip to hold the gold, without altering the appearance of the material. When jobs are to be done on satin or velvet, the part of the surface to be printed must be powdered with the white of egg, which has been dried in the sun and ground on the stone with the muller, until it is reduced as fine as it is possible to make it. If leather is to be printed upon, the part of the surface which is to receive the impression must be rubbed over with the white of egg which has been mixed with a small quantity of sugar.

It will be found convenient, as a general thing, to lay the leaf on the face of the form, instead of on the surface of the material.

The tympan should be quite hard, so that the face of the form only could come in contact with it.

CHROMOTYPE-PRINTING.

This kind of work, although generally called by the above name, is not printing, in the strict sense of the word; because, part of it only is done at the printing-press, the remainder being finished by the use of stencils and water-colors. Chromotype-printing is employed to put in the colors of the maps in such jobs as the large cards printed for railroad-companies, and for coloring parts of the borders of large cards. The latter kind of work is called illuminated-printing.

The stencil is formed by pulling an impression of the job on a card, and cutting out the parts intended for one of the colors; a new stencil being cut for each of them. The colors must be laid on with a fine-grained sponge or soft camel-hair brush.

Any color which can be used for maps may be applied to this purpose. The following will answer very well:

Red. — Steep ground brazil-wood in vinegar, and add a small quantity of alum.

Steep cochineal in water, strain it, and add a sufficient amount of gum-arabic to keep it from depositing.

Dissolve litmus in water and add spirits of wine.

Yellow. — Dissolve gamboge in water; or, steep frenchberries in water, strain the liquor and add gum-arabic.

Blue. — Dissolve prussian-blue in water and add some gum-arabic.

To a solution of litmus add distilled vinegar.

Green.— Dissolve verdigris or sap-green in water and add gum-arabic.

A solution of litmus may be rendered green by adding a small quantity of any of the alkalies to it.

Ox-gall can be added, to brighten any of these colors.

EMBOSSED PRINTING.

This description of printing is done by using metalic dies, into the surface of which the lettering has been cut or punched.

The counter-die is made, by cutting a piece of thick smooth leather to the size of the die; the side which is to receive the impression must now be moistened, and being laid upon the surface of the die, a sufficient pressure must be given to it to make the leather go into all the cavities in the plate. The counter is then to be removed from the die and its edges trimmed so that both will be of the same size, after which the leather must be adjusted to its place on the face of the die, and its back covered with a thick mucilage, another impression must be made, so as to transfer the counter to the tympan. A thin sheet of gutta-percha should now be warmed on one side, and laid upon the face of the plate, with the side which has been heated uppermost. An impression must again be made, by which the leather and the gutta-percha will become attached, the result being an elastic counter, which will retain sufficient firmness to throw up any part of the under surface of the card without breaking the parts at the edges of the letters.

When the job is of large size, such as a show-card, the counter-die may be made by pasting ten or twelve sheets of smooth paper together with mucilage, and while they are in a damp state, to press the die into the pulpy mass, and leave it dry before they are separated.

The printer must be careful with reference to the ink. Whatever color is used should be strong in body, and the roller must be passed over the form, in all directions, so as to secure a perfectly uniform coating of ink.

The form must be cleaned, as occasion may require, by the application of spirits of turpentine with a brush.

ADDENDA.

This being the last division of the work, it will contain such matter as could not be given previously, without breaking into the order of the subject; that is, it will include: Tables for the giving out of paper, Suggestions in reference to the Composition of music and algebra, and Plans of the cases for Greek and Hebrew, etc.

GIVING OUT PAPER.

The following tables will be found convenient, as they will enable the printer to give out paper with facility and correctness for book-work, and for jobs, where the sizes vary and the numbers are irregular.

Those for book-work commence at as low a number as 12, and procced up to 10,000. Where the numbers are small, in book-work, the quantity of paper given out is greater than when the numbers are larger. A ream will not hold out in printing five sheets of one hundred copies each, and still less in smaller numbers; for, each sheet, at press, will require a tympan-sheet; and it is more than probable that one or two more will be spoiled in making the form ready.

Those for jobs include the same numbers, and are so arranged as to specify the quantity to a sheet for each number, without giving fractional parts of a sheet. On this account, many of them are exact, and others have a surplus, which in some instances is very large where there are many on a sheet; but, as jobs are generally delivered without surplus, it was thought best to give the quantity of paper that would make the nearest specific number, and leave the amount over the exact number, at the option of the pressman, or to the order of the proprietor of the printing-office.

BOOK-WORK—WHOLE SHEETS.

Number to be Printed.	Number the Paper will make.	Amount in Rms.	Qrs.	Shs.
12	15	0	0	15
25	28	0	1	4
50	54	0	2	6
75	79	0	3	7
100	104	0	4	8
125	129	0	5	9
150	156	0	6	12
175	181	0	7	13
200	206	0	8	14
250	258	0	10	18
300	310	0	12	22
350	360	0	15	0
375	387	0	16	3
400	412	0	17	4
450	462	0	19	6
500	516	1	1	12
600	618	1	5	18
700	722	1	10	2
750	774	1	12	6
800	826	1	14	10
900	928	1	18	17
1000	1032	2	3	0
1250	1290	2	13	18
1500	1548	3	4	12
1750	1806	3	15	6
2000	2064	4	6	0
3000	3096	6	9	0
4000	4128	8	12	0
5000	5160	10	15	0
6000	6192	12	18	0
7000	7224	15	1	0
8000	8256	17	4	0
9000	9288	19	7	0
10000	10320	21	10	0

BOOK-WORK—HALF SHEETS.

Number to be Printed.	Number the Paper will make.	Amount in Rms.	Qrs.	Shs.
12	16	0	0	8
25	30	0	0	15
50	56	0	1	4
75	80	0	1	16
100	104	0	2	4
125	130	0	2	17
150	158	0	3	7
175	182	0	3	19
200	206	0	4	7
250	258	0	5	9
300	310	0	6	11
350	360	0	7	12
375	386	0	8	1
400	412	0	8	14
450	462	0	9	15
500	516	0	10	18
600	618	0	12	21
700	722	0	15	1
750	774	0	16	3
800	824	0	17	4
900	928	0	19	8
1000	1032	1	1	12
1250	1290	1	6	21
1500	1548	1	12	6
1750	1806	1	17	15
2000	2064	2	3	0
3000	3096	3	4	12
4000	4128	4	6	0
5000	5160	5	7	12
6000	6192	6	9	0
7000	7224	7	10	12
8000	8256	8	12	0
9000	9288	9	13	12
10000	10320	10	15	0

BOOK-WORK—QUARTER SHEETS.

Number to be Printed.	Number the Paper will make	Amount in Rms.	Qrs.	Shs.
12	16	0	0	4
25	32	0	0	8
50	56	0	0	14
75	80	0	0	20
100	108	0	1	3
125	132	0	1	9
150	160	0	1	16
175	184	0	1	22
200	208	0	2	4
250	260	0	2	17
300	312	0	3	6
350	360	0	3	18
375	388	0	4	1
400	412	0	4	7
450	464	0	4	20
500	516	0	5	9
600	620	0	6	11
700	724	0	7	13
750	776	0	8	2
800	824	0	8	14
900	928	0	9	16
1000	1032	0	10	18
1250	1292	0	13	11
1500	1548	0	16	3
1750	1808	0	18	20
2000	2064	1	1	12
3000	3096	1	12	6
4000	4128	2	3	0
5000	5160	2	13	18
6000	6192	3	4	12
7000	7224	3	15	6
8000	8256	4	6	0
9000	9288	4	16	18
10000	10320	5	7	12

ADDENDA. 213

BOOK-WORK—THIRD OF A SHEET.

Number to be Printed.	Number the Paper will make.	Amount in Rms.	Qrs.	Shs.
12	15	0	0	5
25	30	0	0	10
50	57	0	0	19
75	81	0	1	3
100	105	0	1	11
125	129	0	1	19
150	156	0	2	4
175	180	0	2	12
200	207	0	2	21
250	258	0	3	14
300	312	0	4	8
350	360	0	5	0
375	387	0	5	9
400	414	0	5	18
450	462	0	6	10
500	516	0	7	4
600	618	0	8	14
700	723	0	10	1
750	774	0	10	18
800	825	0	11	11
900	927	0	12	21
1000	1032	0	14	8
1250	1290	0	17	22
1500	1548	1	1	12
1750	1806	1	5	2
2000	2064	1	8	16
3000	3096	2	3	0
4000	4128	2	17	8
5000	5160	3	11	16
6000	6192	4	6	0
7000	7224	5	0	8
8000	8256	5	14	16
9000	9288	6	9	0
10000	10320	7	3	8

JOB-WORK—ONE ON A SHEET.

Number to be Printed	Number the Paper will make	Amount in Rms.	Qrs.	Shs.
12	12	0	0	12
25	25	0	1	1
50	50	0	2	2
75	75	0	3	3
100	100	0	4	4
125	125	0	5	5
150	150	0	6	6
175	175	0	7	7
200	200	0	8	8
250	250	0	10	10
300	300	0	12	12
350	350	0	14	14
375	375	0	15	15
400	400	0	16	16
450	450	0	18	18
500	500	1	0	20
600	600	1	5	0
700	700	1	9	4
750	750	1	11	6
800	800	1	13	8
900	900	1	17	12
1000	1000	2	1	16
1250	1250	2	12	2
1500	1500	3	2	12
1750	1750	3	12	22
2000	2000	4	3	8
3000	3000	6	5	0
4000	4000	8	6	16
5000	5000	10	8	8
6000	6000	12	10	0
7000	7000	14	11	16
8000	8000	16	13	8
9000	9000	18	15	0
10000	10000	20	16	16

ADDENDA.

JOB-WORK—TWO ON A SHEET.

Number to be Printed.	Number the Paper will make	Amount in Rms. Qrs. Shs.
12	12	0 0 6
25	26	0 0 13
50	50	0 1 1
75	76	0 1 14
100	100	0 2 2
125	126	0 2 15
150	150	0 3 3
175	176	0 3 16
200	200	0 4 4
250	250	0 5 5
300	300	0 6 6
350	350	0 7 7
375	376	0 7 20
400	400	0 8 8
450	450	0 9 9
500	500	0 10 10
600	600	0 12 12
700	700	0 14 14
750	750	0 15 15
800	800	0 16 16
900	900	0 18 18
1000	1000	1 0 20
1250	1250	1 6 1
1500	1500	1 11 6
1750	1750	1 16 11
2000	2000	2 1 16
3000	3000	3 2 12
4000	4000	4 3 8
5000	5000	5 4 4
6000	6000	6 5 0
7000	7000	7 5 20
8000	8000	8 6 16
9000	9000	9 7 12
10000	10000	10 8 8

JOB-WORK—THREE ON A SHEET.

Number to be Printed.	Number the Paper will make.	Amount in Rms.	Qrs.	Shs
12	12	0	0	4
25	27	0	0	9
50	51	0	0	17
75	75	0	1	1
100	102	0	1	10
125	126	0	1	18
150	150	0	2	2
175	177	0	2	11
200	201	0	2	19
250	252	0	3	12
300	300	0	4	4
350	351	0	4	21
375	375	0	5	5
400	402	0	5	14
450	450	0	6	6
500	501	0	6	23
600	600	0	8	8
700	702	0	9	18
750	750	0	10	10
800	801	0	11	3
900	900	0	12	12
1000	1002	0	13	22
1250	1251	0	17	9
1500	1500	1	0	20
1750	1752	1	4	8
2000	2001	1	7	19
3000	3000	2	1	16
4000	4002	2	14	14
5000	5001	3	9	11
6000	6000	4	3	8
7000	7002	4	17	6
8000	8001	5	11	3
9000	9000	6	5	0
10000	10002	6	18	22

JOB-WORK—FOUR ON A SHEET.

Number to be Printed.	Number the Paper will make.	Amount in Rms.	Qrs.	Shs.
12	12	0	0	3
25	28	0	0	7
50	52	0	0	13
75	76	0	0	19
100	100	0	1	1
125	128	0	1	8
150	152	0	1	14
175	176	0	1	20
200	200	0	2	2
250	252	0	2	15
300	300	0	3	3
350	352	0	3	16
375	376	0	3	22
400	400	0	4	4
450	452	0	4	17
500	500	0	5	5
600	600	0	6	6
700	700	0	7	7
750	752	0	7	20
800	800	0	8	8
900	900	0	9	9
1000	1000	0	10	10
1250	1252	0	13	1
1500	1500	0	15	15
1750	1752	0	18	6
2000	2000	1	0	20
3000	3000	1	11	6
4000	4000	2	1	16
5000	5000	2	12	2
6000	6000	3	2	12
7000	7000	3	12	22
8000	8000	4	3	8
9000	9000	4	13	18
10000	10000	5	4	4

JOB-WORK—FIVE ON A SHEET.

Number to be Printed.	Number the Paper will make.	Amount in Rms.	Qrs.	Shs.
12	15	0	0	3
25	25	0	0	5
50	50	0	0	10
75	75	0	0	15
100	100	0	0	20
125	125	0	1	1
150	150	0	1	6
175	175	0	1	11
200	200	0	1	16
250	250	0	2	2
300	300	0	2	12
350	350	0	2	22
375	375	0	3	3
400	400	0	3	8
450	450	0	3	18
500	500	0	4	4
600	600	0	5	0
700	700	0	5	20
750	750	0	6	6
800	800	0	6	16
900	900	0	7	12
1000	1000	0	8	8
1250	1250	0	10	10
1500	1500	0	12	12
1750	1750	0	14	14
2000	2000	0	16	16
3000	3000	1	5	0
4000	4000	1	13	8
5000	5000	2	1	16
6000	6000	2	10	0
7000	7000	2	18	8
8000	8000	3	6	16
9000	9000	3	15	0
10000	10000	4	3	8

JOB-WORK—SIX ON A SHEET.

Number to be Printed.	Number the Paper will make.	Amount in Rms.	Qrs.	Shs.
12	12	0	0	2
25	30	0	0	5
50	54	0	0	9
75	78	0	0	13
100	102	0	0	17
125	126	0	0	21
150	150	0	1	1
175	180	0	1	6
200	204	0	1	10
250	252	0	1	18
300	300	0	2	2
350	354	0	2	11
375	378	0	2	15
400	402	0	2	19
450	450	0	3	3
500	504	0	3	12
600	600	0	4	4
700	702	0	4	21
750	750	0	5	5
800	804	0	5	14
900	900	0	6	6
1000	1000	0	6	23
1250	1254	0	8	17
1500	1500	0	10	10
1750	1752	0	12	4
2000	2004	0	13	22
3000	3000	1	0	20
4000	4002	1	7	19
5000	5004	1	14	18
6000	6000	2	1	16
7000	7002	2	8	15
8000	8004	2	15	14
9000	9000	3	2	12
10000	10002	3	9	11

JOB-WORK—EIGHT ON A SHEET.

Number to be Printed.	Number the Paper will make.	Amount in Rms.	Qrs.	Shs.
12	16	0	0	2
25	32	0	0	4
50	56	0	0	7
75	80	0	0	10
100	104	0	0	13
125	128	0	0	16
150	152	0	0	19
175	176	0	0	22
200	200	0	1	1
250	256	0	1	8
300	304	0	1	14
350	352	0	1	20
375	376	0	1	23
400	400	0	2	2
450	456	0	2	9
500	504	0	2	15
600	600	0	3	3
700	704	0	3	16
750	752	0	3	22
800	800	0	4	4
900	904	0	4	17
1000	1000	0	5	5
1250	1256	0	6	13
1500	1504	0	7	20
1750	1752	0	9	3
2000	2000	0	10	10
3000	3000	0	15	15
4000	4000	1	0	20
5000	5000	1	6	1
6000	6000	1	11	6
7000	7000	1	16	11
8000	8000	2	1	16
9000	9000	2	6	21
10000	10000	2	12	2

JOB-WORK—NINE ON A SHEET.

Number to be Printed.	Number the Paper will make.	Amount in Rms.	Qrs.	Shs.
12	18	0	0	2
25	27	0	0	3
50	54	0	0	6
75	81	0	0	9
100	108	0	0	12
125	126	0	0	14
150	153	0	0	17
175	180	0	0	20
200	207	0	0	23
250	252	0	1	4
300	306	0	1	10
350	351	0	1	15
375	378	0	1	18
400	405	0	1	21
450	450	0	2	2
500	504	0	2	8
600	603	0	2	19
700	702	0	3	6
750	756	0	3	12
800	801	0	3	17
900	900	0	4	4
1000	1008	0	4	16
1250	1251	0	5	19
1500	1503	0	6	23
1750	1755	0	8	3
2000	2007	0	9	7
3000	3006	0	13	22
4000	4005	0	18	13
5000	5004	1	3	4
6000	6003	1	7	19
7000	7002	1	12	10
8000	8001	1	17	1
9000	9000	2	1	16
10000	10008	2	6	8

JOB-WORK—TWELVE ON A SHEET.

Number to be Printed.	Number the Paper will make.	Amount in Rms.	Qrs.	Shs.
12	12	0	0	1
25	36	0	0	3
50	60	0	0	5
75	84	0	0	7
100	108	0	0	9
125	132	0	0	11
150	156	0	0	13
175	180	0	0	15
200	204	0	0	17
250	252	0	0	21
300	300	0	1	1
350	360	0	1	6
375	384	0	1	8
400	408	0	1	10
450	456	0	1	14
500	504	0	1	18
600	600	0	2	2
700	708	0	2	11
750	756	0	2	15
800	804	0	2	19
900	900	0	3	3
1000	1008	0	3	12
1250	1260	0	4	9
1500	1500	0	5	5
1750	1752	0	6	2
2000	2004	0	6	23
3000	3000	0	10	10
4000	4008	0	13	22
5000	5004	0	17	9
6000	6000	1	0	20
7000	7008	1	4	8
8000	8004	1	7	19
9000	9000	1	11	6
10000	10008	1	14	18

JOB-WORK—SIXTEEN ON A SHEET.

Number to be Printed	Number the Paper will make.	Amount in Rms.	Qrs.	Shs.
12	16	0	0	1
25	32	0	0	2
50	64	0	0	4
75	80	0	0	5
100	112	0	0	7
125	128	0	0	8
150	160	0	0	10
175	176	0	0	11
200	208	0	0	13
250	256	0	0	16
300	304	0	0	19
350	352	0	0	22
375	384	0	1	0
400	400	0	1	1
450	464	0	1	5
500	512	0	1	8
600	608	0	1	14
700	704	0	1	20
750	752	0	1	23
800	800	0	2	2
900	912	0	2	9
1000	1008	0	2	15
1250	1264	0	3	7
1500	1504	0	3	22
1750	1760	0	4	14
2000	2000	0	5	5
3000	3008	0	7	20
4000	4000	0	10	10
5000	5008	0	13	1
6000	6000	0	15	15
7000	7008	0	18	6
8000	8000	1	0	20
9000	9008	1	3	11
10000	10000	1	6	1

JOB-WORK—EIGHTEEN ON A SHEET.

Number to be Printed.	Number the Paper will make.	Amount in Rms.	Qrs.	Shs.
12	18	0	0	1
25	36	0	0	2
50	54	0	0	3
75	90	0	0	5
100	108	0	0	6
125	126	0	0	7
150	162	0	0	9
175	180	0	0	10
200	216	0	0	12
250	252	0	0	14
300	306	0	0	17
350	360	0	0	2
375	378	0	0	21
400	414	0	0	23
450	450	0	1	1
500	504	0	1	4
600	612	0	1	10
700	702	0	1	15
750	756	0	1	18
800	810	0	1	21
900	900	0	2	2
1000	1008	0	2	8
1250	1260	0	2	22
1500	1512	0	3	12
1750	1764	0	4	2
2000	2016	0	4	16
3000	3006	0	6	23
4000	4014	0	9	7
5000	5004	0	11	14
6000	6012	0	13	22
7000	7002	0	16	5
8000	8010	0	18	13
9000	9000	1	0	20
10000	10008	1	3	4

JOB-WORK—TWENTY ON A SHEET.

Number to be Printed.	Number the Paper will make.	Amount in Rms.	Qrs.	Shs.
12	20	0	0	1
25	40	0	0	2
50	60	0	0	3
75	80	0	0	4
100	100	0	0	5
125	140	0	0	7
150	160	0	0	8
175	180	0	0	9
200	200	0	0	10
250	260	0	0	13
300	300	0	0	15
350	360	0	0	18
375	380	0	0	19
400	400	0	0	20
450	460	0	0	23
500	500	0	1	1
600	600	0	1	6
700	700	0	1	11
750	760	0	1	14
800	800	0	1	16
900	900	0	1	21
1000	1000	0	2	2
1250	1260	0	2	15
1500	1500	0	3	3
1750	1760	0	3	16
2000	2000	0	4	4
3000	3000	0	6	6
4000	4000	0	8	8
5000	5000	0	10	10
6000	6000	0	12	12
7000	7000	0	14	14
8000	8000	0	16	16
9000	9000	0	18	18
10000	10000	1	0	20

JOB-WORK—TWENTY-FOUR ON A SHEET.

Number to be Printed.	Number the Paper will make	Rms.	Qrs.	Shs.
12	24	0	0	1
25	48	0	0	2
50	72	0	0	3
75	96	0	0	4
100	120	0	0	5
125	144	0	0	6
150	168	0	0	7
175	192	0	0	8
200	216	0	0	9
250	264	0	0	11
300	312	0	0	13
350	360	0	0	15
375	384	0	0	16
400	408	0	0	17
450	456	0	0	19
500	504	0	0	21
600	600	0	1	1
700	720	0	1	6
750	768	0	1	8
800	816	0	1	10
900	912	0	1	14
1000	1008	0	1	18
1250	1272	0	2	5
1500	1512	0	2	15
1750	1752	0	3	1
2000	2016	0	3	12
3000	3000	0	5	5
4000	4008	0	6	23
5000	5016	0	8	17
6000	6000	0	10	10
7000	7008	0	12	4
8000	8016	0	13	22
9000	9000	0	15	15
10000	10008	0	17	9

JOB-WORK—THIRTY-TWO ON A SHEET.

Number to be Printed.	Number the Paper will make.	Amount in Rms.	Qrs.	Shs.
12	32	0	0	1
25	32	0	0	1
50	64	0	0	2
75	96	0	0	3
100	128	0	0	4
125	128	0	0	4
150	160	0	0	5
175	192	0	0	6
200	224	0	0	7
250	256	0	0	8
300	320	0	0	10
350	352	0	0	11
375	384	0	0	12
400	416	0	0	13
450	480	0	0	15
500	512	0	0	16
600	608	0	0	19
700	704	0	0	22
750	768	0	1	0
800	800	0	1	1
900	928	0	1	5
1000	1024	0	1	8
1250	1280	0	1	16
1500	1504	0	1	23
1750	1760	0	2	7
2000	2016	0	2	15
3000	3008	0	3	22
4000	4000	0	5	5
5000	5024	0	6	13
6000	6016	0	7	20
7000	7008	0	9	3
8000	8000	0	10	10
9000	9024	0	11	18
10000	10016	0	13	1

JOB-WORK—THIRTY-SIX ON A SHEET.

Number to be Printed	Number the Paper will make	Rms.	Amount in Qrs.	Shs.
12	36	0	0	1
25	36	0	0	1
50	72	0	0	2
75	108	0	0	3
100	108	0	0	3
125	144	0	0	4
150	180	0	0	5
175	180	0	0	5
200	216	0	0	6
250	252	0	0	7
300	324	0	0	9
350	360	0	0	10
375	396	0	0	11
400	432	0	0	12
450	468	0	0	13
500	504	0	0	14
600	612	0	0	17
700	720	0	0	20
750	756	0	0	21
800	828	0	0	23
900	900	0	1	1
1000	1008	0	1	4
1250	1250	0	1	11
1500	1512	0	1	18
1750	1764	0	2	1
2000	2016	0	2	8
3000	3024	0	3	12
4000	4032	0	4	16
5000	5004	0	5	19
6000	6012	0	6	23
7000	7020	0	8	3
8000	8028	0	9	7
9000	9000	0	10	10
10000	10008	0	11	14

JOB-WORK—FORTY ON A SHEET.

Number to be Printed.	Number the Paper will make.	Amount in Rms.	Qrs.	Shs.
12	40	0	0	1
25	40	0	0	1
50	80	0	0	2
75	80	0	0	2
100	120	0	0	3
125	160	0	0	4
150	160	0	0	4
175	200	0	0	5
200	200	0	0	5
250	280	0	0	7
300	320	0	0	8
350	360	0	0	9
375	400	0	0	10
400	400	0	0	10
450	480	0	0	12
500	520	0	0	13
600	600	0	0	15
700	720	0	0	18
750	760	0	0	19
800	800	0	0	20
900	920	0	0	23
1000	1000	0	1	1
1250	1280	0	1	8
1500	1520	0	1	14
1750	1760	0	1	20
2000	2000	0	2	2
3000	3000	0	3	3
4000	4000	0	4	4
5000	5000	0	5	5
6000	6000	0	6	6
7000	7000	0	7	7
8000	8000	0	8	8
9000	9000	0	9	9
10000	10000	0	10	10

JOB-WORK—FORTY-EIGHT ON A SHEET.

Number to be Printed.	Number the Paper will make.	Amount in Rms.	Qrs.	Shs.
12	48	0	0	1
25	48	0	0	1
50	96	0	0	2
75	96	0	0	2
100	144	0	0	3
125	144	0	0	3
150	192	0	0	4
175	192	0	0	4
200	240	0	0	5
250	288	0	0	6
300	336	0	0	7
350	384	0	0	8
375	384	0	0	8
400	432	0	0	9
450	480	0	0	10
500	528	0	0	11
600	624	0	0	13
700	720	0	0	15
750	768	0	0	16
800	816	0	0	17
900	912	0	0	19
1000	1008	0	0	21
1250	1296	0	1	3
1500	1536	0	1	8
1750	1776	0	1	13
2000	2016	0	1	18
3000	3024	0	2	15
4000	4032	0	3	12
5000	5040	0	4	9
6000	6000	0	5	5
7000	7008	0	6	2
8000	8016	0	6	23
9000	9024	0	7	20
10000	10032	0	8	17

ADDENDA. 231

JOB-WORK—SIXTY-FOUR ON A SHEET.

Number to be Printed.	Number the Paper will make.	Amount in Rms.	Qrs.	Shs.
12	64	0	0	1
25	64	0	0	1
50	64	0	0	1
75	128	0	0	2
100	128	0	0	2
125	128	0	0	2
150	192	0	0	3
175	192	0	0	3
200	256	0	0	4
250	256	0	0	4
300	320	0	0	5
350	384	0	0	6
375	384	0	0	6
400	448	0	0	7
450	512	0	0	8
500	512	0	0	8
600	640	0	0	10
700	704	0	0	11
750	768	0	0	12
800	832	0	0	13
900	960	0	0	15
1000	1024	0	0	16
1250	1280	0	0	20
1500	1536	0	1	0
1750	1792	0	1	4
2000	2048	0	1	8
3000	3008	0	1	23
4000	4032	0	2	15
5000	5056	0	3	7
6000	6016	0	3	22
7000	7040	0	4	14
8000	8000	0	5	5
9000	9024	0	5	21
10000	10048	0	6	13

JOB-WORK—SEVENTY-TWO ON A SHEET.

Number to be Printed.	Number the Paper will make.	Amount in Rms.	Qrs.	Shs.
12	72	0	0	1
25	72	0	0	1
50	72	0	0	1
75	144	0	0	2
100	144	0	0	2
125	144	0	0	2
150	216	0	0	3
175	216	0	0	3
200	216	0	0	3
250	288	0	0	4
300	360	0	0	5
350	360	0	0	5
375	432	0	0	6
400	432	0	0	6
450	504	0	0	7
500	504	0	0	7
600	648	0	0	9
700	720	0	0	10
750	792	0	0	11
800	864	0	0	12
900	936	0	0	13
1000	1008	0	0	14
1250	1296	0	0	18
1500	1512	0	0	21
1750	1800	0	1	1
2000	2016	0	1	4
3000	3024	0	1	18
4000	4032	0	2	8
5000	5040	0	2	22
6000	6048	0	3	12
7000	7056	0	4	2
8000	8064	0	4	16
9000	9000	0	5	5
10000	10008	0	5	19

ADDENDA. 233

JOB-WORK—NINETY-SIX ON A SHEET.

Number to be Printed.	Number the Paper will make.	Amount in Rms.	Qrs.	Shs.
12	96	0	0	1
25	96	0	0	1
50	96	0	0	1
75	96	0	0	1
100	192	0	0	2
125	192	0	0	2
150	192	0	0	2
175	192	0	0	2
200	288	0	0	3
250	288	0	0	3
300	384	0	0	4
350	384	0	0	4
375	384	0	0	4
400	480	0	0	5
450	480	0	0	5
500	576	0	0	6
600	602	0	0	7
700	768	0	0	8
750	768	0	0	8
800	864	0	0	9
900	960	0	0	10
1000	1056	0	0	11
1250	1344	0	0	14
1500	1536	0	0	16
1750	1824	0	0	19
2000	2016	0	0	21
3000	3072	0	1	8
4000	4032	0	1	18
5000	5088	0	2	5
6000	6048	0	2	15
7000	7008	0	3	1
8000	8064	0	3	12
9000	9024	0	3	22
10000	10080	0	4	9

JOB-WORK—ONE-HUNDRED-AND-TWENTY-EIGHT ON A SHEET.

Number to be Printed.	Number the Paper will make.	Amount in Rms.	Qrs.	Shs.
12	128	0	0	1
25	128	0	0	1
50	128	0	0	1
75	128	0	0	1
100	128	0	0	1
125	128	0	0	1
150	256	0	0	2
175	256	0	0	2
200	256	0	0	2
250	256	0	0	2
300	384	0	0	3
350	384	0	0	3
375	384	0	0	3
400	512	0	0	4
450	512	0	0	4
500	512	0	0	4
600	640	0	0	5
700	768	0	0	6
750	768	0	0	6
800	896	0	0	7
900	1024	0	0	8
1000	1024	0	0	8
1250	1280	0	0	10
1500	1536	0	0	12
1750	1792	0	0	14
2000	2048	0	0	16
3000	3072	0	1	0
4000	4096	0	1	8
5000	5120	0	1	16
6000	6016	0	1	23
7000	7040	0	2	7
8000	8064	0	2	15
9000	9088	0	2	23
10000	1011?	0	3	7

DIMENSIONS OF PRINTING-PAPER.

	Inches Wide.	Inches Long.		Inches Wide.	Inches Long.
Letter	10 ×	15	Royal-and-Half	25 ×	29
Fools-Cap	14 ×	17	Double-Medium.	23 × 24 × 25 ×	36 $37\frac{1}{2}$ 38
Crown	15 ×	20			
Folio-Post	16 ×	21			
Demy	17 ×	22	Imperial-and-Half	20 ×	32
Medium	$18\frac{1}{2}$ ×	$23\frac{1}{2}$			
Royal	19 × 20 ×	24 25	Double-Super-Royal	27 ×	42
Super-Royal	21 ×	27	Double-Imperial	32 ×	44
Imperial	22 ×	32			

FRACTIONAL PARTS OF A BUNDLE.

	Sheets.		Sheets.
Seven-eighths	840	Three-eighths	360
Four-fifths	768	One-third	320
Three-fourths	720	One-fourth	240
Two-thirds	640	One-fifth	192
Five-eighths	600	One-sixth	160
Three-fifths	576	One-eighth	120
One-half	480	One-tenth	96
Two-fifths	384	One-twelfth	80

FRACTIONAL PARTS OF A REAM

	Sheets.		Sheets.
Seven-eighths	420	Three-eighths	180
Four-fifths	384	One-third	160
Three-fourths	360	One-fourth	120
Two-thirds	320	One-fifth	96
Five-eighths	300	One-sixth	80
Three-fifths	288	One-eighth	60
One-half	240	One-tenth	48
Two-fifths	192	One-twelfth	40

A TABLE

Showing the number of lines contained in 1000 m, in all measures from 10 m to 100 m wide:

M wide.	Lines long.	M wide.	Lines long.	M wide.	Lines long.
10·0	100·00	27·0	37·03	44·0	22·72
10·5	95·24	27·5	36·36	44·5	22·47
11·0	90·91	28·0	35·71	45·0	22·22
11·5	86·96	28·5	35·09	45·5	21·97
12·0	83·33	29·0	34·48	46·0	21·74
12·5	80·00	29·5	33·90	46·5	21·50
13·0	76·92	30·0	33·33	47·0	21·27
13·5	74·07	30·5	32·79	47·5	21·05
14·0	71·43	31·0	32·26	48·0	20·83
14·5	68·02	31·5	31·75	48·5	20·62
15·0	66·66	32·0	31·10	49·0	20·41
15·5	64·52	32·5	30·77	49·5	20·20
16·0	62·20	33·0	30·30	50·0	20·00
16·5	60·61	33·5	29·85	50·5	19·80
17·0	58·82	34·0	29·42	51·0	19·62
17·5	57·14	34·5	28·98	52·0	19·23
18·0	55·56	35·0	28·57	53·0	18·87
18·5	54·05	35·5	28·17	54·0	18·51
19·0	52·63	36·0	27·78	55·0	18·18
19·5	51·28	36·5	27·40	56·0	17·85
20·0	50·00	37·0	27·02	57·0	17·54
20·5	48·78	37·5	26·66	58·0	17·24
21·0	47·62	38·0	26·31	59·0	16·95
21·5	46·51	38·5	25·97	60·0	16·66
22·0	45·45	39·0	25·64	61·0	16·39
22·5	44·44	39·5	25·32	62·0	16·13
23·0	43·48	40·0	25·00	63·0	15·87
23·5	42·55	40·5	24·69	64·0	15·55
24·0	41·66	41·0	24·39	65·0	15·38
24·5	40·82	41·5	24·10	66·0	15·15
25·0	40·00	42·0	23·81	67·0	14·92
25·5	39·22	42·5	23·53	68·0	14·71
26·0	38·46	43·0	23·26	69·0	14·49
26·5	37·74	43·5	22·99	70·0	14·28

ADDENDA.

M wide.	Lines long.	M wide.	Lines long.	M wide.	Lines long.
71·0	14·08	81·0	12·38	91·0	10·98
72·0	13·88	82·0	12·19	92·0	10·87
73·0	13·70	83·0	12·05	93·0	10·75
74·0	13·51	84·0	11·90	94·0	10·63
75·0	13·33	85·0	11·76	95·0	10·51
76·0	13·15	86·0	11·63	96·0	10·41
77·0	12·98	87·0	11·49	97·0	10·31
78·0	12·82	88·0	11·36	98·0	10·20
79·0	12·66	89·0	11·23	99·0	10·10
80·0	12·50	90·0	11·11	100·0	10·00

In referring to the foregoing table, it will be seen that the measures are calculated by n, up to 50 m, and by m for all the widths above that number.

A TABLE

Showing the number of m, in the various kinds of types, which will occupy the same space as 1000 m, in all the sizes from pica to nonpareil, inclusive :

Pica,	1000	750	640	520	400	340	250
Small-Pica,	1320	1000	850	695	540	455	333
Long-Primer,	1550	1160	1000	810	633	535	390
Bourgeois,	1900	1425	1225	1000	775	655	480
Brevier,	2433	1833	1566	1285	1000	840	615
Minion,	2880	2160	1850	1500	1180	1000	730
Nonpareil,	4000	3000	2560	2080	1600	1360	1000

COMPOSITION OF ALGEBRA.

This is the most difficult description of work which a compositor has to perform, both on account of the accuracy required in justification, and the want of the necessary sorts in almost every printing-office.

The lower-case letters: a, b, c, x, y, z, etc., are used in the formulas. They should be set in italic, if the lines in which they are placed be roman, and vice versa. When capital letters are inserted, the roman should be employed in all cases. It would be a great convenience if the lower-case letters, used for this purpose, were cast to the size of the figures; because, in all fractional formulas, this would make both parts range correctly without it being necessary to justify every letter.

The signs: $+$, $-$, $\div$, $\times$, $=$, $\therefore$, etc., which are used in algebraic work, should be cast twice the thickness of a figure; and, in fact, every thing used in the examples to the questions should be exact parts of an m-quad. The smaller signs, used in exponents and series, should be on the body in such a position that they would fall in their proper place between the superior and inferior letters, when turned in either direction, as:

$$x^m + ax^{m+1} , \qquad \dot{S}_{m-1}$$

The radical sign should be kerned at the top, so that it could be joined to a space-rule, as:

$$\sqrt{a+b} = x$$

and the larger radical sign should be made in the same manner, and also be as wide as two lines and the space-rule which is run between them.

In setting two or more lines, the similar expressions in each should be placed one above the other, as:

$$8x + 9y + 8z = 2700$$
$$12x + 12y + 10z = 3600$$

$$ax + by + cz = d$$
$$a'x + b'y + c'z = d'$$
$$a''x + b''y + c''z = d''$$

When an equation is too long for the measure of the page, it should be divided either at the sign $\times$ or $=$, and each part must be justified in the centre of the line which it occupies.

Such words as: **Hence** or **Therefore**, when used in this kind of work, should be placed in the commencement of the line, and when a figure is put in as a direction to some other formula, it should be put between parentheses or brackets, at the outer end of the line.

The short part of a fraction should be justified in the centre of the long, without reference to either being divisor or dividend, and the space-rule which separates them should be equal in length to the larger part, as:

$$\frac{cb - y}{a} = \frac{B}{0\cdot00001}$$

In putting together such examples as the above, the most expeditious method of proceeding is, to look along the line, and compose the longer part of each fraction, with the signs which may be between them, as:

$$cb - y = 0\cdot00001$$

The line so composed should be placed on a galley, and each of these portions can be put in the composing-stick, as required, and the remainder of the compound line can be finished with very little trouble and without loss of time.

COMPOSITION OF MUSIC.

The type-founders differ so much in the cut of their music-types that no special directions can be given to assist a compositor in setting up this kind of work; yet, it may be well to state, that the stems should be two-and-one-half m in length, in order to make the page look well; and, when more than one clef is used, that which contains the longer notes should be justified so that these would fall precisely under the first of those which occupy the same time in the other clef, instead of in the centre.

Some of these founts are made so that the line is on the upper edge of the body, while others have the line in the centre. Another class of music-founts is cast so that the lines, which in this kind are made of thin brass-rule, can be put into their places after the line or page has been composed; and, there is yet another kind, in which the notes and the lines are made up in separate pages, the press being built in such a manner that the form could be reversed, after the first impression on each sheet, and the notes printed over the lines, and vice versa. The last comes the nearest in appearance to punched music.

COMPOSITION OF GREEK

The greek alphabet contains twenty-four letters, which are arranged in the following order:

Figure.	Name.	Power.	Figure.	Name.	Power.
A α	Alpha,	a.	N ν	Nu,	n.
B β ϐ	Beta,	b.	Ξ ξ	Xi,	x.
Γ γ	Gamma,	g.	O o	Omicron,	o short.
Δ δ	Delta,	d.	Π π ϖ	Pi,	p.
E ε	Epsilon,	e short.	P ρ	Rho,	r.
Z ζ	Zeta,	z.	Σ σ ς	Sigma,	s.
H η	Eta,	e long.	T τ	Tau,	t.
Θ ϑ θ	Theta,	th.	Υ υ	Upsilon,	u.
I ι	Iota,	i.	Φ φ	Phi,	f.
K κ	Kappa,	k.	X χ	Chi,	ch.
Λ λ	Lambda,	l.	Ψ ψ	Psi,	ps.
M μ	Mu,	m.	Ω ω	Omega,	o long.

Beside the letters shown above, some greek founts have a long γ and τ, as well as an initial σ. The ζ, ρ, and φ are also made of other shapes beside those given; but, as such sorts only encumber the case, and are of no practical use, it would be as well to leave them out.

The character β is used at the commencement of words, and ϐ in the middle, as: βάρϐαρος.

The two letters ϑ and θ are used in the same manner, as: ϑύμιον, βάθρα.

The letter σ is used at the beginning and in the middle of words, and ς at the end, as: σύμβασις. The final ς will sometimes be found in the middle of words. In all such cases the word is compound, as: προςέφη.

The ligatures ﬅ and ϗ are the only ones made at present. The first represents the letters st, and the latter the word kai.

ADDENDA.

The following are the aspirates and accents, with the various combinations which they form:

' Lenis.	˜ Circumflex.
' Asper.	῭ Circumflex-lenis.
´ Acute.	῭ Circumflex-asper.
` Grave.	¨ Diæresis.
″ Lenis-acute.	΅ Diæresis-acute.
″ Asper-acute.	̀¨ Diæresis-grave.
″ Lenis-grave.	῀ Circumflex-diæresis.
″ Asper-grave.	῾' Asper-lenis.

The letter v is the only vowel which takes all the above accents.

The vowel ι takes all of the accents, with the exception of the asper-lenis.

The a, η, and ω do not take the diæresis; and for this reason the accents placed over these letters are twelve in number. The accents over the a, η, and ω are the same as over the a, η, and ω, with the exception of the asper-lenis, which makes their number eleven only.

The vowels ε and o do not take the circumflex, the diæresis, or the asper-lenis, which reduces the number used over these letters to eight.

The circumflex-diæresis and the asper-lenis not being often required, are never cast, but must be made by the compositor.

In giving a plan of the greek cases, the system heretofore followed has been departed from. Instead of the capitals being arranged in alphabetic order, they are placed, as near as possible, in the boxes which would contain the letters of like sounds in the english alphabet. The lower-case has been altered in the same manner, and the boxes for the γ, ζ, ρ, τ, and ϕ have been duplicated, so that, if these sorts be cast of both shapes, there will be a box for each.

The following is the plan of the greek cases:

PRINTER'S MANUAL:

GREEK UPPER-CASE.

ADDENDA.

GREEK LOWER-CASE.

ς	᷿ρ	ϛ	m quads.	Quads.	
ς	᷿ρ	ϛ	n quads.		
ς	θ		σ	:	‚
ς	ϑ	ϖ	π	'	.
ϛ	η		ε	ρ	
ϛ				ρ	
ϛ	ι		ο	α	
ϛ					
ε	e		ν	Thin spaces.	Thick spaces.
ε					
ε	δ		μ	⊦	
ε				⊦	
ε	γ		λ	υ	
ε	γ				
ε	β	ϙ	κ	ϕ	.
ε	φ	φ	ς	ς	ξ	χ

The letters of the greek alphabet are used as numerals. Those from 1 to 999 have a minute-mark or acute accent placed after them, so that they can be distinguished from the ordinary letters, as in the following example:

1	2	3	4	5	6	7	8	9	10
α'	β'	γ'	δ'	ε'	ς'	ζ'	η'	θ'	ι'
11	12	13	14	15	16	17	18	19	20
ια'	ιβ'	ιγ'	ιδ'	ιε'	ις'	ιζ'	ιη'	ιθ'	κ'
21	22	30	40	50	60	70	80	90	100
κα'	κβ'	λ'	μ'	ν'	ξ'	ο'	π'	ϟ'	ρ'
200	300	400	500	600	700	800	900		
σ'	τ'	υ'	φ'	χ'	ψ'	ω'	ϡ'		

From the number 1000 to 999,999 the letters are used in the same manner, the only difference being, that the minute-mark is placed before, and at the bottom of, the letters, in the following manner:

1000	2000	3000	4000	5000	6000	7000	8000	
͵α	͵β	͵γ	͵δ	͵ε	͵ς	͵ζ	͵η	etc.

To designate the number 1,000,000, and all others of higher denomination, the letters are used as in the latter example, the only difference being, that two minute-marks are used instead of one, as may be seen below:

1,000,000	2,000,000	3,000,000	4,000,000	5,000,000	
͵͵α	͵͵β	͵͵γ	͵͵δ	͵͵ε	etc.

The signs of punctuation used in the greek are: the comma, period, semi-colon, and the period reversed. The comma and the period are used in the same manner as in the latin and english. The semi-colon is used as an interrogation-point; and the reversed period in place of the colon. In some editions of greek works published in Germany, the exclamation-point is used.

The apostrophe is often used to cut off a vowel at the end of a word, when the next commences with a vowel. In such cases the apostrophe should have a space put after it, so that it may not be mistaken for the lenis.

COMPOSITION OF HEBREW.

There are twenty-two letters in the hebrew alphabet, which are read from the right to the left, as follows:

Power, TH SH R KH TZ F O S N M L K Y T CH Z V H D G B A
Figure, אבגדהוזחטיכלמנסעפצקרשת
Name, Tauv, Sheen, Raish, Kooph, Tzauday, Pay, Oyin, Saumek, Noon, Mem, Laumed, Kaph, Yood, Teth, Cheth, Zauyin, Vauv, Hay, Dauleth, Gimmel, Bayth, Auleph,

The letters given below, which are used as finals, differ in shape from those of the same power in the alphabet:

TZ F N M K
ץףןםך

As the division of words is not allowed in the hebrew, the following letters are cast broad, so that the compositor will be enabled to justify his lines, without any trouble:

TH M L H A
ת ם ל ה א

There are several letters which might be inserted, one for another, on account of their similarity in appearance. The whole of them are given in the next line, so that a glance will show the difference between them:

בכ: גנ: דרך: החת: טמ: סם: יוזן: עצץ:

Some hebrew founts have four distinct alphabets cast to them: the first being the simple letter (ה) without any point or mark; the second, (הּ), having a point within the body of the letters; the third, (ה֗), a point at the top; and, the fourth, (הּ֗), one at the top, and another within the letter. But, as the two latter alphabets are not often used, and only encumber the case, they had better be left out, with the exception of a few sorts which are placed above the alphabet in the upper-case; the other points, which are not often used, being justified in the line with the superior accents.

Beside the points mentioned on the preceding page, there are seven vowel-points cast on a body half that of the size of the types, so that they can be justified under the letters. The names and shapes are given below:

kamets, patach, sheva, chirek, segol, tseri, kybbutz.

Some of these vowels may be combined, as follows:

chatef-kamets, chatef-segol, chatef-patach.

There are also twenty-four tonic signs, cast like the preceding, some of which are justified at the top of the letters and the others at the bottom of the line. These which are placed at the top are the following:

segolta, little sakeph, great sakeph, rebia, paschta *or* kadma, sarka,

shalshelet, paser, karne-phara, great telischa, little telishcha, geresh,

double gerish *or* guershaim   jethib.

Those accents which are justified below the line are:

silluk, athnach, tiphcha, merka, double merka, munach, tebir,

mahpach, darga, iarach.

There is another accent, called Pesik, which is placed in the line with the letters, as: אִן.

The small circle (°) is used as a mark of reference, and is justified in the line with the superior points.

There are two punctuation-marks used in the body of hebrew work. The one most commonly used is shaped like our colon, (:), and the other is like a period, (˙), with the nick turned inward. Both of them are used in the same manner as the roman period. When either of these points are inserted, it should have a thick space put between it and the preceding word.

ADDENDA.

The **Makkeph** (̠) is used between two words, to show that they are compound.

A sign like a minute-mark (') is sometimes employed to show that a letter has been cut off at the end of a word; and when two (") are inserted, it denotes that the word which precedes it, and that which follows, form one or more compound words.

The only ligature used is the אל, which represents the two letters: Auleph and Laumed.

As the hebrew reads from right to left, the types must be composed in a manner somewhat different from the usual method. Printers generally hold the composing-stick so that they can commence at the outer end of the line, and set the types from the right to the left. This mode, beside being inconvenient, compels the compositor to lift the line in order that the superior points may be justified in their proper position. The most expeditious method of proceeding is, to commence at the nearer end of the stick, and set the types with the nicks inward, and justify the line to the measure by means of spaces, and the broad letters, after which the superior points must be justified in their places, when the line will appear as follows:

לָכֵן יִתֵּן אֲדֹנָי הוּא לָכֶם אוֹת: הִנֵּה הָעַלְמָה הָרָה

The line of text, and that which contains the points, must now be turned, by using the composing-rule and a lead, so that the nicks will be upward. The vowel-points are next to be justified under the letters to which they belong, and the following will be the appearance of the line:

לָכֵן יִתֵּן אֲדֹנָי הוּא לָכֶם אוֹת: הִנֵּה הָעַלְמָה הָרָה

The line of letters should be looked over carefully, before the points are justified above and below it; because if a word, or even a letter, should be doubled or left out, the correction of the line will cause the loss of much time.

The common alphabet, in the lower-case, and the one in the upper-case, have been put in the boxes to which they correspond in the roman.

The plan of the cases is given on the next two pages:

The points should be justified under the centre of the square letters, and, when a letter descends more on one side than the other, the point must be placed exactly under the lower part.

When two points are put under a letter, and they are broader than it, the letter must have a space put on each side, so that the points will not run under the types which come before or after it.

ADDENDA.

HEBREW LOWER-CASE.

[Hebrew typecase layout diagram]

The letters and points should be made to even portions of an m, so that they could be justified, one under the other, with the least possible trouble.

The ascending and descending letters should not be allowed to hang more than half an m above or below the body on which they are cast; because, they will make the lines crooked, or else become broken, should they be justified one above the other.

250   PRINTER'S MANUAL:

The letters of the alphabet are used for numbers, in a manner nearly like they are employed in the greek:

א	ב	ג	ד	ה	ו	ז	ח	ט	י	יא	יב
1	2	3	4	5	6	7	8	9	10	11	12

יג	יד	טו	טז	יז	יח	יט	כ	כא	ל	לא	מ
13	14	15	16	17	18	19	20	21	30	31	40

מא	נ	נא	ס	סא	ע	עא	פ	פא	צ	צא	ק
41	50	51	60	61	70	71	80	81	90	91	100

קא	ר	ש	ת	ך	ם	ן	ף	ץ	א̈	בא̈	
101	200	300	400	500	600	700	800	900	1000	2000	

In the above list of numerals it will be seen that the ones which represent 15 and 16 do not follow the regular order, the first being composed of the characters for 9 and 6, and the second, of those for 9 and 7. This is done, by the Jews, to obviate the necessity of employing, for an ordinary purpose, a combination of letters which are of the most sacred meaning.

COMPOSITION OF INTERLINEAR WORK.

In work of this kind, the lines must be spaced so that the translation will be under the centre of the text. In order to do this correctly the compositor must set up the longest word or phrase in both until the first line is filled, when it will appear like:

Omnes the villages *atque omnia* the buildings, which *quisque*

The words of the translation must now be taken out, and the short words of the text justified in the centre of the spaces, in the following manner:

Omnes   vici   atque omnia   aedificia,   quae quisque
All   the villages   and   all   the buildings, which any one

When the translation can be placed as above.

TECHNICAL TERMS.

In the following list, it is not the intention to insert Technical Terms alone; but, to give place to any other matter which may be deemed of interest. At the same time, reference will be given to the page on which any subject that has heretofore been treated of may be found: making this division a Vocabulary of Technical Terms, as well as a General Index to the work.

A

Abbreviations, 34.
Abbreviations, Commercial, 42.
Accents, etc., 43.
Addenda, 209.
Advy.— A term used, in daily newspaper-offices, as a short method of saying the word: Advertisement.
Algebra, Composition of, 237.
Algebraical Signs, 39.
Angles, Mitering, 53.
Ascending Letters.— This term includes the whole of the capitals, and the following small letters: b, d, f, h, k, and l.
Asterisk.— This mark, (*), when used singly in the body of a work, is intended to direct the reader to some note in the margin or at the bottom of the page. Three or four asterisks placed, without spaces between them, denote the omission of some letters in a word; but, when separated at the distance of an m- or n-quad, are intended to mark some deficiency in the manuscript.
Astronomical Signs.— The signs of the zodiac should be cast uniform in size, so as to save the trouble of justifying them, when used to show the moon's place, in almanacs. The other signs should be fitted up as

closely as the face will allow, because it will often be necessary to get them into the least possible space. [For a list of these signs, see page 38.]

Author's Proof.— After the errors made in composition have been corrected, a clean proof is printed and sent to the author, who makes such alterations as he may deem necessary.

B

Backs.— The backs are those pieces of furniture, in a form of book-work, placed between the sides of the pages and the cross of the chase, in quartos, octavos, and duodecimos; and form the margin of part of the fore-edge of a book, in all the sizes except folio and quarto.

Bank.— A table placed at the side of a hand-press, to receive the sheets before and after they are printed.

Balsam of Copaiva, 180.

Bearers, 144, 156, 162.

Beveled Furniture, 57.

Black-Inks, 151, 183, 185, 186, 196, 198, 199.

Blanket, 155.

Blue Inks, 194, 200.

Bolts.— The pieces of furniture put between the heads of the pages, in a form of Twelves.

Book-Leads, 55.

Brass Rule for Job-Work, 50.

Bronzes, Metal-Leaf and, 203.

Brown Inks, 196, 201.

C

Canada Balsam, 181.

Case-Rack.— A frame made with grooves on the inside, in which the cases can be placed, when not in use. When these racks are intended to contain job-cases, the grooves should be inclined in such a manner that the cases would, when drawn out, be in the same position as if laid on a Stand.

Cases, 59, 66.

Casing the Letter, 60.

Casting Rollers, 171.

Casting up Copy, 62.

Changeable Printing-Inks, 198.
Chases, 58, 135, 144.
Chromotype-Printing, 207.
Citrine Ink, 201.
Clear Up. — When a work is finished, it is cleared up by distributing the head- and foot-lines, and tying up the matter into proper lengths, so that it can be put away by the foreman.
Cleaning Rollers, 173.
Colored Printing-Inks, 187.
Colon, 10.
Colors, Dry, 203; Diagram of, 200.
Comma, 6.
Complementary Colors, 202.
Commercial Abbreviations, 42.
Composing, 64.
Composing-Rule, 65; -Stick, 64.
Composition, 59; of Algebra, 237; of Book-work, 64; of Column-work, 142; of Figure-work, 142; of Greek, 240; of Hebrew, 245; of Interlinear Work, 250; of Music, 239; of Newspapers, 145; of Tables, 142; of Title-Pages, 141; for Rollers, 169.
Compound Colors, 200; Words, 21.
Copper-Faced. — This term is applied to types which have a coating of copper deposited upon their faces, to keep the type-metal from being worn by the machines used in printing daily newspapers. It is different from Electrotype, which means the depositing of a thin copper sheet into a mould, exactly counter to the original — the back of the copper being afterward filled with an inferior metal.
Correcting, 136.
Correction-page, 138.
Copy, 62.
Crimson Ink, 198.
Cross. — The Long-Cross and Short-Cross are two bars of iron crossing each other at right-angles and dovetailed into the rim of the chase. Both of them should be movable, so that the chases will answer for Twelves, Eighteens, and Twenty-Fours, as well as the regular forms.
Cutting Furniture, 129.

D

Dash, 12.
Dimensions of Printing-Paper, 235.
Distributing, 61.
Division of Words, 18.
Dry Colors, 203, 204.

E

Electrotyping, 144. [See Copper-Faced.]
Elisions, 44.
Embossed Printing, 208.
Exclamation, 13.

F

Face of Types, 49.
Flock, 205.
Folios, 68.
Forms, Locking up, 132; Making ready, 154, 164; Washing, 163, 165, 205.
Fount.— The whole of the letters, spaces, points, etc., in a printing-office, which are cast in the same mould and with the same face. [See pages: 48, 49, 50.]
Frisket, 155.
Furniture, Beveled, 57; Cutting, 129; Metal, 56; Wooden, 57.

G

Galleys, 67.
Geometrical Signs, 40.
Giving out Paper, 209.
Green Inks, 194, 201.
Guide, The, 65.
Gutters.— The pieces of furniture put in between an odd and even page in a form of book-work, which give the back-margin when the book is folded and cut.

H

Head-lines, 68.
Head- and Foot-lines, 68.
Hight-to-Paper, 49.
Hot Printing, 206.

I

Imposing Forms, 69.
Indelible Ink, 199.
Indian-Red, 180.
Indigo, 179.
Inks, Black, 151, 183, 185, 186, 196, 198, 199.
Inks, Colored, 187; Blue, 194, 200; Brown, 196, 201; Citrine, 201; Crimson, 198; Green, 194, 201; Olive, 202; Orange, 192, 201; Purple, 195, 201; Red, 189, 200; Russet, 201; Yellow, 193, 200.
Interrogation, 13.
Ivory-Black, 178.

J

Job-work, 141.

L

Lamp-Black, 177.
Latin and French Phrases, 23.
Leads, 54; Weight of, 55; Lengths for Book-work, 55; Lengths for Job-work, 55.
Length of Pages, 67.
Lining of Types, 50.
Linseed-Oil, 176.
Locking up the Form, 132.

M

M.— A square equal to the body of any size of type.
Making Margin, 120.
Making ready the Form, 154.
Making Rollers, 168.
Making up, 67.
Margin, Making, 120.
Materials, 45.
Measure.— The number of m in the width of a page.
Medical Signs, 40.
Metal Furniture, 56.
Metal Leaf and Bronzes, 203.
Mitering Rules, 52.

N

Names of Types, 46.
Newspapers, 145.
Nicks, 49.

Number of Lines contained in 1000 m, in all measures from 10 m to 100 m wide, 236.
Numerals, Roman, 40.

O

Olive Ink, 202.
Orange Inks, 192, 201.

P

Paper, 152; Giving out, 209; Dimensions of, 235; Parts of a Bundle of, 235; Parts of a Ream of, 235; Wetting, 153.
Paper for Blanket, 155, 162, 164.
Period, 11.
Phrases and Signs, 23.
Points and Marks, 14.
Position at Case, 64.
Preserving Rollers, 173.
Press, The, 149.
Pressing Sheets, 167.
Press-Work, 149.
Primary Colors and their Compounds, 199.
Printing of Book-Forms, 154; Bronzes, 203; Cards, 165; Chromotype, 207; Dry Colors, 203; Embossed, 208; Engravings, 160; Flock, 205; Hat-Tips, 206; Job-Work, 164; Leaf and Bronzes, 203; Leather, 207; Parchment, 153; Satin or Velvet, 206.
Proof, Taking, 136.
Proportion of Sorts in a Fount, 48.
Proportions of Types, 63, 237.
Prussian-Blue, 179.
Printing-Inks, 175—201.
Punctuation, 5.
Purple Inks, 195, 201.

Q

Quadrats.— These, as well as Spaces, are cast to the size of the body of the type, but varying in width from one-sixth of an m to three m, so as to facilitate justification. Their hight varies with the kind of work for which they are used: those for letter-press being between three-fourths and five-eighths of an inch high, while those used for stereotype-work must be as high as the square parts of body upon which the faces are cast.

Quoins.— These are made of widths, varying from two inches to a quarter of an inch, so that any required size may be obtained when locking up a form. They should be of the same hight as the other furniture; and their bevel should be similar to that of the side- and foot-stick, so as to make the edges of the quoins next to the chase exactly parallel with the edges of the beveled furniture which is placed against the outer sides and feet of the pages.

Quotations, 55.

R

Red Inks, 189, 200.
Rollers, Casting, 171; Making, 168; Preserving, 173; Recasting, 172.
Roman Numerals, 40.
Rosin, 176.
Rules, Brass, 50; Mitering, 52; Space, 53.
Running-Title, 68.
Russet Ink, 201.

S

Signs, Algebraical, 39; Astronomical, 38; Geometrical, 40; Medical, 40.
Schedule, 140.
Secondary Colors, 201.
Semicolon, 10.
Signatures.— The letters of the alphabet as well as the roman numerals are used for marking the first page of each sheet in a work. When letters are employed, the J, V, and W are usually left out, which makes the alphabet fall short of the numbers. It would be better to insert the whole of the letters except J, as by doing so the alphabet would consist of twenty-five letters — four of these alphabets will be equal to one hundred signatures; but it will be best to use figures in all cases. [See page 68.]

Sizes of Types, 45.

Slice. — The inner bottom of a large galley, which is so made that it can be drawn out.

Smalts and Dry Colors, 204.

Sorts. — This word is applied to any letter, point, mark, space, or quad, which is either deficient or redundant, in a fount of types. A work is said to Run on Sorts, when a greater number of any particular kind is required than that furnished by the type-founder.

Spacing, 65.

Space Rules, 53.

Stands, 58.

Stereotyping, 144.

Stick and Rule, 64.

Stone, 58.

T

Table showing the number of m, in the various kinds of types, which will occupy the same space as 1000 m, in all the sizes from Pica to Nonpareil, 237.

Taking the Proof, 136.

Tertiary Colors, 201.

Two-line Letters, 47.

Tympan, 150, 162.

Types, Face of, 49; Hight-to-Paper of, 49; Nicks of, 49; Lining of, 50; Proportions of, in a Fount, 48; Relative Proportions of, 237; Sizes of, 45; Weight of, 50.

W

Words, Compound, 21; containing *ei* and *ie*, 15; Division of, 18; ending in *-ing*, *-ed*, and *-er* or *-or*, 16; Plurals of, 16.

Washing the Form, 163, 165, 205.

Weight of Types, 50.

Wetting Paper, 153.

Wooden Furniture, 57.

Y

Yellow Inks, 193, 200.

MACHINERY.

It will be impossible to give special directions to put up every kind of printing-machinery, in the space allotted to us in this work; yet there are points of similarity in all machines of this kind, so that, by a little attention thereto, any pressman may succeed in putting them up correctly.

Some regard should be had for the strength of the foundation upon which a press is to be placed: if light, it should be strengthened by timbers placed under the floor, or the floor doubled. The bearing-points of a hand-press are small, and most of the weight will be sustained by a small portion of the floor. For cylinder-machines, too much care can not be bestowed on the foundation, without which the best constructed press will never give satisfactory work, and will soon be seriously injured. All large drum- and double cylinder machines should be placed in the lower parts of the building.

Any machine, after it has been running a week or so, should be thoroughly examined in every part, as the jarring is apt to affect the foundation, and loosen the bolts; all of which should be restored to their places, or much damage to the press will be the result.

None but the best quality of oil should be used on printing-machines — sperm, or winter-strained lard-oil. It will be found advantageous occasionally to use coal-oil, as it acts as a solvent of the gum in other oils, and washes it away, thereby keeping the oil-holes and wearing parts of the press clean.

HAND-PRESS.

To put up a hand-press, place it on its back, with the foot end slightly elevated, key on the legs, place it on its feet, put the frame in its place, then the ribs or bed-ways on their bearings, screw in the bolt that holds the ribs to its place, but not so tightly as to spring the cross-piece through which the bolt passes, put the support of the outer end of the ribs in its place, but not so as to force the ribs up, put on the bed of the press, run it under the frame, so that it shall bear upon the legs of the press, see now that the frame and its bed is level, which can be ascertained by a spirit-level, or a few drops of water; the press should be leveled by underlaying the feet; the outer end of the ribs should bear lightly on the adjusting-nut, but no attempt should be made to level the press by forcing up the outer end of the ribs.

CYLINDER-PRESS.

Particular attention should be given to the foundation of the cylinder-press — it can not be too firm; the parts that support the bed (the roller-ways) should be placed in their position, then put on the side pieces, screw all together

firmly, now **examine** if the frame and bed-ways bear evenly
on the foundation: this can be ascertained by raising one
side or end of the frame, near the center, with a lever,
and observing, in letting down, that both corners touch the
foundation at the same time; also see that the bed-ways
are level, both length, and breadthwise. If the bottom of
the frame does not bear evenly, thin pieces of iron should
be driven under, until it bears evenly all over; the outer
corners, especially, should bear firmly. After all is adjusted,
it adds much to the firmness of the press to pour melted
lead under any opening that may exist; put in the pul-
leys and shaft, universal-joint and pinion, put on the bed,
then the cylinder, rollers, and fountain; be particular that
the distributing-rollers are so placed that the traversing-screw
on the roller does not go too far on one side, so as to butt
against the frame: if not free to move, the teeth of the
pinion or the rack must break. Some presses have a heavy
iron foundation; if this is properly leveled, the frame will
also be level.

THE ADAMS PRESS.

The same rule should be observed in leveling the above
press. The winter, or the lower heavy piece that receives
the toggles, should be placed in position first, and raised so
that the side-pieces can be placed in position, place under
the winter the piece that sustains the springs, then adjust
the side frames to their places by the cross-pieces, see that
the rod that supports the bellows just under the edge of the
bed, on the fly side of the press, is put in its place before

the sides are too far closed, now put the toggles in their places, adjust the bed by raising it over the frames, and slide it into the grooves in the inside of the frame, or leave one side off till the bed is in its place, and let it rest on supports put under it; put on the driving-wheel, and the piece that moves the toggles (called the goose-neck), then adjust the pitman or rod that connects the driving wheel with the goose-neck, put in the bellows, then the rollers, nipper-frame and fly.

In the above directions for putting up printing-machines, it will be found, if you proceed in the order in which the parts are named, no difficulty will occur by the interfering of one piece with another.

The List of Titles

1. Balston, Thomas. *James Whatman, Father & Son.*

2. Balston, Thomas. *William Balston, Paper Maker, 1759–1849.*

3. Hunter, Dard. *Papermaking in Pioneer America.* New introduction by Leonard Schlosser.

4. Munsell, Joel. *Chronology of the Origin and Progress of Paper and Paper-Making.* Fifth edition, with additions. New introduction by Henry Morris.

5. Arnett, John Andrews (i.e. Hannett, John). *Bibliopegia; or, The Art of Bookbinding in all its Branches.* New introduction by Bernard C. Middleton.

6. Nicholson, James B. *A Manual of the Art of Bookbinding, Containing Full Instructions in the Different Branches of Forwarding, Gilding, and Finishing.* New introduction by Sidney F. Huttner.

7. Hullmandel, Charles Joseph. *The Art of Drawing on Stone, Giving a Full Explanation of the Various Styles, of the Different Methods to be Employed to Ensure Success, and of the Modes of Correcting, as well as of the Several Causes of Failure.* New introduction by Joan Friedman.

8. Burch, Robert M. *Colour Printing and Colour Printers.* New introduction by Joan Friedman.

9. Brightly, Charles. *The Method of Founding Stereotype as Practised by Charles Brightly.* Bound with Hodgson,

The List of Titles

Thomas. *An Essay on the Origin and Progress of Stereotype Printing*. New introduction by Michael L. Turner.

10. De Vinne, Theodore L. *The Printers' Price List, a Manual for the Use of Clerks and Book-Keepers in Job Printing Offices*. New introduction by Irene Tichenor.

11. R. Hoe & Co. *Catalogue of Printing Presses and Printers' Materials, Lithographic Presses, Stereotyping and Electrotyping Machinery, Binders' Presses and Materials*. New introduction by Frank E. Comparato.

12. Berry, W. Turner & A.F. Johnson. *Catalogue of Specimens of Printing Types by English and Scottish Printers and Founders, 1665–1830*. New introduction by James Mosley.

13. Morison, Stanley. *John Bell, 1745–1831, Bookseller, Printer, Publisher, Typefounder, Journalist, &c.* New introduction by Nicolas Barker.

14. Morison, Stanley. *John Fell, the University Press and the "Fell" Types*. New introduction by Nicolas Barker.

15. American Type Founders Company. *Specimens of Type, Brass Rules and Dashes, Ornaments and Borders, Society Emblems, Check Lines, Cuts, Initials and Other Productions of the American Type Founders Co.* New introduction by Alexander S. Lawson. Bibliographical note by John Bidwell.

16. Legros, Lucien Alphonse and John Cameron Grant. *Typographical Printing-Surfaces: The Technology and Mechanism of their Production*.

17. Stower, Caleb. *The Printer's Manual, an Abridgment of Stower's Grammar, Comprising all the Plans in that Work for Imposing Forms, Several Tables and other Useful Articles*. New introduction by John Bidwell. Bound with Grattan, Edward. *The Printer's Companion: Being Practical Directions for Filling the Various Situations in a Printing Office*. New introduction by Clinton Sisson.

The List of Titles

18. Van Winkle, Cornelius S. *The Printers' Guide; or, an Introduction to the Art of Printing, Including an Essay on Punctuation and Remarks on Orthography.* New introduction by Carey S. Bliss.

19. Adams, Thomas F. *Typographia; or, The Printer's Instructor. A Brief Sketch of the Origin, Rise, and Progress of the Typographic Art, with Practical Directions for Conducting Every Department in an Office, Hints to Authors, Publishers, &c.* New introduction by John Bidwell.

20. Lynch, Thomas. *The Printer's Manual, a Practical Guide for Compositors and Pressmen.* New introduction by Peter M. VanWingen.

21. Ringwalt, J. Luther (editor). *American Encyclopaedia of Printing.* New introduction by Daniel Traister.

22. Southward, John. *Practical Printing, a Handbook of the Art of Typography.*

23. Thompson, John S. *The Mechanism of the Linotype: A Complete and Practical Treatise on the Installation, Operation and Care of the Linotype, for the Novice as well as the Experienced Operator.* Bound with Thompson, John S. *History of Composing Machines, a Complete Record of the Art of Composing Type by Machinery.* New introduction by Bruce L. Johnson.